THE ROUGH GUIDE TO
Nirvana

by
Gillian G. Gaar

ROUGH GUIDES

www.roughguides.com

Credits

The Rough Guide to Nirvana

Text editing & picture research: Kate Berens
Typesetting: Umesh Aggarwal
Proofreading: Andrew McCulloch
Production: Rebecca Short & Vicky Baldwin

Rough Guides Reference

Director: Andrew Lockett
Editors: Kate Berens, Peter Buckley, Tracy Hopkins,
Matthew Milton, Joe Staines, Ruth Tidball

Publishing Information

This first edition published June 2009 by
Rough Guides Ltd, 80 Strand, London WC2R 0RL
375 Hudson St, 4th Floor, New York 10014, USA
Email: mail@roughguides.com

Distributed by the Penguin Group:
Penguin Books Ltd, 80 Strand, London WC2R 0RL
Penguin Putnam, Inc., 375 Hudson Street, NY 10014, USA
Penguin Group (Australia), 250 Camberwell Road, Camberwell, Victoria 3124, Australia
Penguin Books Canada Ltd, 90 Eglinton Avenue East, Suite 700, Toronto, Ontario M4P 2Y3, Canada
Penguin Group (New Zealand), cnr Rosedale and Airborne Roads, Albany, Auckland 1310, New Zealand

Printed in Singapore by SNP Security Printing Pte Ltd

© Gillian G. Gaar, 2009
264 pages; includes index

A catalogue record for this book is available from the British Library

ISBN 13: 978-1-85828-945-8
ISBN 10: 1-85828-945-9

1 3 5 7 9 8 6 4 2

Contents

Foreword

When Krist Novoselic, Kurt Cobain and Dale Crover walked into Reciprocal Recording in January 1988, I didn't know what to expect. This "band" had no name. Dale (who I knew from the Melvins) was apparently just "sitting in" on the drums. Who were these guys? But as the tape rolled, and they blazed their way through nine-and-a-half songs in just a few hours, I began getting more excited; this was the best "out of left field" thing I'd heard in a while.

They were tight, the bass was rock solid, every song had a killer guitar riff, and Kurt's vocals really made an impression on me, an opinion I shared with Dale, who agreed exactly with me on that point. I couldn't make out what the lyrics were about, but the intensity of Kurt's delivery got to me. There was something going on here, some X-factor. I begged to keep a cassette copy, which I shared with the guys at Sub Pop Records and with my journalist girlfriend Dawn Anderson.

That cassette led to them getting signed by Sub Pop and then by major label DGC; it led to world tours and magazine covers; it led to *Nevermind* knocking Michael Jackson off the top of the US album charts. Their trajectory went from wildly improbable, to amazing... and then to a tragedy. What was left was their music, which has refused to go away, because there is something real there that people want, something that the sterile, overproduced corporate-machine-made cotton candy that dominates our pop charts is lacking. I was lucky enough to play a small part in bringing Nirvana's music into the world, from that first demo, to recording *Bleach* and "Sliver," to the *In Utero* demos, to working (with writer and researcher Gillian Gaar) on piecing together the *With The Lights Out* box set. In this book, the *Rough Guide to Nirvana*, Ms. Gaar has nicely summarized twenty years of Nirvana history. Don't forget to crank up Nirvana's music while you read it!

JACK ENDINO
Producer/engineer
www.jackendino.com

Seattle record producer Jack Endino was a key player in the grunge movement. A founding member of the band Skin Yard, he's worked on more than 300 records to date, by bands ranging from Screaming Trees to Hot Hot Heat. He played a critical role in Nirvana's career, among other things producing their seminal debut album *Bleach*.

Acknowledgements

My first thanks go to Richie Unterberger who got the ball rolling. The three main Nirvana texts, Michael Azerrad's *Come As You Are*, Charles R. Cross's *Heavier Than Heaven* and Everett True's *Nirvana*, have each laid the groundwork for future writers and are essential reading for anyone interested in the band. Over the years I've been fortunate enough to interview many involved in Nirvana's story, and have drawn on my interviews with Krist Novoselic, Chad Channing, Dan Peters, Aaron Burckhard, Mark Pickerel, Bruce Pavitt, Jonathan Poneman, Steve Fisk, Craig Montgomery, Butch Vig, Steve Albini, Charles Peterson, John Goodmanson, Jon Snyder, Lori Goldston, William Arnold and Earnie Bailey for this book. Jeff Burlingame, Jacob McMurray and Enrico Vincenzi each provided valuable additional assistance. I've relied on help from my online friends, Rasmus Holman of nirvanaclub, Alex Roberts of livenirvana, and Kris Sproul and Mike Ziegler of nirvanaguide, for many years now, and I'm always glad to have them on my side. I am most grateful for Jack Endino's consistent support and friendship. Thanks to all who provided photographs and/or artwork. Among the Rough Guide crew, Andrew Lockett, Ruth Tidball, Peter Buckley and Kate Berens helped make the whole process easier. My drop-in visitors, Mingus, Amon and Griffin, helped lift my spirits. Special thanks as always to my mother, Marcella Gaar, who always helps to keep the home fires burning.

This book is dedicated to the memory of my father, John Milton Gaar, who never liked rock music ("I like *real* music"), but would be pleased I have another book out. Thanks, dad.

Photo credits

Inside front cover © Jeff Kravitz/FilmMagic/Getty Images; p.v © Lance Mercer; pp.1, 159, 223 detail from De Formato Foetu by Adriaan van de Spiegel (1578–1625); p.5 © Harley Soltes/Time Life Pictures/Getty Images; pp.6, 7, 16, 17, 19, 21, 33, 35, 37, 61, 83, 121, 140, 147, 244, 245, 247 © Gillian G. Gaar; p.11 © George Chin/Redferns; pp.27, 39, 46, 47, 50 © JJ Gonson/Redferns; p.52 © Brigitte Engl/Redferns; p.57 © 2008 Jon Snyder; p.63 © Kirk Weddle/Corbis; pp.67, 87, 95 © Mick Hutson/Redferns; p.69 © Marty Temme/WireImage/Getty Images; p.71, 79 © Steve Pyke/Premium Archive/Getty Images; p.72 © Peter Pavkis/Redferns; p.75 © George Chin/Redferns; p.89 © Ke.Mazur/WireImage/Getty Images; p.99 © Joe Giron/Corbis; p.100 © Tibor Bozi/Corbis; p.107 © Ebet Roberts/Redferns; p.110 © Trapper Frank/Corbis Sygma; pp.112, 117 © Jeff Kravitz/FilmMagic/Getty Images; p.115 © Frank Micelotta/Getty Images; p.122 © Steve Catlin/Redferns; p.123 © Rafaella Cavalieri/Redferns; pp.127, 134, 138 © Curt Doughty; p.151 © Neal Preston/Corbis; p.154 © Gary Hershorn/Reuters/Corbis; p.156 © Gary Wolstenholme/Redferns; p.157 © Karen Mason Blair/Corbis; p.172 © Paul Bergen/Redferns; p.191 © Michel Linssen/Redferns.

The Publishers have made every effort to identify and to contact the correct rights holders in respect of images featured in this book. If despite these efforts any attribution is missing or incorrect, the Publishers will correct such, once they have been brought to their attention, in any subsequent printings.

Part One:
The Story

Early days
1967–87

Early days
1967–87

The members of Nirvana were all born in the shadow of the Baby Boom generation, in the mid- to late 1960s. But it was the punk and metal they discovered in their teens that would shape the music they ultimately made. Living far from any of the nation's cultural centres, they were free to mix and meld their musical influences as they pleased. And for two-thirds of the band, their musical ambitions took them out of their small town surroundings, a milieu Kurt Cobain once described as "*Twin Peaks* without the excitement".

Home town story

Aberdeen, Washington, one hundred miles southwest of Seattle and a half-hour's drive from the Pacific coast, was a town in slow economic decline at the time of *Nevermind*'s release in 1991, with perennially grey skies (average rainfall being nearly 84 inches a year) adding to the overall gloom. But the town was quite different when **Kurt Donald Cobain** was born in Aberdeen's Grays Harbor Community Hospital on February 20, 1967, with jobs in the timber industry (there were 37 mills in the area) providing employment for most of the local population. Cobain spent

Kurt Cobain later referred to his early childhood (pre-divorce) as "blissful times".

his first two and a half years living in the smaller, adjoining town of **Hoquiam**, where his father, Don, worked as a mechanic at the local Chevron station; Wendy, his mother, was a homemaker. The family relocated to Aberdeen in 1969, and Cobain's sister Kim was born when he was three.

Cobain later described his childhood – at least until the age of nine – as "blissful times". As the first-born child in his generation, with two uncles on his father's side and six aunts and uncles on his mother's, Cobain was at the centre of an extended family that doted on him. His artistic talent was evident at a young age, and encouraged by the family, who readily provided art supplies and toy instruments. There were already a few musicians in the family on Cobain's mother's side: her brother Chuck played in a local band called The Beachcombers, her sister Mari was a country musician, and a great-uncle, Delbert, had moved to California, changed his name to Del Arden, and established a career as a singer.

Mari Earl holds the distinction of being the first person to put a guitar in Cobain's hands, when he was two. "He turned it around the other way, 'cause he was left-handed," she recalled. A Beatles fan from a young age, Cobain was recorded singing "Hey Jude", along with the theme to the *The Monkees* TV show, and Arlo Guthrie's "Motorcycle Song", delighting in how Guthrie rhymed "pickle" and "motor*sickel*". "You could just say, 'Hey Kurt, sing this!' and he would sing it," Mari Earl told *Goldmine*. "He had a lot of charisma from a very young age." After getting his start on a child's Mickey Mouse drum set, he took up drums more seriously in the fifth grade, later joining the school band; a picture in the book *Cobain* shows Kurt as a preppy-looking junior high student, sitting behind his snare at a school assembly.

"That legendary divorce"

But Cobain's childhood idyll was shattered at age nine, when his parents divorced. However much he downplayed it later, it was the key event of his young life – perhaps of his entire life – bringing to the surface all his feelings of shame and inadequacy. "I desperately wanted to have the classic, you know, typical family," he told journalist Jon Savage in July 1993, two months before the release of *In Utero*, whose opening track sarcastically dismissed

the by-then "legendary" divorce as "a bore". To his own biographer, Michael Azerrad, he spoke of "feeling like I wasn't worthy anymore". The situation wasn't helped by the fact that the divorce was far from amicable.

After living with his mother for about six months, Cobain moved in with his father in **Montesano**, eleven miles east of Aberdeen. Father and son initially bonded, at least until Don remarried in 1978, something Cobain regarded as a betrayal; instead of being the centre of his father's attention, he was now "one of the last things on his list", Cobain told Azerrad. Don's new wife had two children from a previous marriage, and the couple soon had a son of their own.

Cobain's aunt, Mari Earl (pictured right) was the first to hand him a guitar, when he was two years old

Bridge over the Wishkah River in Aberdeen, Washington: the unassuming logging town from which Nirvana emerged.

Don was given full legal custody of Cobain in 1979, but he nonetheless became increasingly difficult to deal with, complaining, refusing to do his chores and sequestering himself in his room. In spring of 1982, he left his father's house and was passed among various relatives before finally moving back in with his mother that fall.

Alongside this turbulence in his personal life, Cobain's creative life had been steadily developing. He'd continued drawing and painting, with some of his artwork reproduced in school publications, and made short films using his father's Super-8 camera. But increasingly music became his dominant interest. For his fourteenth birthday, his uncle Chuck gave him the choice between a bicycle and guitar. He chose the guitar, a cheap, secondhand model, and one of the first songs he learned was the garage rock classic "Louie Louie". Chuck arranged for Cobain to take lessons with another local musician, **Warren Mason**, at Aberdeen's music store, Rosevears (today, a star with Cobain's name is embedded in the sidewalk in front of the shop). Mason set Cobain up with a $125 Ibanez, and taught him "Stairway to Heaven" and AC/DC's "Back in Black". Though the lessons were curtailed after a few months when they began to interfere with Cobain's schoolwork, he'd learned enough by then to continue on his own, and subsequently spent hours practising in his room.

Musical foundations

Cobain never lost his taste for the kind of pop melodicism exemplified by **The Beatles**, but his musical interests were also broadening. Given his immediate environment, he was mostly exposed to the top-forty rock of local radio stations, buttressed by albums his father received via his membership of the Columbia House Record and Tape club. **Queen, Led Zeppelin, Aerosmith** and **Journey** were favourites, along with new wave acts like the **B-52's** and **The Cars**. On 29 March 1983, he travelled to Seattle with friends to see his first concert, Sammy Hagar. Though he later told journalist Gina Arnold the show "didn't thrill me", he nonetheless bought the T-shirt, proudly wearing it to school the following day.

But his musical interests were about to shift in a new direction. During the summer of 1983, he attended a concert by a local band called the **Melvins** in the unlikely locale of the Thriftway grocery store's parking lot in Montesano,

where the band's guitarist, **Roger "Buzz" Osborne,** worked. For Cobain, the Melvins' blast of unadulterated punk was a revelation: "This is what I was looking for," he later wrote in his journal. He quickly befriended the group, a relationship that was to prove invaluable to his musical education, and eventually his career. Osborne passed on mix tapes of punk acts like **Black Flag** and Flipper, a photo book of the Sex Pistols and back issues of *Creem* to his young acolyte, and Cobain soon began going to Melvins' practice sessions, held at the Aberdeen home of their drummer, **Dale Crover.**

The iconoclastic group had attracted a little band of teenage followers, somewhat derisively

Montesano's Thriftway car park hosted the Melvins gig in summer 1983 that introduced Cobain to punk, the revelation he'd been looking for.

The young Cobain's favourite songs

"Hey Jude" – The Beatles

The Fab Four were one of the first bands – maybe the first band – Cobain developed a strong affinity for. He was known to go around his neighbourhood as a child singing this song while banging on a bass drum strapped to his chest. His aunt Mari recorded him singing the song on a home tape deck.

"Theme from *The Monkees*" – The Monkees

Aunt Mari also captured Cobain singing this ditty from the TV series of America's premier pre-Fab Four on her tape deck. Excerpts of both this and "Hey Jude" can be heard in the film *Kurt & Courtney*.

"The Motorcycle Song" – Arlo Guthrie

Another song Cobain would sing aloud as a child. Guthrie's countercultural, anti-authoritarian stance was a good fit for a kid who was already shouting "Corn on the cops!" at passing police cars, and

would later have a sticker on his guitar reading "Vandalism: Beautiful as a Rock in a Cop's Face."

"Seasons In The Sun" – Terry Jacks

As the first record Cobain purchased, it was a decidedly morbid choice. The music was typical of the easy listening pop of the early 1970s, but the lyrics (originally written by Jacques Brel, translated into English by Rod McKuen and further tweaked by Jacks) are sung from the perspective of a young man making his farewells to loved ones as he faces death in ambiguous circumstances – is he dying of an illness or about to commit suicide? Nirvana occasionally performed the song live and recorded a rather ramshackle version in Rio in January 1993 (which appears on the *With The Lights Out* DVD).

"Don't Bring Me Down" – Electric Light Orchestra

While in the seventh grade at Montesano Junior High School, Cobain was profiled in the student newspaper, the *Puppy Press*, in its "Meatball of the

referred to as "Cling-Ons", one of whom was a lanky 6'7" Croatian, **Krist Novoselic** (then giving his first name the Americanized spelling of "Chris"). Novoselic was born 16 May 1965, in Compton, California. His father, Krist Novoselic, Sr., had fled what was then Yugoslavia in 1955 to escape the Communist rule of Marshal Tito, eventually arriving in America in the early 1960s. He first worked as a fisherman on the East Coast, before settling in Gardena, California, working as a truck driver

for the Sparklets drinking water company. His wife Maria moved to the US to join him, and the couple had two more children after Krist, Robert and Diana.

In 1979, the family moved to Aberdeen, where living expenses were lower; Krist's father took a job as a machinist, and Maria worked in local stores, later setting up her own hair salon. "It was a culture shock," Krist said of the move. "Aberdeen was not only geographically isolated, it was culturally isolated. I missed

Month" column. Cobain cited this rousing number (ELO's first song to not feature a string section) as his current favourite; Meat Loaf was his designated "favourite rock group".

"Louie, Louie" – The Kingsmen

The first song to be mastered by many an aspiring guitarist, Cobain first played it on the drums while a member of his junior high school band. In 1985, there was a failed attempt to make it the official state song of Washington.

"Back in Black" – AC/DC

According to his guitar teacher, Warren Mason, one of the first songs Cobain wanted to learn was this tribute to the band's late singer, Bon Scott. Its distinctive guitar riff was a powerful draw; "That's pretty much the 'Louie, Louie' chords and that's all you need to know," he later told his biographer, Michael Azerrad.

"Stairway to Heaven" – Led Zeppelin

Warren Mason said his student was keen to learn how to play this monumental song, though Cobain later denied it, perhaps embarrassed by his early mainstream rock leanings. But it's worth noting that Nirvana included a few Zeppelin songs in their set in their early years.

"My Best Friend's Girl" – The Cars

Cobain became interested in new wave acts after seeing the B-52's on the TV show *Saturday Night Live*. This song was one of the first he learned to play, and one of the last he ever played live: it opened Nirvana's final show on 1 March 1994.

"Hunting Tigers out in Indiah" – The Bonzo Dog Band

An early sign of Cobain's interest in quirky, off-the-wall songs, he taught himself to play this track after receiving the album *Tadpoles* as a Christmas present when he was fifteen.

the weather and the culture of California. Everybody in Aberdeen was listening to Kenny Rogers!" Novoselic had more of a penchant for hard rock acts like Black Sabbath, Led Zeppelin and Aerosmith (though he shared with Cobain an affinity for The Beatles). His musical horizons expanded when he was sent to live with relatives in Yugoslavia for a year, and discovered punk and ska. Once back home in Aberdeen, he tuned in every Sunday to Seattle radio station KZOK's punk/new wave show, "Your Mother Won't Like It", which spun tunes by the likes of **The Ramones**, the **New York Dolls** and **The Stooges**, carefully recording each programme on cassette.

KZOK promoted the first concert Novoselic attended, a **Scorpions** show on 16 July 1982, at Seattle's Hec Edmunson Pavilion, which he later described as "totally boring". But after meeting the Melvins' Buzz Osborne through friends in Aberdeen, he eventually found some kindred spirits. Osborne also introduced him to

The Melvins

In a sense, the Melvins could be considered Nirvana's doppelgängers: a power trio from a small Washington state town few people had heard of, playing a style of music no one quite knew what to call. In fact, the two bands' paths crossed numerous times over the years, and they occasionally worked together.

The Melvins were formed in 1983 by three friends from Montesano High School (Mike Dillard on drums, Matt Lukin on bass, and Roger "Buzz" Osborne on guitar and vocals), largely as a means to alleviate the boredom of being stuck in "a nasty dull rainy dark hell hole filled with dumb redneck simpletons", as Osborne put it in the liner notes of *Mangled Demos from 1983*. Their name came from a fellow employee at the Montesano Thriftway, where Osborne worked as a clerk. The band started out playing covers of classic rock acts like The Who, but switched to a faster, hardcore style after Osborne discovered punk. Playing punk rock was daring enough in a region that preferred metal acts like Iron Maiden and the Scorpions. But by 1984 (when Dillard had been replaced by Dale Crover), the Melvins had advanced their sound further by starting to play more slowly, in stark contrast to the breakneck pace of orthodox hardcore punk. In fact, the band was simply carving out its own niche, blending a punk sensibility with the hard riffing of heavy metal to create the music that would later be dubbed "grunge".

Kurt Cobain had seen Osborne and Lukin around when he lived in Montesano, and first saw the Melvins play at the summer 1983 parking lot gig; Novoselic had met them around the same time through mutual friends. In addition to introducing them to other punk acts via Osborne's record collection, the band also served to show Cobain and Novoselic that you didn't have to conform to prevailing music trends but could dare to create music that was entirely your own. Most importantly, they proved that however idiosyncratic the music, with enough drive and dedication it would surely find an audience. The Melvins didn't find particularly receptive audiences awaiting them, however, and local gigs were as likely to be interrupted by heckling as applause. But they doggedly plugged away, eventually landing shows in Seattle (with Cobain tagging along as a roadie), and increasingly out of state.

The Melvins' first recordings appeared on C/Z Records' legendary *Deep Six* compilation (see p.000), released in 1985, which featured four of their songs. Their next records were *Six Songs* (later expanded and subsequently retitled *8 Songs*, *10 Songs* and ultimately *26 Songs*), released on C/Z in 1986, and their first full-length album, *Gluey Porch Treatments*, released on Alchemy Records in 1987. Both offer an excellent introduction to the band's trademark heavy, grinding, dirge rock. Their use of a dropped-D tuning made an immediate impression on bands when they started to play Seattle. Kim Thayil of Soundgarden later recalled to *Guitar World* how Osborne had explained the tuning to him and Mark Arm (then of Green River) at a party; "And then we D-tuned and started experimenting. We've never stopped," he added. Osborne said the tuning was a trick he'd picked up from a "metal kid" in Aberdeen.

In his first published interview, Cobain admitted he was afraid Nirvana would be seen as "a Melvins rip-off", and songs like "Paper Cuts" and "Sifting" clearly reveal the band's influence (Crover even plays drums on the former). But Nirvana already had more of a pop element to their music than the Melvins ever would. Nonetheless, Cobain and Novoselic drafted Crover to play on their first professional demo. The Melvins relocated to San Francisco in 1988, but the two bands remained in touch, and in 1990 played some shows together. Dale Crover even returned to the drummer's seat in Nirvana on a short West Coast tour. But the biggest boost the Melvins ever gave to Nirvana came when Dave Grohl called Osborne to say that his band, Scream, had broken up. Osborne gave him a suggestion that would change his life forever: call Nirvana.

Grohl had discovered the Melvins while on a European tour with Scream in the late 1980s. While hanging out in Amsterdam, he stumbled upon *Gluey Porch Treatments* in a friend's record collection. "It really fucking blew my mind", he later recalled to *Mojo*, deeply impressed by music "heavier than Black Sabbath or any metal record I had heard"; he claimed to listen to the record every day for the next two years. He later became friends with the band, hence the call to Osborne. After Grohl joined the group, Cobain proudly described him as "a baby Dale Crover".

Connections between the two bands remained strong throughout the rest of Nirvana's career. After the success of *Nevermind*, Nirvana's patronage led to the Melvins signing a major label deal with Atlantic Records, and during the summer of 1992, Cobain produced six tracks on their debut album for the label, *Houdini*, released in 1993. The album achieved the highest chart placing of the band's career, reaching number 29 on *Billboard*'s "Heatseekers" chart. Nirvana also continued to share bills

with the band right up to their very last show, on 1 March 1994.

Though the Melvins were dropped by Atlantic in 1997, they'd established enough of a following to keep them busy, and had released over twenty albums at the time of writing, not counting numerous side projects. Their 2000 album *The Crybaby* featured a tribute to their one-time comrades – a cover of "Smells Like Teen Spirit", with former teen idol Leif Garrett on lead vocals. As Cobain had once used footage of Garrett in an early video made for the song "School", it was a gesture he undoubtedly would have appreciated.

They continue to tour regularly; Novoselic found himself sharing a stage with them once again, when playing with Flipper, who joined them on a UK tour in 2006. In an interview in 2004, Osborne noted while being in the Melvins hadn't made him rich, "I get to make a racket for a living, and that's pretty fucking cool". It may well have been the path that Cobain might have preferred over his own worldwide success.

The Melvins' connections to Nirvana run deep; Buzz Osbourne (centre) introduced Cobain to punk, while Dale Crover (right) would drum with Nirvana on several occasions.

Flipper, a band he was initially slow to appreciate, though he was eventually won over in a big way. "It was a revelation," he told journalist Gina Arnold. "It was art." He was soon joining the Melvins on trips to Seattle to see other punk bands, a necessity given Aberdeen's isolation. Cobain accompanied the gang on some of these trips, going to a Black Flag concert in Seattle with Osborne and other friends.

When Cobain returned to his mother's house in the fall of 1982, he began attending **J.M. Weatherwax High School**, more commonly known as Aberdeen High School, where Novoselic was also a student. Novoselic would graduate in 1983 (the same year his parents divorced), becoming the only member of Nirvana to graduate from high school. Though Cobain maintained an active interest in art and reading (when skipping lessons he could often be found at the Aberdeen Library), school bored him. He'd also become a regular drug user, primarily pot and alcohol. And he was as argumentative with his mother as he'd been with his father. She was embroiled in her own difficulties with her new boyfriend (whom she would later marry, have a daughter with, and then divorce). On one occasion, Cobain was able to use this to his advantage: after a fight, his mother threw her boyfriend's guns into the nearby Wishkah River; Cobain retrieved them the next day, and promptly pawned them, using the money to buy an amplifier.

The breaking point came in the spring of 1984, when Cobain's mother caught him in bed with a teenage girl and kicked him out; he later moved back in with his father, and then with the family of his friend, **Jesse Reed**. Neither arrangement worked out, and by the following year he'd dropped out of high school. His living arrangements remained haphazard (he was evicted from one apartment and kicked out of another friend's house), and he was erratically employed at various maintenance jobs, including a janitorial position at his old high school. He was also **arrested** for the first time in 1985 for vandalism; though he later claimed he'd spray-painted the inflammatory slogan "God is gay", he'd actually spraypainted the more bizarre phrase "Ain't got no how watchamacallit".

First recordings, first bands

Cobain managed to keep working on his music through all the turmoil. His aunt Mari, who had married and moved to Seattle, recalled him visiting her home in 1982 and using her equipment to make a tape called "**Organized Confusion**", on which he played guitar and drums. He rejected the offer of her drum machine, telling her "I want to keep my music pure", and improvised a drum set with an empty suitcase and a pair of wooden spoons. He'd begun jamming with Novoselic while living at Reed's house, and was also writing his own songs. None of this material has surfaced, though *Heavier Than Heaven* cites a country and western song about a classmate who'd killed himself, called "Ode to Beau", while Eric Shillinger (another friend Cobain

The Fecal Matter tape

After years making home demos, Cobain made a more advanced recording in December 1985, at his aunt Mari's home in Seattle, using her four-track tape deck to record a collection of songs entitled *Illiteracy Will Prevail*, credited to a group called Fecal Matter. For years this recording was known as "the Fecal Matter demo"; it wasn't until the booklet in the *With The Lights Out* box set reproduced Cobain's hand-drawn cover of the cassette tape that anyone realized the tape actually had a title. (It's also on the cover of *Silver: The Best Of The Box*, see p.181.)

Most people learned of the tape's existence when Michael Azerrad wrote about it in *Come As You Are*, and for years it was the Holy Grail among Nirvana collectors. In 1997, a recording purporting to be the tape surfaced on the collector's circuit, but it proved to be a fake. Only one track, an early version of "Spank Thru", has been officially released, on the *Sliver: The Best Of The Box* compilation. But since 2006, excerpts from the tape have appeared online.

They represent the earliest known example of Cobain's songwriting and as such are fascinating to listen to. Musically the tape veers between heavy metal riffing and high-speed punk, while Cobain's bawling vocals at times have a trace of an English accent. Though it's hard to discern all the lyrics, when they are intelligible they reveal a clear sense of humour at work, and a contempt for any person or institution that adheres to conventional mores; one song makes sarcastic reference to the conservative belief that homosexuality is not innate but a "choice". Cobain later summarized his writing of this period as his "trying to be Mr Political Punk Rock Black Flag Guy", but even as a punk rocker, he was far from being an angry one, retaining a degree of empathy for his song's characters, however small-minded they may be. The tape also featured a brief sound collage, with excerpts from the film *Reefer Madness*; Cobain would later create sound collages that ran close to half an hour.

Most interesting are the songs that went on to be performed by Nirvana. "Downer" and "Spank Thru" were later recorded for Nirvana's first demo in 1988; the two songs are both slower here (probably an indication of Cobain's skill level on guitar at the time), and have him singing in a deeper voice, but the lyrics are largely identical.

Cobain dubbed off copies of the tape on a home stereo, and illustrated the cassette's j-card with a drawing of a large pile of excrement with flies buzzing around it and a few song titles. He passed out copies to friends, including Krist Novoselic, prompting Novoselic to suggest the two form a band. It's not known how many other copies exist, or if there are any plans for an official release of the entire tape one day.

---

had briefly lived with) told a Nirvana website he recalled a parody of Madonna's "Material Girl" called "Venereal Girl", with appropriately rude lyrics.

In 1985, Cobain formed a band called **Fecal Matter** with Dale Crover playing bass, and another friend, **Greg Hokanson**, playing drums. But only Crover accompanied Cobain to Seattle, where the two recorded a demo called *Illiteracy Will Prevail* at Aunt Mari's house. Though rough, the recording was fairly accomplished for someone whose previous

The Story

experience had been limited to the school band and jam sessions with friends. The songs were immersed in punky thrashing, without the melodic pull of Cobain's later work. Lyrically, the sneering putdowns of mainstream society reflected a punk sensibility, but were also indicative of Cobain's growing social consciousness.

Cobain later practised the Fecal Matter songs with Buzz Osborne and Mike Dillard, but the band broke up before playing a show. Cobain continued playing with whomever he could, jamming with Novoselic and other friends. Both were also venturing into the realm of live performance. Novoselic briefly played with the Melvins when the band shared the bill with another Aberdeen band, Metal Church, on 4 May 1984. Novoselic and Cobain were also on-and-off members of the **Stiff Woodies**, a loose-knit group with a revolving line-up that included various Melvins. The band played a few parties, and also performed a brief set on KAOS, the radio station at **Evergreen State College** in Olympia.

Olympia, the state capital of Washington, was fifty miles east of Aberdeen, but a world away in attitude. This was largely due to Evergreen, a freethinking institution where students were able to design their own courses (alumni include Matt Groening, creator of *The Simpsons*, and Michael Richards, who played Kramer in *Seinfeld*). Nirvana would have numerous associations with Olympia and Evergreen in the future, beginning with Cobain's first public performance (Stiff Woodies parties aside), at GESCCO (Greater Evergreen Student Community Cooperative Organization). On 5 May 1986, Cobain appeared as the opening act at a Melvins/Danger Mouse show there, delivering spoken-word readings while Osborne and Crover backed him. The one-off trio had wanted to call themselves Brown Towel, but the name was printed as "Brown Cow" on flyers promoting the show. As Crover later described Cobain's performance, "Kurt was just jumping around the stage reading, singing, and screaming" – already, the building blocks for Nirvana's own performances were in place.

The roots of
Nirvana
1987–88

The roots of Nirvana
1987–88

Ever since he'd picked up a guitar, Cobain had been wanting to start a band, but the opportunity had so far eluded him. But he was about to form a permanent musical alliance with someone that would last the rest of his life, and with whom he'd already been jamming for some time: Krist Novoselic.

First live shows

The same year Cobain made his live debut, Krist Novoselic and his girlfriend, Shelli Dilly, moved to Arizona, though they returned to Aberdeen after a few months. Cobain had

Cobain's rented house in Aberdeen, which was little more than "a shack" according to Novoselic, gave the band somewhere to practise at last.

given him a copy of the Fecal Matter demo, and Novoselic eventually suggested they move beyond jamming and get a band together. Since September 1986, thanks to a loan from his mother, Cobain had been renting a small house a few blocks from her home, so the nascent band now had somewhere to practise. "It was a little shack," says Novoselic. "It was like a little half house." With Cobain on guitar, and Novoselic on bass, they began rehearsing with drummer **Aaron Burckhard**, whom they'd met at Melvins' practices, in early 1987.

From the very start, Cobain was driven, showing a commitment to work largely absent in other areas of his life. "It was like practice, practice, practice, all the time," says Burckhard. "It kind of got to me. I just wasn't into practising a lot. 'Cause we weren't doing any shows, all we were doing was playing at his house. But we always had people over to watch us practise and whatnot." The band eventually secured a date to play a party in Olympia, only to arrive and find the next-door neighbour screaming at the partygoers that she had just called the police. "So we couldn't play," says Burckhard. "We just partied and went back home."

They had better luck in March, when they played a house party in the small town of **Raymond**, 29 miles south of Aberdeen. Amazingly, a recording was made of this unknown band – so new they didn't even have a name – which has since been bootlegged extensively. The "show" comes across as more of a rehearsal, with extended pauses between songs while seemingly everyone present shouts out comments along with occasional whoops of encouragement. Even four years later, Cobain was describing the show as one of Nirvana's best, bragging to journalist Gina Arnold that the band had played Flipper's **"Sex Bomb"** for an hour while their girlfriends began making out with each other, "and that really started freaking out the rednecks! And that was the idea of punk rock to us in the first place, was to abuse your audience. And what better audience to have than a redneck audience?"

In truth, the band's entire set was less than an hour long, and aside from a cover of Led Zeppelin's "Heartbreaker", played at the audience's request, consisted wholly of original material, including most of the songs they'd go on to record for their first professional demo. Though the band had practised all of the songs from the Fecal Matter demo,

In March 1987, a party at this house in the nearby town of Raymond was the setting for Nirvana's first live performance.

"Downer", "Spank Thru" and occasionally "Anorexorcist" were the only tracks from the tape they'd perform live; Cobain was already coming up with new songs. "Kurt was the lead songwriter," Novoselic says of the band's creative process. "He had riffs and a vocal line he'd be hammering out. Sometimes it was just a riff and vocal melody, sometimes it was a couple riffs, more like a song. Then it depended on what everybody's input was."

After a show the following month at GESCCO, they were asked to do a live radio show on the university station **KAOS**. The band, now billing themselves as **Skid Row**, performed two new additions to their set, the disturbing "Floyd The Barber" and a cover of Shocking Blue's "Love Buzz", which Novoselic had discovered. In the space of a month, the band's confidence had grown immeasurably, and a tape of the

The Story

Flipper

When Krist Novoselic joined Flipper in 2006, it closed a circle of influence that had begun when he first discovered the band in the early 1980s. He and Cobain were introduced to the punk band by the Melvins' Buzz Osborne, Novoselic later recalling being particularly taken with their full-length debut *Generic Flipper* (also known as *Album*), though he admitted it took him a few listens before having what he later described in his column for the *Seattle Weekly* as an "epiphany". "The music drew me into a universe where bleak was beautiful," he wrote. "Mainstream convention was shattered. Flipper were too weird and dangerous for the world. And if the world didn't get it, that was just another loss for humanity."

Flipper was founded by Ricky Williams (vocalist), Ted Falconi (guitar), Will Shatter (bass, vocals) and Steve DePace (drums) in San Francisco in 1979; Williams was soon replaced by Bruce Lose, who would share bass duties with Shatter. More dissonant drone than punk thrash, their definitive work is considered to be 1982's *Generic Flipper*, which features the classic "Sex Bomb", a surprisingly lengthy number considering the entire lyric consists of a mere seven words. While some songs evince a bleak world view ("Life Is Cheap", "Way of the World"), others display a sarcastic sense of humour, and even, in "Life", a positive message of hope amidst the caterwauling sound. *Generic Flipper* was

followed by *Gone Fishin'* in 1984, and the group also released two live albums during this period, *Blow'n Chunks* (1984) and *Public Flipper Ltd. Live 1980–1985* (1986), the latter title a swipe at Public Image Ltd., whom the group believed had appropriated their title and cover design for P.i.L.'s own 1986 release called *Album*.

The band broke up when Shatter died in December 1987 of a drug overdose, but reformed in 1990 with John Dougherty on bass, signing to Def American and releasing the album *American Grafishy* in 1993 (Lose changing his last name to "Loose" as it was "less negative"). Then Dougherty died of a drug overdose in 1995, and the band went on hiatus again, making only the occasional appearance on compilations.

In 2005, they were asked to play some benefit shows for legendary New York club CBGB's, bringing in Bruno DeSmartass on bass. But DeSmartass left after a year, meaning the group was once again in need of a bass player when contacted by Sonic Youth's Thurston Moore, who was curating one of that year's All Tomorrow's Parties events in the UK. DePace mentioned to Moore they'd be interested in working with Novoselic; Moore duly called Novoselic, who quickly accepted the offer.

Wth Novoselic on board, the newly revitalized Flipper played a few warm-up shows in the US, before heading to the UK in December 2006 to play at All Tomorrow's Parties and join the Melvins for a short tour. Energized by the experience, they began to work on new material, and recorded an album in the summer of

KAOS show secured them some gigs at the Community World Theater in **Tacoma**, a city midway between Olympia and Seattle. The audiences were small but receptive, according to

Burckhard. "But Kurt was always the type not to gloat about it," he adds. "He had this attitude like, 'Yeah, it was a good show, let's show up for practice tomorrow'."

Krist Novoselic performing as part of a reformed Flipper in 2008.

2007, with Jack Endino producing. The band continued to play live shows, and celebrated the release of the *Flipper Live* DVD, a collection of shows from 1980 and 1981, by playing an in-store gig at Amoeba Records in San Francisco on 18 February 2008. Novoselic's tenure in the group was short-lived, however; in September 2008, it was announced he was leaving the band due to "Responsibilities at home [that] will prevent him from being able to take the time necessary to get out on the road to promote our upcoming releases." The release of the Endino-produced Flipper album was pending at the time of writing.

Cobain moved to Olympia in the spring, moving in with his new girlfriend, Tracy Marander, while Novoselic and his girlfriend relocated to Tacoma. Burckhard was still in living in Aberdeen, and with everyone so spread out, the band went on hiatus. When Cobain and Novoselic decided to revive the group, it was without Burckhard, who by his own admission

The Story

wasn't as dedicated to practice. In October 1987, the two ran a "Musicians Wanted" ad in Seattle's music paper, *The Rocket*: "SERIOUS DRUMMER WANTED. Underground attitude, Black Flag, Melvins, Zeppelin, Scratch Acid, Ethel Merman. Versatile as heck." The ad brought no results, so they worked again with Dale Crover on a temporary basis until a permanent drummer could be found.

The Dale Demo

Cobain had been studying the studio ads in *The Rocket*, and set up a demo session with **Reciprocal Recording** in Seattle. Reciprocal was already becoming the studio of choice for a slowly burgeoning Seattle music scene: in 1987 both Green River's *Dry As A Bone* and Soundgarden's *Screaming Life* EPs had been recorded at the studio for Seattle-based Sub Pop Records. Both records were produced by the same person, **Jack Endino**, who also played guitar in the band Skin Yard.

Though Cobain said he chose Reciprocal because it was the cheapest he could find, Crover recalled that Cobain had wanted to record there because he'd liked the *Screaming Life* record. It was Endino that took Cobain's call to the studio. Cobain introduced himself as a friend of the Melvins, explained that he wanted to make a demo "really fast", and added that Crover would be on drums; as Endino thought highly of the Melvins himself, that was all the recommendation he needed. Cobain had given no name for his band, and Endino misspelled his name as "Kurt Kovain"

in his calendar. Due to Crover's involvement, the tape from this session has come to be known as the "**Dale Demo**".

The band duly arrived at Reciprocal around noon on 23 January 1988, and quickly got to work, recording and mixing ten songs in six hours. The songs, in order, were "If You Must", "Downer", "Floyd The Barber", "Paper Cuts", "Spank Thru", "Hairspray Queen", "Aero Zeppelin", "Beeswax", "Mexican Seafood" and "Pen Cap Chew", all of which the band had been playing steadily over the last year. As a demo, it was substantially better than the KAOS radio session the previous April, largely because Crover was on drums – the band's music required a hard-hitting drummer to fully come across. Indeed, "Floyd The Barber" and "Paper Cuts" would be pulled from the demo for the *Bleach* album, with "Downer" later surfacing as an extra track on the *Bleach* CD.

The songs were recorded live with Cobain overdubbing his vocal; the last song recorded, "Pen Cap Chew", was given a fade-out ending as the tape had run out, and the band didn't want to spring for the cost of another reel. The development of the band's, and particularly Cobain's, skills in performance and arranging is easy to trace by comparing the versions of "Downer" recorded for the Fecal Matter demo (also with Crover on drums), the KAOS performance and the Dale Demo. On Fecal Matter, the vocals alternate between a lazy mutter and low-grade yowling, and overall the tempo drags. There's a noticeable improvement on all fronts by the time of the KAOS performance, but the song really comes to life on the Dale Demo, with more confident vocals and the tempo bumped up to the point that this version of the song is only half as long as the original. All those hours of practice Cobain had put the band through were paying off.

The band had to leave by 6pm in order to get to Tacoma for a show that night at the Community World Theater. Endino only charged them for five hours work plus the cost of the tape, the final bill being $152.44. Having made a quick mix of the demo for the band to take with them, Endino asked if he could hold on to the master to make a further mix for himself. The band agreed, little suspecting the repercussions this request would have on their career. The next day, they filmed some primitive videos of themselves miming to songs from the demo at Aberdeen's RadioShack, brief clips of which were later broadcast on the TV programme *American Journal* after Cobain's death (with Eric Harder, the man who'd taped the band, shown handing over a copy to Courtney Love). Though admittedly amateurish (one of the "special effects" was created by blowing cigarette smoke across the camera lens), the videos show Cobain throwing himself around the shop with gusto, leaping in the air and dropping to his knees.

Jack Endino (left) produced Nirvana's first recording session, the "Dale Demo", in January 1988 – and wrote the foreword to this book.

Deep Six: The record that launched grunge

In late 1984, a handmade poster reading "Seattle Scene Found Dead" began appearing on telephone poles in the city. And it almost seemed like it was true. None of the bands from Seattle's punk/new wave scene of the early 1980s managed to make waves outside the city, though a few would go on to bigger things (Duff McKagan of The Fastbacks, 10 Minute Warning and The Fartz later joined Guns N' Roses; Paul Barker and Bill Rieflin of The Blackouts later joined Ministry). *The Rocket* struck a similar note about the paucity of Seattle's music scene in its January 1985 issue, featuring the usual top ten listings for the previous year; for "Best Venue", the magazine listed "Your living room".

But there were already a crop of new bands percolating in the city's underground, often playing in spaces that weren't much bigger than a living room. Chris Hanzsek, a record producer and engineer who'd moved to Seattle from Boston, had been

producing local acts like Green River and The Accused. In 1985, he and his girlfriend, Tina Casale, decided to start a record label, which they called C/Z Records. The label's first release was a compilation spotlighting various local bands: *Deep Six*.

What the record did, albeit inadvertently, was to capture the roots of the scene that would later be dubbed "grunge". Of the six bands featured on the album, only Green River and The U-Men had released records before. The U-Men were the album's biggest name: they'd been together for three years and were widely regarded as one of the top alternative acts in the city; but they were also stylistically quite different from the other *Deep Six* bands, with the rockabilly swing of their track "They" reminiscent of groups like The Cramps.

This stood in contrast to the rest of the album, which emphasized fuzzy guitars and vocals put through various forms of distortion. Indeed, it's

Soon after recording the Dale Demo, Crover departed for San Francisco, where Osborne had decided to relocate the Melvins. The band duly placed another ad in *The Rocket*: "DRUMMER WANTED: Play hard, sometimes light, underground, versatile, fast, medium, slow, versatile, serious, heavy, versatile, dorky, nirvana, hungry." There were still no takers, but Crover had previously recommended a drummer called **Dave Foster**, another Aberdonian, and Cobain and Novoselic decided to take him on. Foster

played his first show with the band the same month the *Rocket* ad ran, at a house party in Olympia. The ad had hinted at the band's new name, which they used for the first time on a Cobain-designed poster for a 19 March show at the Community World Theater: Nirvana. In an effort to clarify just who they were, Cobain had added the helpful subtitle "Also Known As: Skid Row, Ted Ed Fred, Pen Cap Chew, Bliss". He had chosen the name in part because he liked the Buddhist definition of the concept the vocal performances that are the primary distinguishing characteristic of each group: the Melvins are the most recognizably "grunge", both the heaviest and most intimidating; Green River its usual bawling bratty self; Malfunkshun's metal-lite is saved by an appealing mix of braggadocio and parody; Soundgarden and Skin Yard are the most conventional in this context, Soundgarden's Chris Cornell already staking his claim as one of Seattle's most powerful hard rock vocalists, and Skin Yard's edginess striking a disquieting note.

The album was released in mid-1986 to massive indifference (aside from a few positive local reviews); though only a few thousand copies were pressed, it took nearly three years to sell most of them. But it was the first hint of things to come as most of the acts went on to then unimaginable success. The sole exception was the unfortunate U-Men, destined to never receive their due; they would split up before the decade was over. Soundgarden became the first band of the grunge era to sign to a major label. The Melvins have persevered against all odds and continue to tour and

record today. Green River split into two factions, Mark Arm and Steve Turner forming Mudhoney (who also still tour and record), and Jeff Ament, Stone Gossard and Bruce Fairweather forming Mother Love Bone with Andrew Wood from Malfunkshun. Mother Love Bone were on the verge of releasing their major label debut in 1990 when Wood died of a drug overdose; Ament and Gossard went on to form Pearl Jam. A reunited Green River played two shows in July 2008 as part of Sub Pop's twentieth anniversary celebrations.

Skin Yard never made it to the majors. But guitarist Jack Endino would go on to work with all the major grunge acts of the era as the producer of choice for Sub Pop. And after releasing a Melvins EP, Hanszek and Casale broke up and handed the label over to Skin Yard's bassist, Daniel House. The label's last release was a Skin Yard compilation in 2002.

Deep Six was reissued on CD in 1994, jointly released by C/Z and A&M, with different cover artwork. Both the vinyl album (designed by Reyza Sageb, see opposite) and CD are now out of print – and highly sought after collector's items.

(which he explained to *Flipside* as "Freedom from pain and suffering in the external world"), and in part because he liked the incongruity of giving a gnarly rock band a mellow name.

Sub Pop comes calling

With a final name now in place, Cobain set about looking for ways to boost the band's

profile, dubbing copies of the Dale Demo and sending them off to record labels and anyone else who might be interested (a major reason why the demo has been bootlegged so extensively). Among the labels to receive copies were Touch and Go (Cobain offered to pay recording and production costs for their own record), Alternative Tentacles, and SST (whose co-owner, Black Flag guitarist Greg Ginn, wrote it off as "not that original. It wasn't bad, but it wasn't great either").

"World Domination": the story of Sub Pop

The Sub Pop record label started life as a fanzine in 1979 when Bruce Pavitt (originally from Park Forest, a suburb of Chicago), then a student at Evergreen State College in Olympia, put out around two hundred copies of a zine he called *Subterranean Pop*. The zine covered alternative American music, and by issue three the name had been shortened to the punchier *Sub Pop*. Issues five, seven and nine were cassette zines, largely featuring acts from the Pacific Northwest.

On graduating from Evergreen, Pavitt relocated to Seattle in 1983, working at a record store before taking a job at Yesco (later acquired by Muzak), a company that produced bland background music tapes for use in shopping malls and other businesses. His last zine came out in the same year, but he kept the Sub Pop name alive by using it as the title for both a show on the University of Washington's radio station KCMU and a column in *The Rocket*.

He was also interested in making Sub Pop a proper record label focusing on the music of the region. "I wanted it to be a Northwest record label the same as Motown was a Detroit label," he says. "I wanted to establish an identity." Still, when *Sub Pop 100* was released in 1986, most of the acts featured on the record weren't based in the Northwest, though Sonic Youth, Scratch Acid and Naked Raygun were probably more of a draw than any local bands at the time.

Pavitt next planned to release an EP by Green River (funded by a loan from his family), and was also interested in securing Soundgarden for the label, but simply didn't have enough money. It was then that Soundgarden's guitarist Kim Thayil suggested Pavitt team up with a mutual acquaintance, Jonathan Poneman. Poneman had moved to Seattle from Toledo, Ohio, and had briefly played guitar in a band called The Treeclimbers. But he soon realized his skills were more suited to off-stage work, hosting his own radio show on KCMU (eventually becoming the station's programme manager), and booking local shows. He was also a fan of Soundgarden, and, best of all, had cash he was willing to invest in a start-up label. Green River's *Dry As a Bone* EP and Soundgarden's "Hunted Down"/"Nothing To Say" single duly appeared in June 1987, and Sub Pop was on its way.

In addition to having a good instinct about which local bands were worth signing, Pavitt and Poneman understood the value of hype in promoting what was in reality a minuscule scene at the time. To help foster a sense of community, Sub Pop's records had a uniform look and sound, and were mostly recorded at Reciprocal Recording with Jack Endino in the producer's chair. The label specialized in EPs to take full advantage of the graphic possibilities of a 12-inch cover, while the record's wider grooves would make the music sound better. Photographs, primarily shot by Charles Peterson, were in black and white, which made them easier for fanzines to reproduce. The records were also released on coloured

Cobain didn't think to send a copy to **Sub Pop Records**, as the label was just getting off the ground, but someone else did. Jack Endino had been impressed by the band. "I just liked the songs," he says. "I liked the band; I thought they were really good. Good drumming, good ideas, great screaming, you know? Excellent screams." He gave a copy vinyl and in limited editions to enhance their desirability, a strategy that reached its apex with the "Sub Pop Singles Club", a subscription for a year's worth of singles only available to club members. In a typical example of extravagance, the 1988 compilation *Sub Pop 200* was issued as a three-EP box set, even though the songs would have fit on two albums, because it made a bigger splash.

In promoting the label, Pavitt and Poneman made hyperbole into an art form. The booklet in *Sub Pop 200* featured a picture of an impressive multistorey building billed as "Sub Pop World Headquarters", though the label only occupied a few offices in the building. The Sub Pop Singles Club was promoted with the slogan "We're ripping you off big time". And if the label wasn't boasting about its plans for "World Domination", it was sending up its own pretensions by producing T-shirts that proudly read "LOSER" on the front, with the label's logo on the back (a parody version of this shirt was also produced, reading "SUGAR" on the front, with the label's logo reconfigured to read "Soda Pop", and the tagline "Super Sugar Big Buzz", a play on the title of Mudhoney's EP *Super Fuzz Big Muff*). "Bruce and I were obviously indulging in what was to become the national pastime in the 90s – irony," says Poneman.

But by 1991, the label was in serious financial trouble. Soundgarden had long since left, and the label's other moneymakers, Mudhoney and Nirvana, were on the verge of doing so. Meanwhile, negotiations with CBS over a proposed distribution deal (which ultimately fell through) had run up a hefty legal bill. Owing money to everyone, the label responded in typical style, producing T-shirts that read "Sub Plop" on the front (taken from a headline about the label's troubles in *The Rocket*) and "What part of 'We have no money' don't you understand?" on the back.

Sub Pop was saved when Mudhoney loyally agreed to give the label one more album, 1991's *Every Good Boy Deserves Fudge*. And when Nirvana's *Nevermind* took off, Sub Pop was doubly rewarded, as it received two percent of the album's sales thanks to a clause in the buy-out contract with DGC, and sales of *Bleach* also soared, eventually making it the label's first platinum album. "On one level it didn't surprise me when the bands became popular, because as a fan I thought they should be popular," Poneman says. "But on the other hand, in the real world stuff like that rarely seemed to happen. And so that it actually happened, with our friends, in our own community, right before our eyes, seemed miraculous."

In 1995, Warner Bros bought a 49 percent share in the company; in 1997, Pavitt resigned. But Poneman has kept the label going through sheer tenaciousness, and Sub Pop has recently enjoyed successes with Modest Mouse, The Postal Service and The Shins, whose 2007 album *Wincing the Night Away* debuted on the Billboard charts at number two, the highest chart position achieved by both the band and the Sub Pop label to date.

to his then-girlfriend, **Dawn Anderson,** who was the editor of a new Seattle music monthly, *Backlash*; she would soon write the first article published on Nirvana. He gave another copy to Shirley Carlson, a DJ at KCMU, the University of Washington's radio station. And he gave a third copy to **Jonathan Poneman** at Sub Pop.

Poneman was also impressed by the demo, particularly Cobain's vocals. The demo's first song, "If You Must", begins with a mid-tempo series of drumbeats, followed by quiet bass and guitar lines. It was what happened next that floored Poneman. "Kurt's doing this slurring, quiet vocal over this dark, dissonant guitar", he told journalist Carrie Borzillo-Vrenna. "And then suddenly, he goes into his classic roar into this chorus. The first time I heard that I just went 'Ohhhhh my God'." He immediately contacted **Bruce Pavitt**, telling him, "You have got to listen to this tape!" Ironically, "If You Must" was a song Cobain always professed to dislike (at one point referring to it as "sickening and dumb"), and Nirvana would drop it from their set list by the end of the year.

Pavitt was not as instantly won over as his partner, but agreed to consider them, and so some Seattle shows were arranged. "It seems like you could play Tacoma and Olympia, but until you played Seattle you didn't make that crucial step up to the big city," says Novoselic. But Nirvana would get off to a shaky start in the "big city". There is some uncertainty as to when their first Seattle show took place. It was long thought to be on 24 April 1988, at a club called The Vogue, but Pavitt and Poneman told journalist Everett True the band had played an earlier show at the **Central Tavern**. The show only drew a handful of people, including Pavitt and Poneman, but it was enough to make Cobain nervous; he threw up before the show. Pavitt still wasn't overwhelmed, though he did choose "Love Buzz" as the band's strongest song. The label then added Nirvana to The Vogue's "Sub Pop Sunday" bill on 24 April, a show that drew around twenty people (with Cobain again vomiting beforehand). His unease was evident to the audience, and Dawn Anderson later wrote that Cobain was so nervous "he was shaking in his flannels". Photographer **Charles Peterson** was so unimpressed he didn't bother taking any pictures. "I thought they were atrocious," he recalls. "I just thought, 'This is a joke. This is not going to go anywhere'." Ironically, Peterson's later photos of the band would appear on almost every Nirvana release.

Cobain was well aware the performance was not up to standard, and equally aware of the audience's scrutiny. "We felt like we were being judged," he told Anderson a few months later. "It was like everyone should've had scorecards." Undeterred, Poneman met with Cobain and Novoselic at Seattle's Café Roma, and agreed that Sub Pop would put out a single of "Love Buzz". The two would have preferred one of their own songs as the single's A-side, but the desire to have a record released at all won out.

Another new drummer

Tellingly, Dave Foster was not at the meeting with Poneman: his days with the group were numbered. Cobain was already uncomfortable with the drummer's appearance, which was far too conventional for the alternative crowd he was now hanging out with in Olympia. Confrontation wasn't Cobain's style, but Foster inadvertently engineered his own exit, engaging

Another drummer: Chad Channing played with Nirvana from 1988 to 1990 and is pictured here at an April 1990 show in Boston.

in a brawl with a young man who turned out to be the son of the mayor of Cosmopolis, another of Aberdeen's neighbouring towns. After serving a two-week jail term, he lost his driver's licence and was unable to attend practice sessions. Cobain and Novoselic then got back in touch with Aaron Burckhard, who starting rehearsing with them again. One night after practice, Burckhard borrowed Cobain's car to get more beer. But he stopped off at a tavern on the way back, and ended up getting arrested for drunk driving, with Cobain's car being impounded. That got him booted from the band for good.

Cobain and Novoselic took out yet another *Rocket* ad ("Heavy, light punk rock band: Aerosmith, Led Zeppelin, Black Sabbath, Black Flag, Scratch Acid, Butthole Surfers. Seeks drummer"), even though they already had their eye on someone else. They had met drummer **Chad Channing** when Nirvana shared the bill with Channing's previous band Tick-Dolly-Row at the Community World Theater, and had been especially impressed by his large North drum kit, which featured drums with unique flared shells. After a show at Evergreen, when Foster was still in the band, Cobain

The Story

and Novoselic asked Channing if he'd like to jam with them. Channing agreed, and after a few practice sessions realized he was now a member of Nirvana, though neither Cobain or Novoselic explicitly told him "You're in".

Channing was born 31 January 1967 in Santa Rosa, California; his father's work as a DJ meant the family moved frequently throughout Channing's childhood. He'd started to play drums while recovering from an accident that had shattered his thigh bone when he was thirteen, and joined his first band in 1982. He then went on to play in Mind Circus, which he described as "very Melvins-ish" (Ben Shepherd, later in Soundgarden, played guitar for the group), and the speed metal band Stone Crow. Channing had been impressed by the Nirvana shows he'd seen, and already had the sense this band might have a future. "The only feeling I had when I first started getting involved with them, was that the band was going to go somewhere," he told Everett True, though adding, "Exactly how far, I wasn't sure."

Recording "Love Buzz"

Nirvana had little time to break in their new drummer; barely a month after he'd joined, the band headed back into Reciprocal on 11 June for their first proper recording session. Though only scheduled to record a single, they worked on a lot of new material, some of which would be re-recorded for *Bleach*. At the first session, the band laid down "Blandest", then being considered for the B-side, first takes of "Love Buzz" and "Big Cheese" (also under consideration as a B-side), and early versions of three new songs, "Mr Moustache" and "Blew", neither of which had final lyrics, and "Sifting", which was entirely instrumental.

If cassette copies of the sessions had not been made, some of the takes would have been lost for good, as new tracks were simply recorded over previous takes the band didn't like, so that they wouldn't have to buy a new reel of tape. "We did that routinely. I fitted new tracks over unwanted old takes right in the middle of the reels if necessary," Endino says. Thus, when the band returned to the studio on 30 June, a re-recording of "Spank Thru" (with Endino on backing vocals) was recorded over "Blandest", and a second take of "Big Cheese" was recorded over the first take of "Love Buzz". The band also recorded a new version of "Floyd The Barber" and two more takes of "Love Buzz", one an instrumental.

The second take of "Love Buzz" was chosen for the single, and the second take of "Big Cheese" was selected as the B-side over "Blandest" at Endino's suggestion, as he felt it was a stronger song. Poneman also asked that Cobain's vocal for "Love Buzz" be re-recorded. Overdubs and mixing were done in a three-hour session on 16 July.

Cobain later called "Love Buzz" "the wimpiest recording we've ever done", though it's actually an appealing number, which settles into a hypnotic groove almost immediately, demonstrating that despite their allegiance to punk and hard rock, the band's pop sensibilities would never be buried completely. The 7-inch has a different mix from the version that appeared on *Bleach*, including a sound collage Cobain had put together during the song's instrumental break. Cobain also devised a sound collage for the song's intro, which he'd originally wanted to run for 45 seconds, but which was trimmed back to 10 seconds. "Big Cheese" emphasized the darker, heavier side to the band, though it was livelier than the sinister "Blandest".

The band's first **photo session**, for the single's cover, was shot by Alice Wheeler, another Evergreen student who was friends with Bruce Pavitt and Tracy Marander. It took place at Never Never Land, a park near the Tacoma Narrows Bridge, so named for its statues of fairytale characters. Cobain was the most prominent in both shots, standing in front of Novoselic and Channing on the front cover (see opposite), and pictured alone underneath the bridge on the back, a clear, if inadvertent, indication of his dominant role in the band. Wheeler shot on infra-red film, giving the pictures a fuzzy, soft look, and lending the band members a boyish appeal at odds with the music's hard edge. The single also featured the first of several variations on the way Cobain spelled his name, crediting him as "Kurdt Kobain".

The band had hoped the single would be issued right away, and were somewhat annoyed when Pavitt telephoned Cobain and asked for a loan to enable its release. They were further dismayed when informed that the single would be the first in a new subscription-only series Sub Pop was launching later in the year, the **Sub Pop Singles Club** (though the single was also briefly available through mail order and in a few Seattle shops). With no further recording dates set, Cobain continued sending out tapes, now including the new single, to prospective labels and other interested parties. One version of the tape, labelled *Kurdt's Kassette*, featured "Floyd The Barber", "Spank Thru", "Hairspray Queen", "Mexican Seafood", "Beeswax", "Beans" (a short jokey number with a distorted vocal), "Paper Cuts" and a sound collage on side one, and "Big Cheese", "Love Buzz", "Aero Zeppelin", "Pen Cap Chew" and another sound collage called "Montage of Heck" on side two. With a few exceptions, like the heavy "Paper Cuts", the tape highlighted the more melodic side of the band.

Better than the Melvins

But even before the single's release the band was beginning to develop a live following and was now playing shows on a more regular basis. On 23 July, they opened for their first out of town act, Leaving Trains, at the Central (coincidentally, the Trains' lead singer, "Falling" James Moreland, would marry, and soon divorce, aspiring actress and rock musician Courtney Love the following year; and one of the show's co-promoters, Nikolas Hartshorne, then a medical student, would conduct Cobain's autopsy). In August, the **first article** on the band, written by **Dawn Anderson**, would

appear in her magazine *Backlash*. Anderson started the article in jocular fashion: "Ah, Aberdeen – a town where there's nothing to do but drink fish-beer and worship Satan" (a reference to Schmidt Beer, whose cans had pictures of different animals). But the most famous line in the article, considered a daring statement at the time, was "The group's already way ahead of most mortals in the songwriting department and, at the risk of sounding blasphemous, I honestly believe that with enough practice, Nirvana could become... *better than the Melvins!*" (emphasis Anderson's).

Sub Pop soon decided to put out another track from the recording session, adding "Spank Thru" to their various artists compilation, *Sub Pop 200*, set for release at the end of the year. This version was lighter, having more of a pop swing than the Dale Demo version, though Cobain still worked in some nice screams going into the chorus. On 28 October, the band played their biggest show to date, opening for the Butthole Surfers at Union Station (a former train station) in Seattle, a point of pride for the band, and especially Cobain, since the Butthole Surfers were on Touch and Go Records, the label he had most wanted to be on. Two days later they played a show at **Evergreen's K Dorm**, which has famously gone down as the first show where Cobain smashed a guitar, though both Channing and Slim Moon (Cobain's neighbour, a musician and future founder of the Kill Rock Stars label) recall him "trashing" an instrument at earlier shows. But on this occasion he completely destroyed it, sending fragments flying around the room that the audience quickly snatched up.

The year would end on a high note for the band. "Love Buzz" was released in November, and gained positive notices as far away as England, where Everett True made it Single of the Week in *Melody Maker*. *Sub Pop 200* followed in December, with BBC Radio 1 DJ John Peel writing in *The Observer*, "It is going to take something special to stop *Sub Pop 200* being the set of recordings by which all others are judged". By the time Nirvana performed at the *Sub Pop 200* record release party on 28 December, they'd also taken another big step in their career: they'd begun to record their debut album.

From Aberdeen to the world

1988–89

From Aberdeen to the world
1988–89

December 1988 was the busiest month so far for Nirvana, and indicated how far they'd come in the space of a year; they were now regularly playing shows at venues from Olympia to Seattle, they'd solved their revolving drummer problems (at least for the moment), and they'd released their first single. Now they were ready to build on those accomplishments.

Recording Bleach

Sessions for *Bleach* began on 24 December at Reciprocal. Apart from the lyrics, the songs were fairly well worked out, due to the band's intensive practising ("We would practise from eight in the evening till six in the morning, and we did that every single night," Channing remembers). The band had been listening to Celtic Frost and, aiming to achieve a similar heaviness, re-recorded "Mr Moustache" and two new songs, "Scoff" and "Sifting", in what they thought was the key of D. But afterwards they realized they had tuned down to C, and unfortunately for future historians and collectors, decided to record new versions of the songs in D over their initial attempts. They again tackled a track from the Dale Demo, "Hairspray Queen", but decided the re-recording wasn't as good as the original. "Basically, whenever they tried to do

something that used to be a Dale song, it just didn't sound that good," says Endino.

Musically, the songs had so far not been too dissimilar to those Nirvana had previously recorded. But lyrically, Cobain was paring himself down, in stark contrast to the stream-of-consciousness lyrics of songs like "Downer". This was partly due to his admitted lack of interest in spending much time on them ("When I write a song the lyrics are the least important subject", he would tell journalist Ian Tilton in July 1989), and lyrics for the new songs on *Bleach* were sometimes hastily scrawled out on the way to the studio. But neither did Cobain need many words to convey the feelings of suffocation, frustration and rage that ran through the album.

But with the next song they recorded, "**About A Girl**", Nirvana stepped outside familiar territory. Despite its bitter lyric, melodically "About A Girl" was an unabashed pop song, and Cobain worried about how well it would sit alongside the hard thrashing rock he presumed was Sub Pop's primary interest. "I remember he warned me, 'Okay, some people aren't going to like this song,'" Endino recalls. "'But I want to do this anyway. This is a direction I want to do more songs like.' And it came out fine." The song would quickly come to be seen as a highlight of the album, and would remain in the band's set list through to their very last show, long after most of the songs on *Bleach* had fallen by the wayside.

"Blew", "Swap Meet", "Negative Creep", "School" and "Big Long Now" were more in keeping with the band's usual style. Endino was particularly impressed by the vocal on the last song, but Cobain decided to drop it from the album, telling Endino, "We have enough slow heavy songs". Recording was completed in six sessions and wrapped up on 24 January 1989. "Love Buzz" was remixed for the US version of the album, minus its sound collage intro, while "Big Cheese" was used on the UK version. Two songs from the Dale Demo, "Floyd The Barber" and "Paper Cuts", were remixed for the album (with background vocals added to the latter song), with "Downer", also from the Dale Demo, added to the *Bleach* CD.

In between recording, the band played a few shows. On 1 December, they opened for Canadian punkers **D.O.A.** at Seattle club The Underground, sharing the bill with Coffin Break. On 21 December, they played the closest thing to a hometown show they'd ever do, performing at the Eagles Hall in Hoquiam (which saw

Novoselic stripping down to his underwear). And they returned to The Underground on 28 December for the first party celebrating the release of *Sub Pop 200*. **Jesse Bernstein**, a gravelly voiced poet who also appeared on the record, was the master of ceremonies. "Don't say MC," he corrected an audience member, "I'm not that hip." He then introduced the band with

Bleach was recorded on this 8-track tape machine in six sessions at Reciprocal Recording, from December 1988 to January 1989.

The Story

a flourish – "Freeze-dried music – Nir-VANA!" – after which the group obligingly tore into "School". Most of the set consisted of songs that would appear on *Bleach*, though in the case of "Mr Moustache" the lyrics weren't finalized. And with new songs to perform, songs from the Dale Demo like "Mexican Seafood" and "Hairspray Queen" would soon be dropped from the band's set list.

In January 1989, Nirvana signed their first **recording contract**. During a late-night party with Minneapolis band Babes in Toyland, Novoselic had gone next door to Bruce Pavitt's, and pounded on his window, shouting, "You fuckers, we want a contract!" He ran into Pavitt returning from visiting the Babes himself, and a contract was quickly drafted by Jonathan Poneman. The contract called for three albums, offering the band advances of $6000 for the first, $12,000 for the second and $24,000 for the third. It was the first extended contract Sub Pop had with a band – and would have unimagined consequences later on.

The band also played their first out of state shows in January (two gigs at the club Satyricon in Portland, Oregon), then went on a short tour of California in February. While in San Francisco, where the AIDS crisis was particularly devastating, they saw numerous public awareness signs reading "Bleach Your Works" posted around the city, urging IV drug users to clean their needles with bleach to help staunch the spread of the disease. Mulling the phrase over, the band decided to call the album *Bleach* (having originally considered the decidedly more misanthropic "Too Many Humans").

The tour also marked the debut of a second guitarist, **Jason Everman**, a friend who'd generously paid the recording costs for *Bleach* and was credited on the cover, though he didn't play on the album (Cobain would again be credited as "Kurdt Kobain").

Sub Pop: Rock City

Meanwhile, Sub Pop, always searching for ways to boost the label's profile, asked their UK

publicist, Anton Brookes, to find a journalist to send over and write up the label in one of the influential British music weeklies. Writer Everett True and photographer Andy Catlin from **Melody Maker** were duly dispatched to the city. Although True had given the "Love Buzz" single a good review, and would go on to be one of the band's biggest champions, he was unimpressed by his first Nirvana show, a 25 February date at the HUB (Husky Union Building) Ballroom on the campus of the University of Washington.

Nonetheless, the first two articles spawned by his visit, a two-page spread on Mudhoney in *Melody Maker*'s 11 March issue, and a two-page spread on Sub Pop's other acts ("Sub Pop: Rock City") the following week, gave the label the major coverage they'd hoped for. True later revealed that the section in his article describing Nirvana hadn't been written by him at all; he'd simply taken a quote from Jonathan Poneman, who'd eschewed Sub Pop's penchant for hype by describing the group simply as "four guys in their early twenties from rural Washington who want to rock", and attributed it to himself.

A picture Tracy Marander took at a 1 April show at Olympia's Reko/Muse Gallery provided the **cover art** for *Bleach*, a reverse-negative with Cobain in mid-headbang, with the band's name above the picture, the album title below. As Grohl later noted, it conveyed a somewhat one-dimensional image of "big burly unshaven logger, drinking guys... almost like a metal band." Future album covers would reflect Cobain's sensibilities to a much greater degree. Ironically, given his interest in art and design,

One of Seattle's oldest theatres, the Moore played host to Sub Pop's "Lame Fest" featuring Tad, Mudhoney and Nirvana in June 1989.

Cobain had no say in the design of Nirvana's logo, which made its first appearance on the *Bleach* cover. The album's cover was designed by Lisa Orth, who worked at *The Rocket* and used it as a base for her freelance work. In the rush to finish the cover, she told *The Rocket*'s typesetter (Grant Alden, who was also the magazine's managing editor) to use whatever typeface was currently set up in his machine. It happened to be Onyx.

Bleach was released that June, and in a line that was often quoted due to its prescience, Sub Pop's catalogue boasted, "Hypnotic and righteous heaviness from these Olympia pop stars. They're young, they own their own van, and they're going to make us rich!" Though not officially announced as such, Nirvana's appearance at Sub Pop's first "Lame Fest" show ("Seattle's lamest bands in a one-night orgy of sweat and insanity!"), on 9 June at The Moore Theatre, served as a de facto record release party. Built in 1907, the Moore was one of Seattle's oldest theatres, a former vaudeville house and

The Story

Grunge

In *Hype!*, Doug Pray's documentary of the Seattle music scene, Leighton Beezer, a member of such Northwest outfits as The Thrown-Ups, Blunt Objects and Stomach Pump, gives a concise definition of grunge in just eighteen seconds. He first plays a trademark Ramones riff on his guitar, in the upbeat chugging style of Chuck Berry. "That's punk rock," he explains. "And one day they just sort of started going, um..." he continues, playing a riff from Green River's "Come On Down", with a similar rhythm but a noticeably minor key sound. "And that's grunge!" he concludes. It's an excellent demonstration of the genre that will now forever be associated with the "Seattle Sound" – though not all grunge bands hailed from Seattle, any more than all Seattle bands played grunge.

Initially, the term "grunge" was used to describe dirt or filth, as in saying how "grungy" something was. Indeed, when the word was used by rock journalists like Lester Bangs in the 1970s, it referred to a raw, gritty quality in a band's sound. Mark Arm is believed to be the first to use the term in reference to a Seattle band, in a satirical letter he sent to short-lived Seattle music paper *Desperate Times* in 1981, when they solicited their readers to nominate the most overrated band in Seattle: "I hate Mr Epp and the Calculations! Pure grunge! Pure noise! Pure shit!" The joke was that Arm was in Mr. Epp, but he signed the letter using his real name, Mark McLaughlin. The term was soon picked up by Sub Pop's co-founder Bruce Pavitt, who used it freely in promoting the label: Green River's *Dry As A Bone* EP was called "ultra-loose GRUNGE that destroyed the morals of a generation", while Mudhoney were described as "ultra sludge, grungy glacial, heavy special, dirty punk" (perhaps not coincidentally, both bands also featured Mark Arm).

Gradually, "grunge" passed from being a term used to describe an element of the music to describing the music itself, thereby inventing a new genre. Journalists previously had used a string of terms to describe the nascent Seattle bands – "thrash-noise-metal" – since no one word seemed to fully embody the sound of a music that encompassed different genres. The one thing all grunge bands did have in common was a wide range of influences. The Melvins started out playing Jimi Hendrix and The Who covers. Mudhoney covered Sonic Youth. And Kurt Cobain, describing Nirvana's music in an early band bio, wrote that the group sounded like "Black Sabbath playing The Knack, Black Flag, Led Zeppelin and the Stooges, with a pinch of Bay City Rollers" – almost exactly the same influences he cited in the record company bio that accompanied the release of *Nevermind*. For a music that drew on such a variety of styles, an all-purpose, all-encompassing tag like "grunge" fit the bill nicely.

The grunge aesthetic was also rooted in egalitarianism. Bands tended to not stand on ceremony, even after they'd become successful; there were no massive stage sets or special visual effects, no extended guitar or drum solos, no rock star pretensions, on or offstage. And though often seen as a music mired in despair and alienation, grunge had a decidedly sarcastic bent, as expressed in songs like Mudhoney's "Touch Me, I'm Sick", Soundgarden's "Big Dumb Sex" and Nirvana's "Lithium". Shows were also celebratory events that, at least in the beginning, made little distinction between audience and performer. At early shows, a good percentage of the club audience was made up of performers from other bands anyway; perhaps that's why gigs often ended with half of the audience also on the stage (if there was one), with moshing and crowd-surfing other accepted means of participation.

Throughout the 1980s and into the early 90s, grunge was allowed to develop in relative isolation.

Then in late 1991, Nirvana's *Nevermind* blew the lid off the whole scene. In the wake of Nirvana's success, other Northwest records soon followed them up the charts, including Pearl Jam's *Ten*, Soundgarden's *Badmotorfinger* and Alice In Chains' *Dirt*. Grunge had officially gone mainstream.

After that, in the eyes of the media, grunge became a matter of style over substance. The fact that there were bands in Seattle playing something other than grunge, and that there were other local labels besides Sub Pop, was conveniently overlooked. Meanwhile, major record labels, operating under the premise that nothing succeeds like success, streamed into Seattle to sign any band that hadn't been picked up yet; opportunistic bands also relocated to Seattle, buying distortion pedals and flannel shirts in an attempt to pass themselves off as the genuine article. Producers like Jack Endino were continually hit up with requests from bands wanting to sound like the new grunge icons. Even bands touted by acts like Nirvana in interviews received offers, with the Melvins and Meat Puppets among those signed to a major label following Nirvana's endorsement.

But when those bands, and other Seattle signings like Mudhoney, Tad, Hammerbox and Seven Year Bitch, didn't have the same runaway success, they were summarily dropped. Then came the imitators (Candlebox, Stone Temple Pilots, Silverchair, Bush), which lasted longer but weren't seen as having the same sort of cultural impact. And though a "grunge backlash" wasn't long in arriving, grunge's real decline was due simply to the passage of time. From late 1993 through early 1994 there was another run of success from Seattle

Flannel Shirts

bands – Nirvana's *In Utero*, Pearl Jam's *Vs.*, Alice In Chains' *Jar Of Flies* and Soundgarden's *Superunknown* all topped the US album chart – but Cobain's death in April 1994 left a void that would never truly be filled. Then Pearl Jam, trying to figure out how to stage a tour without utilizing Ticketmaster, cut back on their touring schedule. And while continuing to release records, Alice In Chains became increasingly MIA on the road due to lead singer Layne Staley's own struggles with addiction.

Green Day were the first beneficiaries of this vacuum, with their major label debut, *Dookie*, becoming the kind of 10 million-plus seller *Nevermind* had been. In the UK, the rise of bands like Oasis, Blur and Pulp ushered in the era of Britpop. It was the inexorable cycle of a new music trend rising, gaining popularity, then giving way to another new trend rising in its wake.

And what of grunge's legacy? The success of the grunge bands did lead to a momentary opening in the major label mindset as far as alternative bands were concerned; no longer dismissed as cult acts, labels quickly set up alternative music departments in their A&R divisions, lest some other potential moneymaker get away. As a result, for a brief period, there was a modicum of diversity in mainstream music. And like the punk movement in the 1970s, grunge's DIY ethic spurred many budding musicians into picking up instruments themselves, suddenly grasping that you didn't have to be a hair metal virtuoso to make music. Grunge as a style and a genre has passed into music history. But the recordings remain, continuing to provide fresh inspiration.

The Story

more recently home to the Seattle International Film Festival, and one of the largest venues Nirvana had yet played – though they were third on the bill to Tad and Mudhoney. Though marred by sound problems, *Backlash* reported that the show was "totally intense. Hair explosions, prat falls, jumps, body writhing and a trash-a-thon finale that left instruments and bodies strewn about the stage". Not everyone was so impressed. The critic at the *Seattle Times* demonstrated the generation gap was still alive and well in his assessment: "If this is the future of rock and roll, I hope I die before I get much older." Clearly, civic pride in the band's accomplishments was some years away.

Also in June, the band had their only recording session with Jason Everman. The session (which may have spanned two days but was more likely one) was produced by Evergreen student Greg Babior at a studio in the college's music building. The main task was to record a cover of the Kiss song "Do You Love Me", which was originally slated for a split single with Northwest band Alphabet Swill. It turned out to be the most over-the-top track the band ever committed to tape, more in the vein of a comedy record. The first incarnation of "Dive", also recorded at the session, was more interesting. Though the heavy, lurching guitars of the intro recall the material on *Bleach*, a growing pop sensibility was also in evidence, giving the song a lighter edge. Unlike "Do You Love Me", which ultimately wound up on a Kiss tribute album, the recording of "Dive" was purely an exercise; it would remain unreleased until it appeared on *With The Lights Out*.

First US tour

Later that month, Nirvana embarked on their first extended US tour. Straight after a show at The Vogue on 21 June, they drove over 800 miles to San Francisco for a show at the Covered Wagon Saloon the next night. From there the tour continued across the Southwest into Texas, through the Midwest to Illinois and Iowa, up to Minnesota and Wisconsin, then east through Pennsylvania, Massachusetts, New Jersey and New York. It was a typically low-budget venture. Thanks to the label's inconsistent distribution, *Bleach* often wasn't yet for sale in the cities where the band appeared, and some shows drew no more than twenty people. What money the band earned was usually needed to cover gas and food; if they couldn't crash at someone's house, the band often ended up sleeping by the side of the road. They were able to generate some extra income selling T-shirts, which sported a slogan Novoselic had thought up on the back – "Fudge packin, Crack smokin, Satin worshippin mother fuckers" – while the front, designed by Cobain, featured the band's name and an illustration of Dante's Circles of Hell. Occasionally, police officers would ask people wearing the shirts to put them on inside out, to avoid giving offence.

But it was also an adventure, and, for Cobain, the first time he'd travelled beyond the West Coast. To relieve boredom during the long drives, Cobain bought a crucifix that he'd stick out of the van's window to flash at people, sometimes taking pictures of their startled expressions. And though it wasn't apparent at the time, the band were laying the groundwork for their future success. Audiences might have been sparse in some places, but the band generally received a positive reception, especially in smaller towns. "That's the thing about big cities, they weren't really enthusiastic," says Novoselic. "It'd be a lot more fun to play Medford, Oregon or Ellensburg [Washington] than it would some big city. Everybody's kind of jaded, too hip for their own good." *Bleach* was receiving good notices in the alternative press (*CMJ New Music Report* noted "Nirvana could become the coolest thing since toast") and the tour helped attract more attention; in LA they were interviewed by the punk magazine *Flipside* (with Cobain named as "Kirk").

By the time the band made their New York City debut on 18 July at the Pyramid Club, Cobain had become increasingly tired, as would happen with all lengthy Nirvana tours. He'd already phoned his girlfriend saying he wanted to come home; he was especially prone to catching colds; and a recurring stomachache he'd had for a number of years was aggravated by life on the road. Nor had Everman been working out as well as they'd hoped. It was felt his guitar work was steering Nirvana's sound in more of a "rock" direction at a time when the band was developing its more melodic side, but personal differences between Everman and Cobain had as much to do with the growing schism. Everman had expected to have more

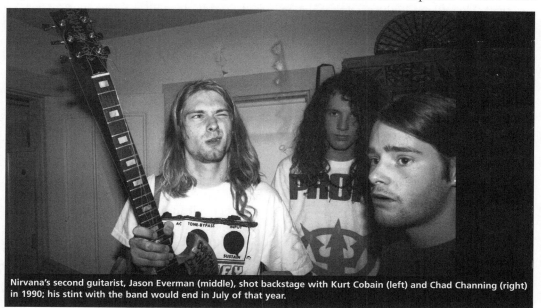

Nirvana's second guitarist, Jason Everman (middle), shot backstage with Kurt Cobain (left) and Chad Channing (right) in 1990; his stint with the band would end in July of that year.

creative input into the group, but Cobain was not willing to cede creative control to anyone. Everman had also committed the cardinal sin of picking up a young woman after one of the band's shows, the kind of thing that flew in the face of the more egalitarian rock culture Cobain was immersed in back in Olympia.

Fed up with the situation, after the Pyramid show Cobain told Novoselic that Everman was out and the tour was over. The band drove straight back to Seattle, and, in typically passive-aggressive fashion, Cobain never actually told Everman he'd been kicked out; he was simply never contacted by anyone in Nirvana again. The band immediately scheduled a new tour that would take them back into the Midwest later in the year, to make up the shows they'd cancelled.

In the interim, Cobain began consulting doctors about his stomach condition, but the cause of the problem remained undetermined. He and Novoselic, along with **Mark Lanegan** and **Mark Pickerel** of Screaming Trees, formed a side project band and recorded Leadbelly covers in August. And Nirvana, stripped down to a three-piece again, went into the studio with a new producer in September to record tracks for an upcoming EP.

Music Source sessions

This was the only time the band would work with **Steve Fisk**, a producer and musician then working out of a Seattle studio called **The Music Source**. Much time was spent trying to get the band's gear in shape; Fisk recalls Channing's drum being "cracked like the Liberty Bell. And the bass amp and the speakers were blown up and rumbling. So it was a lot like recording some dodgy band with broken-up gear where you realize things would sound a lot better if we had this or that – but this is what we have to work with."

The songs were a quantum leap beyond what the band had done before, more akin to power pop than trademark grunge. The band knocked out five songs in one session, with the first two, "Been A Son" (which had yet to be played live) and "Stain", used on the upcoming EP. Next was the disquieting "Polly". Cobain had already done an acoustic home demo of the song, but gave it an electric arrangement on this outing. Then there was a first run-through of "Even In His Youth", which at this point had a raucous intro that would later be used in the "Endless, Nameless" jam. Finally, the band recorded "Token Eastern Song", the title a nod to the Eastern-flavoured groove that ran through the number, in a manner similar to "Love Buzz".

The band returned about a week later to do overdubs and final vocals, but only "Stain" and "Been A Son" were completed. This time, they took full advantage of the studio's 24-track capabilities, working with Fisk on getting a different, lighter sound, especially on the drums. After "Been A Son" was finished, everyone was so pleased with the result they danced on the studio's tables. But though the plan was to go back and do final overdubs for the other tracks, it never happened, and the songs remained in the vaults until the release of *With The Lights Out*.

The make-up tour ran from 28 September to 13 October, and took the band as far east as Ohio. Accompanying them was Ben Shepherd, a Seattle musician the group momentarily considered as a replacement for Jason Everman (and following Everman's short-lived tenure in Soundgarden, Shepherd would replace him on bass in that group too). The tour had its low moments, such as when Cobain collapsed in Minneapolis due to his stomach problems. But overall, it was a less stressful trip than the previous one. The band bought PixelVision cameras (a video camera designed for children) to record their antics for their own amusement, and while in Colorado Cobain picked up a 12-string Stella acoustic for $32.21.

The Heavier Than Heaven tour

Less than a week after the tour ended, Nirvana left for their first trek to **Europe** on 20 October. They would co-headline with **Tad**, swapping the running order each show on what became known as the "Heavier Than Heaven" tour, after the phrase appeared on a poster advertising a UK show. The tour consisted of 36 shows in 44 days, in less than desirable conditions: the two bands, along with tour manager Edwin Heath and soundman Craig Montgomery, were packed into a single van with all their equipment and luggage. "You couldn't really sleep well [in the van] 'cause

there was nine [sic] of us sitting shoulder to shoulder," said Montgomery. "It was tough. There was always somebody getting sick."

The first show was 23 October at The Riverside in Newcastle. After being hit in the head with a beer bottle, Novoselic set about smashing the rental equipment that was supposed to last the entire tour. The band recorded their **first radio session** for the DJ John Peel's programme on BBC Radio 1 on 26 October, then made their London debut on 27 October at the University of London's School of Oriental and African Studies (SOAS). The packed house responded enthusiastically, with a steady succession of fans climbing the speaker stacks at the side of the stage to leap into the audience below; "It's like the crowd have been shot full of electricity," *Melody Maker* observed. Searching for a suitable end to the proceedings, Cobain set off a fire extinguisher.

The next month, the tour moved to mainland Europe. On 1 November they recorded another radio session, this time broadcast live, for VPRO's *Nozems-a-GoGo* show at the studio in Hilversum, the Netherlands. Then it was on to West Germany, where they arrived in **West Berlin** on 11 November, two days after East Germany had announced their citizens could freely enter West Berlin, the first step toward the country's eventual reunification.

The tour next took in Austria, Hungary and Switzerland before arriving in Italy on 26 November for a show at Bloom in Mezzago (a town close to Milan), which saw Cobain singing during Tad's set when singer Tad Doyle was momentarily indisposed. The following

The Story

Nirvana on the radio

Nirvana's handful of national radio appearances were all made on their European tours between 1989 and 1991, helping to build their audience overseas. The first of these came seven days into their first tour abroad, when they recorded a session for BBC Radio 1's legendary *John Peel Show* at the BBC's Maida Vale studio in London on 26 October 1989. In most of their radio sessions, the group opted to highlight their lighter, poppier side. This particular session drew on songs from their first single ("Love Buzz"), first compilation ("Spank Thru") and first album ("About A Girl"). The band also performed a then-unreleased song, "Polly", of which they'd recorded an early version the previous month with Steve Fisk in Seattle; it was at that point a mid-tempo, electric arrangement.

The session's producer, Dale Griffin, recalled the band as being well rehearsed and "very relaxed", and this is evident in the performance, with the songs taken at a brisk pace, giving them all an engaging freshness. The show was first broadcast on 22 November 1989.

On the same tour, they also performed a live session for VPRO's *Nozems-a-GoGo* show at the station's studio in Hilversum, the Netherlands, on 1 November 1989. The band again performed "Love Buzz" and "About A Girl" and another song yet to be recorded, "Dive". The band doesn't sound quite as bright-eyed and bushy-tailed on this outing, but Cobain puts some effort into his guitar antics on "Love Buzz" (especially

after the song's second verse). It's also interesting to hear "Dive" in the process of development: not quite as strong as it would be when it was next recorded, but a clear leap from the version recorded at Evergreen State College the previous June.

By the time Nirvana turned up at the same BBC studio on 21 October 1990, for another Peel session, Dave Grohl was their drummer. It was the band's most unusual session as all the songs were covers: two by the Vaselines ("Son Of A Gun" and "Molly's Lips"), one by the Wipers ("D-7") and one by Devo ("Turnaround"). But it was also perhaps their strongest session so far, the band's up-tempo performance brimming over with optimism. It's as if Grohl's addition to the line-up has given the band a shot of adrenaline, with the rendition of "D-7", which starts out slowly then goes into overdrive halfway through, particularly aggressive. And aside from "Molly's Lips", the songs were all new additions to the band's repertoire. Broadcast on 3 November 1990, it later became the first session to have its songs officially released, when "D-7" appeared on the *Hormoaning* EP and UK "Lithium" single. The other songs would then turn up on *Incesticide*.

Nirvana's final Peel session took place on 3 September 1991 at the end of a short UK/European festival tour. Though "Smells Like Teen Spirit" was due to be released in the UK the following week,

night, tensions came to a head. Though the crowds had been receptive and many of the shows were sold out, everyone was drained by a schedule that allowed scarcely any time off. Cobain's stomach woes were aggravated by the unfamiliar foods and erratic eating schedule, and Doyle himself was prone to stomach

upsets that had him vomiting at the side of the road. When Bruce Pavitt and Jonathan Poneman flew to meet everyone in **Rome**, expecting that seeing some friendly faces from back home would boost morale, they were instead confronted with a group of hungry, tired and ill musicians, who were resentful at the band chose to perform two of *Nevermind*'s lesser numbers, "Drain You" and the "hidden" track "Endless, Nameless", as well as "Dumb", which hadn't been recorded yet. The band was sufficiently tired that rescheduling the session was briefly considered as an option, but it eventually went ahead, and it could be argued that the evident fatigue worked well in the world-weary "Dumb". Nor was "Endless, Nameless" short-changed, running for nearly nine minutes. Producer Dale Griffin conceded the performance was "not their finest hour", but he respected the band's ability to get the job done without complaint, while remaining concerned about Cobain's physical and mental state. The session was first broadcast on 3 November 1991, and "Dumb" and "Endless, Nameless" later appeared on *With The Lights Out*.

The band's last appearance on the BBC was a session for Radio 1's *Mark Goodier's Evening Session*, recorded on 9 November and broadcast on 18 November 1991. The band again opted not to perform "Teen Spirit", but gave a new twist to "Polly", speeding it up to the point that it was renamed "(New Wave) Polly" when it finally appeared on *Incesticide*. The other selection from *Nevermind* was a heavy, powerful performance of "Something in the Way". The band also boosted the tempo on "Been A Son" in sharp comparison with the version that appeared on the *Blew* EP. But the song they spent the longest time working on

was "Aneurysm", creating an interesting effect on the backing vocals, which fade in and out during the verses, giving the track a lighter feel in comparison with the version that appeared on the "Teen Spirit" single. "Been A Son" and "Aneurysm" would also appear on *Incesticide*.

The band's final radio session was a joint production between Dutch radio stations VPRO (for their *Nozems-a-GoGo* programme) and VARA (for their *Twee Meter De Lucht In*), and was recorded in Hilversum on 25 November 1991. Though it was hoped the band would play something from *Nevermind*, they declined, instead recording just two numbers, "Where Did You Sleep Last Night" (an arrangement similar to the one they'd later use on *Unplugged*) and "Here She Comes Now". They also performed a long, desultory jam that the station DJs were unimpressed with. In less than an hour, the band had left the studio, though Krist Novoselic took the time to apologize for the lacklustre performance.

It was a disappointing end to Nirvana's short roster of radio appearances. But for the most part, the band had risen to the occasion, choosing songs that hadn't been recorded yet for each session, in addition to working up new arrangements for songs rather than simply recreate what was already on record. Thus the radio sessions are especially interesting to listen to. Not all of the band's radio performances have been officially released, but they have been extensively bootlegged.

their employers' comfort when they'd spent weeks travelling in a cramped, freezing van.

Cobain finally snapped during Nirvana's set at the Piper Club in Rome, the night Pavitt and Poneman arrived. Ten songs into the set, during "Spank Thru", sound problems caused him to start smashing his guitar in a rage. He

then climbed the speaker stack next to the stage and threatened to jump, but was eventually talked down. Backstage he continued to smash equipment and burst into tears of frustration, expressing unhappiness not just at the strenuous touring conditions but also the very nature of his work. "It was the first time I heard him say, 'I see

The Story

all these people in the crowd and they're fucking idiots,'" Poneman said. He told Poneman he wanted to quit the band and go home.

The next day, thankfully, was a day off. Poneman arranged for Cobain and himself to travel via train, but while waiting at the border to cross into Switzerland, Cobain's passport and wallet were stolen as he slept. Poneman drew on all his powers of persuasion to smooth over the situation with the authorities, and the tour lumbered on. Fortunately, it was nearly over: there remained just two shows in Switzerland, a show apiece in France and Belgium, and a final show back in London on 3 December, at Sub Pop's second "Lame Fest", with the two bands sharing the bill with Mudhoney.

The musicians were late, arriving at **London's Astoria** half an hour before the show was due to start. A coin toss decided the running order for the night, with Nirvana taking the stage first, without the benefit of a soundcheck. "This is the last show of our tour, so we can do whatever the fuck we want!" Novoselic bellowed before "Scoff", later swinging his bass around with such force the strap snapped and the instrument nearly hit Mudhoney drummer Dan Peters in the head. The show ended with an even more elaborate display of destruction than usual, Novoselic holding his bass like a baseball bat and smashing Cobain's guitar to smithereens.

Accounts of the show vary, some finding it sloppy, while others felt Nirvana had stolen the show. Journalist Keith Cameron, who would become one of the band's biggest supporters, called the show "magical". He afterwards asked Cobain what his hopes were for the 1990s: "Our band want to debase every known form of modern music," Cobain replied.

The tour had done much to extend Nirvana's appeal abroad. In the UK especially, media coverage had been more extensive than at home, and they even received their first cover story – albeit shared with Tad – in music paper *Sounds*' 21 October issue. The end of the tour coincided with their first UK-only release, the *Blew* EP (released on Tupelo), featuring "Love Buzz" and two of the tracks recorded with Steve Fisk, "Stain" and "Been A Son", along with the title track. Another track from the Dale Demo session, "Mexican Seafood" had just been released on the first EP in C/Z's *Teriyaki Asthma* series. When the band returned home, issues of the first stateside magazine to put them on the cover, *The Rocket*, were in clubs and record stores all over the greater Seattle area – and this time, they were on the cover alone.

Post-tour, Nirvana took the month of December off, though Cobain attended the sessions for Mark Lanegan's solo album, *The Winding Sheet*, and recorded backing vocals for "Down In The Dark". The year ended with Novoselic marrying Shelli at their Tacoma home, with a drunken celebration following the ceremony. Though no one could have foreseen it, great changes lay ahead for Nirvana in the coming year.

A transitional year
1990

A transitional year 1990

Now that they were an established act, with a number of records and tours under their belt, Nirvana were primed to take the next step in building on their achievements by recording a new album and continuing to tour. There was no thought, yet, of moving to a major label, nor were any personnel changes on the cards. But by the year's end, there would be new developments in both areas.

The single-song session

The year began with one of Nirvana's strangest recording sessions, a two-day stint at Reciprocal on 2 and 3 January 1990, that would result in the band recording a single song that would remain unreleased for fifteen years. "They just said, 'We're going to come in and record something' and Sub Pop said 'Okay,'" Endino recalls. "They just wanted to get this song down. Sub Pop didn't have any plans on releasing it or doing anything with it. I'm not sure why they did it; they spent a bunch of money just to do one song that never went anywhere."

The song in question was then entitled "Sappy", and the group had started performing it during the European tour. "[Cobain] was looking for some kind of different sound," says Endino of the session. "He just had me do stuff I wasn't used to doing. I remember we recorded the vocals from a distance or something, which

Often vocal in condemning the macho redneck side of rock, Cobain could also make a statement with his choice of stage outfit, as at this gig in 1990.

is perfectly fine, but I had never done that before. And he wanted a really boomy sort of weird room sound on the drums." It was the first attempt at a song the band would revisit on three other occasions; this version wouldn't be released until 2005 on *Sliver: The Best Of The Box* CD.

After four shows in the Northwest, Nirvana hit the road again on a West Coast tour that began 9 February in Portland at the Pine Street Theatre, and took them all the way down to Tijuana in Mexico, via a single date in Arizona; in March they played their first Canadian date, in Vancouver. Everett True was along for the ride for some dates, and by the time his story ran, in *Melody Maker*'s 17 March issue, Nirvana were preparing for another US tour, during which they also planned to record their next album for Sub Pop.

Prior to the trip, Cobain arranged a video shoot at Evergreen on 20 March, directed by student Jon Snyder (a friend of Greg Babior, who served as sound technician on the shoot). Cobain brought in videotapes he'd recorded from television, which were projected behind the band as they played. But in a few months' time, the band's line-up would change again, one reason why the video project was never completed.

Spring tour and Smart sessions

The spring tour began on 1 April at Cabaret Metro in Chicago, after which the group

Krist Novoselic backstage on the spring US tour, Massachusetts, April 1990.

drove to Madison, Wisconsin, where recording sessions were scheduled to begin the next day. Sub Pop had arranged for the band to work with producer **Butch Vig** at the studio he co-owned, **Smart Studios**. Vig, who'd started out as a drummer in the band Spooner (later renamed Fire Town), and would later form Garbage, had recently produced Tad's *Eight Way Santa* album. "If you saw Nirvana here in Seattle, it's like Beatlemania," Poneman enthused to Vig, "and they're going to be as big as The Beatles." Vig was understandably sceptical about Poneman's claim, but

The lost videos

On 20 March 1990, Nirvana taped a short set of songs intended for a home video that they could sell on tour. Though bootlegged extensively, the performances remain officially unreleased.

The taping was arranged with Jon Snyder, an Evergreen student who'd seen the band play in Olympia numerous times. He also worked in the college's television studio. "I had gotten myself into a situation where I had keys for everything there at Evergreen that had to do with media and so people would come to me for things," he explains. "I was very excited about filming them. It was so, so cool to me. They were a big part of my world before they became a bigger part of the world at large."

Snyder met with Cobain and Novoselic beforehand to discuss ideas. "They remembered seeing these really funny psychedelic kind of Black Sabbath videos on MTV," Snyder recalls. "And there would always be some weird psychedelic thing going in the background, some really primitive TV Chroma Key effect [a blue screen used for rear projection] with the band against it, floating on something. They wanted to do something like that."

Cobain had plenty of footage he wanted to use: material he'd taped from TV, Super-8 films he'd made of his doll collection, and footage from the silent film *Häxan: Witchcraft of the Ages*. On the day of the shoot, everything was done live: the band was shot by two different cameras as they played live in the studio, with Snyder switching between cameras in the control booth, while Cobain's footage, playing on another machine, was used for the rear projection. The sound was engineered live by Greg Babior, who'd recorded the band at Evergreen the previous year.

The session began with two takes of "School" (the first incomplete), which used footage from a Shaun Cassidy special, a boy–girl tap-dancing team that appeared on *Star Search*, footage of Christian bodybuilders "The Power Team" and assorted commercials – the clean-cut, 1980s-style perms contrasting with the band's scruffy appearance. Novoselic also placed strips of tape all over his legs as the colour of his pants too closely matched the blue of the rear screen, making his legs "disappear" (he also sports a black eye, received in an altercation with a bouncer at a club the previous night).

It was then determined that Novoselic's bass wasn't coming through loudly enough, so the band played a new song, "Lithium", to allow the sound levels

on listening to *Bleach* was impressed by the melodic pull of "About A Girl".

Recording took place 2–6 April, with the band laying down eight songs, evenly split between older material – "Immodium" (which later became "Breed"), "Polly", "Dive" and "Sappy" – and new: "In Bloom", "Lithium", "Pay to Play" (which later became "Stay Away") and a cover of the Velvet Underground's "Here

She Comes Now". The band's main instruction to Vig was that it should "sound really heavy"; he also put plywood planks on the floor to enhance the "live" feel of the room.

Of necessity, recording went quickly, as the band was expected in Milwaukee on 8 April. Unsurprisingly, it was two of the newer songs, "Lithium" and "In Bloom", that gave the group most trouble, with Cobain frustrated to be adjusted. The film crew was excited to hear a new Nirvana song, especially one that sounded so different from the *Bleach* material. "We looked at each other and went, 'Oh my God, they're gonna make it,'" recalls Maria Braganza, one of the camera operators. "Because they'd gone over into pop land. We were like, 'Oh my God, that was so fun, we got to hear a song that nobody else had heard!'" The band also jammed on other material during breaks in filming.

There were then two takes of "Big Cheese" using the *Häxan* footage. These videos are the most effective of the batch, the darkness of the song's lyrics well matched with the black-and-white depiction of witches and demons. The set closed with a single take of "Floyd The Barber", featuring clips Cobain had shot of his dolls and other toys. But the video's most notable feature is a feedback loop effect that creates a staggered image, in this case making each musician look like they've got multiple arms. "It's an incredibly low-tech, cheesy effect," Snyder admits. "It's like the equivalent of putting reverb or echo on your voice. But we thought it looked kinda cool." The song ends with Cobain falling into Channing's drum kit.

The group had planned to film extra footage so they'd have at least an hour's worth of material for the home video. "Pretty ambitious for where they were at the time," Snyder says, "and probably in hindsight totally impossible because of how crazy their lives were. And that's probably why we never got any further than that." Another likely reason the material was never used was that by the end of May Chad Channing was out of the band.

Snyder eventually made videos of "School" and "Lithium", which each featured additional live footage and still photos shot by Snyder at Nirvana's 11 October 1990 show at Olympia's North Shore Surf Club. The videos were screened on two episodes of *1200 Seconds*, a programme put together by Evergreen students, which aired on the local community access cable station in the fall of 1990. A clip of "Big Cheese" has appeared in MTV profiles of the group.

In 2002, Snyder sold the footage (along with that of other bands he'd shot while living in Olympia) to Seattle's Experience Music Project museum. It has since been used in the museum's exhibits, and has occasionally been licensed by outside parties: the performance of "Love Buzz" from the North Shore show appeared on the *With The Lights Out* DVD.

enough by Channing's drumming that he got behind the kit to show Channing what he wanted; conversely, Channing handled himself well on "Here She Comes Now", which he'd never even heard before but was captured in one take (the song was destined for a Velvet Underground tribute album).

Cobain was very particular about the kind of sound he wanted. In recording "Polly", he switched from an electric to an acoustic guitar, using the Stella he'd picked up in Denver the previous year (though a twelve-string guitar, Cobain only had six strings on it). Vig suggested using another guitar to "get a nice pristine sound", but Cobain demurred, insisting "No, no, this is the sound, this dark sound". Vig also encountered the complexities of Cobain's personality during the sessions. "We'd be

The Story

working on the songs and he'd be very articulate and all of a sudden, he would just shut down, just go sit in a corner and wouldn't say a thing," he recalled. "And Krist would be, 'He's OK, he just gets really moody sometimes.'"

One of the last shows to feature Channing's drum kit, in Massachussets, 1990.

In general, everyone was satisfied with the results, though there wasn't enough to fill an entire album. The new material marked a clear change in Cobain's evolution as a songwriter. He had told *Sounds* the previous summer, "The early songs were really angry... now [they're] about conflicts in relationships, emotional things with other human beings", and such themes are readily seen in songs like "Polly", "Immodium" and "Lithium".

On their last night in Madison, Nirvana played at Club Underground, sharing the bill with Tad and Victim's Family. Jonathan Poneman had flown in to see the show and listen to the material the band had recorded. Nirvana pushed on with their tour, through Minnesota, Michigan, Ohio, up into Canada, and back into the States through Massachusetts, Pennsylvania and New York.

While in New York City, Bruce Pavitt arranged for the band to be photographed by Michael Lavine, yet another Evergreen student, who shot photos of Sub Pop's bands whenever they visited the city. The band left him a copy of the Smart session demos, which Lavine played for Iggy Pop during another photo session that day. Pop liked the tape so much Lavine took him to the Pyramid show that night, and afterwards introduced him to the band; Cobain was somewhat embarrassed to be wearing a Stooges T-shirt. The band were also embarrassed by their performance and Novoselic shaved his head the next day as "punishment".

The band also shot their first proper video while in New York, using "In Bloom" from the Smart sessions. Directed by Steve Brown, the video was a low-budget affair: the band wear their own clothes, and in lieu of sets, they're shown rehearsing, playing live (at Maxwell's in Hoboken, New Jersey, 28 April), and walking around town. There's a decided charm to the video, with the band coming across as a bunch of friendly, unassuming guys, though Cobain demonstrates an ability to look alternately sweet and demented. In the most inventive shot, they're seen through a hole in the wall, Cobain passing by in one direction, Novoselic in the other, then Channing running directly toward the camera before darting off to the side; Cobain then cautiously pokes his head up.

From New Jersey the tour continued down the East Coast into Florida, then west through Georgia, Ohio, Oklahoma, Nebraska and Colorado, with a final stop on 17 May at The Zoo in Boise, Idaho. Audiences on this tour were bigger than they had been in 1989, evidence of a growing popularity. But though aware of their increasing success, on the surface the band tried to play it down. "We're just here to have fun, write songs and play," Cobain told Bob Gulla in an interview done in Cambridge, Massachusetts, which remained unpublished until 1999. "We're totally comfortable with the level we're on now... I mean, we just want people to like our music. We don't want a big multi-million- dollar promotional deal to bring us into every high school across the country, to make us into multi-million-dollar paper dolls."

Changing drummers – again

Then, at this key juncture, the line-up changed once again, when Channing left the band. Tensions had been growing for some time; Vig had seen it in Cobain's impatience with Channing's work in the studio. For his part, Channing was tired of feeling, as he put it, like little more than a "drum machine". A guitarist and songwriter himself, he had hoped to contribute more to the band, so was not entirely unhappy when Cobain and Novoselic turned up at his home to inform him he was no longer in Nirvana – a courtesy none of the previous drummers had received.

With no drummer, touring plans were put on hold. Meanwhile, Sub Pop was fielding offers from major labels who wished to purchase a share in the indie upstart, and they had offered Nirvana a new thirty-page contract that was substantially more detailed than the two-page effort Poneman had cobbled together the previous year. Cobain and Novoselic felt that if Sub Pop was going to join forces with a major label it would be in the band's better interests to sign with a major directly. They began soliciting advice, meeting with Soundgarden's manager, Susan Silver, who in turn introduced them to Alan Mintz, a music industry lawyer based in Los Angeles (and who later, as Vice President of Content Development/Head of A&R at Starbucks, would bring Paul McCartney to the coffee chain's Hear Music label). They also began

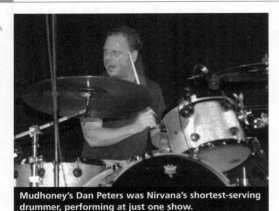

Mudhoney's Dan Peters was Nirvana's shortest-serving drummer, performing at just one show.

shopping the Smart session demos themselves, without informing Sub Pop, dubbing them over cassettes of *Bleach*.

They nonetheless recorded another single for the label, returning to Reciprocal on 11 July to record "Sliver" with a new drummer, Dan Peters from Mudhoney. Peters had run into Shelli and Tracy at The Vogue, and, on learning that Channing had left Nirvana, asked them to pass along word he'd be interested in joining the group, as Mudhoney were currently on hiatus. Soon after he received a call from Cobain. Peters stressed he didn't want to audition; they either wanted him as their drummer or not. He was assured no other drummers were under consideration. On hearing the Smart session demos, he was suitably impressed. "The first song I heard was 'In Bloom' and I was just like Jesus Christ, this is one of the best songs I've ever heard!" he says. "I was psyched. It was definitely something I was excited about. There was something amazing going on."

"Sliver" had developed during the band's practise sessions. "When we started working on it, it just came really easily," says Peters. "Kurt started up the riff and it's obviously a really straight-ahead song … I love that song." The recording was done very quickly, with the basics laid down in just one hour. But it had to be done fast, as Endino had squeezed Nirvana in at Poneman's behest while working with Tad. Nirvana returned on 24 July to record overdubs and Cobain's vocal. "Sliver" was paired with "Dive" from the Vig session, and released as a single in September (but not until January in the UK).

Prior to engaging Peters' services, Cobain and Novoselic had already deputized Dale Crover for a short West Coast tour in August, eight days from Las Vegas, Nevada, to Vancouver, BC, opening for **Sonic Youth**. The New York-based band was proving to be a good source of advice, having just released *Goo*, their first album on a major label, DGC (a subsidiary of Geffen Records), without any resulting loss in hipster credibility.

Dave Grohl arrives

It was at this time that **Dave Grohl** entered Nirvana's orbit. Like Cobain and Novoselic, Grohl came from a divorced family and had been playing in bands since his teens. Born David Eric Grohl on 14 January 1969, in Warren, Ohio, he moved with his family to Springfield, Virginia, when he was three. Grohl's parents divorced when he was seven; though Grohl has said little publicly about the

Sonic Youth

Sonic Youth's Thurston Moore first saw Nirvana when they played Maxwell's in Hoboken, New Jersey, on 13 July 1989. Despite later describing the raggedy trio as looking like the youthful backwoods murderers from Stephen King's *Children of the Corn*, he was nonetheless blown away by the band's performance. "They just incinerated the place," he later told *Spin*. "Not only was every song crushingly great, but at the end, they just smashed their instruments and threw them into the audience... that band knew how to rock." The two bands soon became friendly, and Sonic Youth would help Nirvana navigate their rise from the indie realm to the majors.

Sonic Youth formed in New York City in 1981, the core trio being Moore (vocals and guitar), his wife Kim Gordon (vocals and bass) and Lee Ranaldo (vocals and guitar); the band's current drummer, Steve Shelley, joined in 1985. Part of the city's abrasively inclined "no wave" scene, Sonic Youth quickly became known for their experimentation with guitars, utilizing alternate tunings and as likely to play with a drumstick or screwdriver as a pick. Though they toured erratically during their early years, they made a point of establishing contacts in every place they visited, becoming respected taste-makers and mentors of alternative/underground music and musicians.

Cobain was especially impressed with how Sonic Youth managed to maintain their integrity as they moved to a major label; their landmark double album *Daydream Nation* (which Cobain placed on one of his "Top 50 Albums" lists in his journals) was released in 1988 on Enigma, which was affiliated with Capitol Records; the band subsequently signed directly with major label DGC Records (a subsidiary of Geffen Records). Sonic Youth championed Nirvana to their friends and business associates, and the two bands toured together in August 1990, so it was almost inevitable that they ended up signing with both Sonic Youth's management, Gold Mountain, and their label.

Though musically on different paths – Nirvana's song structure was always more conventional – the two bands admired each other's work. Their camaraderie is evident in pictures Charles Peterson took backstage on 11 April 1991, when Sonic Youth opened for Neil Young in Seattle. They're seen engaging in more tomfoolery while on a short European tour in August that year, this time captured on film by Dave Markey for his documentary *1991: The Year Punk Broke*. "Nirvana were like Sonic Youth's children on that tour," Markey told writer David Browne in *Goodbye 20th Century*, Browne's biography of Sonic Youth. The two never shared a stage again, but did work together on occasion. Cobain provided the cover art for Sonic Youth's *Whores Moaning* EP (a play on Nirvana's *Hormoaning* EP), with video director Kevin Kerslake photocopying a doll from Cobain's collection for the front, and Cobain supplying a disturbing drawing of a young girl pointing a pistol in her mouth for the back. Later, Moore joined Dave Grohl in the band that provided the soundtrack for the 1994 film *Backbeat*, about the early years of The Beatles.

Though Cobain's suicide shocked the members of Sonic Youth, Gordon admitted to Browne: "It was a surprise that he shot himself, but it wasn't a *total* surprise," she said (emphasis Gordon's). Some have thought the Sonic Youth songs "Androgynous Mind" and "Junkie's Promise" reference the Nirvana songs "Stay Away" and "I Hate Myself And Want To Die", respectively, though the band have always denied the connection. But both Moore and Gordon gave the controversial film *Last Days*, "inspired by" Cobain's life, an endorsement by working on the movie. Moore also wrote liner notes for Nirvana's *With The Lights Out*, in which he shared his personal reminiscences, concluding "Nirvana were their generation's greatest voice, and continue to be."

divorce, he told Michael Azerrad that ideologically his parents "were pretty much at other ends of the spectrum". Grohl's father, a former news reporter, moved back to Ohio, working as a speechwriter for the Republican party; his mother remained in Springfield with Grohl and his sister, taking a job as a teacher.

The first instrument Grohl learned to play was the trombone, but as he became increasingly interested in rock music, he switched to guitar at the age of twelve. Grohl had a good grounding in a wide range of rock music, listening to The Beatles and Led Zeppelin, Devo and the B-52's, AC/DC, Motörhead and Rush. While visiting relatives in Illinois, aged thirteen, he was introduced to punk by his cousin, and became an instant convert, though his diverse musical tastes would remain evident (eventually he'd have tattoos of both John Bonham's three-circles logo and Black Flag's logo on his arms).

With Springfield essentially a suburb of Washington, DC, Grohl was soon investigating the city's hardcore scene, and in 1984 joined a local band named Freak Baby. During his short stint with them he made a key connection when the band recorded some demos at a local studio called the Laundry Room. **Barrett Jones**, who ran the studio based in the laundry room of his parents' home, became a good friend of Grohl's, and would work with him on many subsequent projects.

Though Grohl started out in Freak Baby (later renamed Mission Impossible) on guitar, he soon switched to drums. The following year, Grohl formed the band Dain Bramage, but left them in 1987, also dropping out of high school

to join **Scream**, a DC band he'd long admired. He would eventually record two studio and two live albums with the band.

Cobain and Novoselic first saw Scream when the band played Olympia in early August 1990, though their chief memory was not about how well the group played; rather, they were put off by the band members' behaviour at an after-show party, when the Scream crew irritated partygoers by trying to play a Primus tape on the host's stereo. They paid more attention when they saw Scream a few weeks later at the I-Beam in San Francisco, both coming away highly impressed with Grohl's drumming.

As it happened, Scream were then on their last legs as a band. While in LA on tour, the bass player, who'd long grappled with drug problems, disappeared, leaving the group stranded. Grohl, a major Melvins fan who'd been friends with the group since they'd shared a bill with Scream, now reached out to Buzz Osborne, asking for help. Osborne mentioned that Nirvana were looking for a drummer and gave him Novoselic's number. Grohl duly placed a call, only to be informed the group had filled the slot with Dan Peters. But after conferring, Cobain and Novoselic agreed that Grohl's harder-hitting style might be just what they were looking for, and Novoselic called Grohl back, asking him to come and audition. Grohl packed up his drum kit and headed for Washington state, initially staying with Novoselic and his wife in Tacoma.

Peters remained oblivious to these developments, playing what would turn out to be his only show with Nirvana on 22 September at the Motor Sports International Garage, topping a bill that also included the Derelicts, the Dwarves and the Melvins. The space was a former garage briefly used as a performing venue, with a makeshift stage and little in the way of security. It was the largest show the band had played, with an estimated 1500 in attendance – twice the number any Seattle club could accommodate. "There was a keg of beer on the side of the stage, and the whole backstage was just a giant party," Novoselic recalls. "It was insane." The intensity of the crowd's enthusiasm gave Grohl pause; "I didn't know what I was getting myself into at all", he later admitted to Azerrad.

The next day, Novoselic hosted a barbecue at his home. *Sounds*' Keith Cameron and photographer Ian Tilton were there working on another cover story on the band, and Peters was introduced as the band's new drummer, though Grohl can be seen in the background in some of Tilton's pictures. In contrast to his disavowals of five months earlier, Cobain, referred to as "Kurdt Kobain" in the article, told Cameron "It's really not hard to keep your dignity and sign to a major label", pointing to Sonic Youth as an example. He also freely admitted "All my life my dream has been to be a big rock star". Still, Nirvana had so far avoided confronting Sub Pop, who had just released "Sliver", about their intentions to switch labels. Nor was Peters aware the band was in the process of getting a new drummer. Cobain and Novoselic had already been rehearsing with Grohl and although the first session had gone well, the second was not as strong, leaving everyone with lingering doubts. A third rehearsal eliminated those doubts for good; Grohl was Nirvana's

new drummer. All that remained was for the band to tell Peters.

In fact, it would be the listeners of Calvin Johnson's KAOS radio programme *Boy Meets Girl* who would first hear the news, when Cobain appeared as a surprise guest on 25 September. Accompanying himself on acoustic guitar, he performed "Lithium", "Been

Motor Sports Int'l Garage

Contrary to the poster listing, Nirvana were headliners at their largest show yet in Seattle.

A Son" and "Polly", and debuted "Dumb" and "Opinion", the last a song never recorded by Nirvana. Johnson himself joined him on a cover of the Wipers' "D-7", which Nirvana also had yet to perform. Between songs, Cobain announced that Grohl was their new drummer, describing him as a "baby Dale Crover", and admitting they hadn't told Peters yet. Peters got the word soon after, and though not happy about being kept in the dark for so long, ultimately took the news with good grace, going on to play with Screaming Trees, then returning to Mudhoney when they reformed.

Grohl's debut

Grohl made his live debut with Nirvana on 11 October at Olympia's **North Shore Surf Club**.

Unusually, the set opened with three cover songs: "Son Of A Gun" and "Molly's Lips" (both by the Vaselines, one of Cobain's favourite bands) and "D-7". The sound and lights went out repeatedly during the first four numbers, prompting Novoselic to urge that someone needed to pay the electricity bill in a more timely fashion ("You can get government aid and stuff if you can't afford it," he added). It quickly became evident that Grohl's style of drumming was exactly what Nirvana had needed. The songs they'd recorded with Dale Crover had been the most powerful, and Grohl's work was just as strong. His playing infused the group with an energy they'd never consistently had before, and the North Shore audience responded in kind, moshing in front and gleefully body surfing, causing Grohl at one point to flash a big grin at Novoselic. At the end of the set, before the encore, Cobain proudly held up one of Grohl's drums, displaying how it had been destroyed by the sheer force of his playing. Jon Snyder was part of a crew that filmed the show, hoping to get footage to use in a video for "Lithium", and he sensed that the band would soon be leaving their indie rock days behind: "It was clear that it was only going to get bigger from here."

Just over a week after the North Shore show, Nirvana headed back to Britain for a seven-day tour. During a photo session for *New Musical Express*, photographer Martyn Goodacre took a series of headshots of Cobain staring moodily into the camera. A picture from the series first appeared on the cover of *Select*'s July 1993 issue, but it would go on to achieve iconic status when it was widely used after Cobain's death, beginning with the front cover of *NME*'s memorial issue. "A lot of people say it's a very stylized shot, but it's not," Goodacre later told *Uncut*. "I didn't tell him what to do – my usual way is to just start taking pictures and hope they react to the camera."

On 21 October, Nirvana recorded another session for John Peel, broadcast on 3 November, playing all the covers they'd performed at the North Shore, perhaps endeavouring to break their drummer in slowly. Indeed, for the next several months, the band would play relatively few shows. For Cobain, the highlight of the tour came during the band's appearance in Edinburgh, for which his beloved Vaselines reformed. They had broken up in 1989, but on learning that Nirvana had been covering Vaselines songs, they agreed to reunite at Cobain's request. Cobain's patronage of the group would eventually lead to Sub Pop's reissuing all the Vaselines' material on CD.

Moving to the majors

When the band returned to the US, Grohl moved in with Cobain in Olympia. The buzz about Nirvana was steadily growing within the music industry, and their next show, at Seattle's Off Ramp club on 25 November, attracted a horde of A&R scouts. The band debuted a number of new songs, including "Aneurysm", "Oh, The Guilt", "Dumb", "Something In

The Way" and "Radio Friendly Unit Shifter". Crowd response was so ecstatic, the club agreed to extend the show, though in keeping with Washington state's restrictive liquor laws, the house was cleared, the liquor locked up, and everyone re-admitted to watch the band play an extended encore.

Though several labels thought they were in the running to snag the band's signature, the band's lawyer, Alan Mintz, told Charisma Nirvana would sign with them. But before the deal was finalized the band had a change of heart, and they ultimately signed with Sonic Youth's management company, **Gold Mountain** (jointly managed by John Silva and Danny Goldberg), and Sonic Youth's label, DGC, as well (**DGC's** A&R rep, Gary Gersh, had seen Nirvana in New York the previous April at The Pyramid). The band opted for a lower advance than other labels were offering ($287,500) in exchange for a higher royalty rate and more artistic control, though negotiations dragged

Dave Grohl clearly enjoying his debut gig with NIrvana at the North Shore Surf Club, Olympia, October 1990. His drumming was just what the band needed.

on until 30 April 1991. Cobain also signed a deal with Virgin Publishing, naming his publishing company "The End of Music". Each band member was put on a retainer of $1000 a month, meaning the band could cut back on touring while working on new material.

But while his professional fortunes were looking up, Cobain's personal life had become more troubled. He'd split with Tracy Marander, and had then been involved with another Olympia musician, Tobi Vail (who would later form riot grrrl band Bikini Kill). The two shared an interest in making music and occasionally jammed together; Cobain also played guitar on a single by one of Vail's many bands, The Go Team. But the relationship soon fell apart, and Cobain sank into a depression serious enough that Grohl became concerned; Cobain eventually assured Grohl "I'm not always like this".

He'd also begun using heroin that fall, spelling it "heroine" in his journal. The day after first using it, he called Novoselic to tell him; Novoselic was alarmed, and tried to sound a note of caution, citing the number of people they knew who'd used the drug and had died (including Andrew Wood, lead singer of Seattle band Mother Love Bone, who died the previous March, on the verge of releasing their debut album on Polygram; the remaining members formed the band Pearl Jam). Cobain assured Novoselic he wouldn't use it again, but nonetheless continued to do so. At this stage, his usage was minimal, and when questioned about it, he explained that heroin eased his stomach pains and made him feel more "sociable". In reality, it was something that would have an increasingly significant effect on every aspect of his life.

Grohl returned to Virginia for a quick visit in December, during which he recorded some material for a solo project at the Laundry Room, and was back in the Pacific Northwest for Nirvana's final show of the year, a New Year's Eve gig at Satryicon in Portland. But there would be no celebrations into the wee hours welcoming in the new year for the band; the very next day they were expected in the studio for their first session in what would prove to be a momentous year.

The year Nirvana broke

1991

The Story

The year Nirvana broke
1991

In contrast to the previous years, the first part of 1991 was a quiet time for Nirvana. They dramatically cut back on shows (playing only eight gigs from January to May), instead spending hours in rehearsal, almost as if they knew they had to prepare themselves for what lay ahead. In fact, the band, their management and their label all had relatively modest expectations about how successful Nirvana's major label debut would be. Alternative acts weren't hitmakers; John Rosenfelder, in DGC's radio promotion department, told Charles Cross they hoped for sales of 50,000. This actually worked to Nirvana's advantage. Freed from the pressure of churning out hits, they could simply concentrate on making their next album the best it could be.

Return to the (Music) Source

Nirvana's second session at the Music Source in Seattle was the band's first with Grohl, and a chance for the group to see how they worked together. Their soundman, **Craig Montgomery**, produced the session, gaining access to the studio as he was friendly with someone who worked there. "I was young and naïve and I thought that if the session went really great, they might let me work on their record," he says.

The group recorded seven songs, most of them new: "Aneurysm", "Oh, The Guilt" and "Radio Friendly Unit Shifter" had first appeared in the set list little more than a month earlier, and "On A Plain" and "All Apologies" had yet to be performed live. Most songs had scratch vocals ("Oh, The Guilt" was an instrumental), and there were few overdubs, aside from vocals on "Aneurysm" and "Even In His Youth", both of which later appeared on the "Smells Like Teen Spirit" single (with the drums beefed up by samples dropped in by Andy Wallace, who mixed the tracks).

"Token Eastern Song" and "Even In His Youth" offered the first recorded comparison between Dave Grohl's drumming and that of Chad Channing. "Dave was a breath of fresh air," says Montgomery. "He could play solid and steady and could sing and was fun to be around." Grohl's vigorous playing adds a propulsive energy to "Token Eastern Song" in particular, a song the group wouldn't play again. Other songs underscore the musical direction in which Nirvana was now headed. In this early incarnation, "All Apologies" had a light, almost breezy arrangement featuring a tambourine, while Montgomery calls "On A Plain" "a pop song in the tradition of all of the best pop songwriters like Lennon and McCartney. It's not heavy metal, it's Nirvana." As with the Smart Studios sessions, there were plans to finish up the tracks someday, "but we never did," says Montgomery. "Everything started happening so fast. This was just a day of goofing around, basically."

Nirvana released two singles in January. The UK version of "Sliver" finally came out, the CD including live recordings of "About A Girl" and "Spank Thru" from the Portland show the previous February. The second single was their last for Sub Pop, a live version of "Molly's Lips" from the same Portland show, paired with "Candy" by the Fluid, a band from Denver, Colorado. Cobain was reluctant to have the single released, as he felt the band's performance was "ragged", but had to accede as it was part of the buy-out deal with Sub Pop, in which the label was paid $75,000 and would receive two percent of sales of the band's next two albums. The word "Later" was scratched in the single's run-out groove.

The one show Nirvana played that month was an **anti-war concert** at Evergreen on 18 January,

in protest at the Gulf War with Iraq. It was the first political benefit they played ("I made a fiery speech before the show," Novoselic notes proudly. "It was a good one.") Until the end of April, most of their time was spent in intense rehearsal in a new practice space they rented in Tacoma, owned and shared with a lounge band who'd lined the place with thick brown shag carpet. The band diligently practised every day, indulging in lengthy jam sessions that produced what Grohl later said were innumerable potentially great songs, now lost to memory. In an effort to save some of their ideas, they would occasionally record their practice sessions on cassette – and then lose the tape.

The band took a break from rehearsing in March, playing four shows in Canada and one in Idaho. At the 8 March date at **Vancouver**, BC's Commodore Ballroom,

The venue for the first performance of Nirvana's most famous song, Seattle's OK Hotel also starred in the movie *Singles*; it's no longer standing today, a casualty of the 2001 earthquake.

Charles Peterson shot one of the most widely reproduced images of Cobain, seemingly playing his guitar while standing on his head. The moment came during the instrumental break in "Love Buzz", when Cobain, writhing on his back on the stage, suddenly pushed his body up so he was resting momentarily on his shoulders; from Peterson's angle, he appeared to be balancing on his head. "Just that Vancouver show alone, there's probably been more images reproduced from that than all the others put together," he says.

None of the new material was played live (save "Territorial Pissings", which they'd performed at the January anti-war show) until 17 April, at Seattle's **OK Hotel**, when they debuted "Smells Like Teen Spirit". The title was a phrase Kathleen Hanna, who would later join Cobain's then-girlfriend Tobi Vail in the band Bikini Kill, had written on Cobain's apartment wall (Novoselic recalled that his reaction on first reading it had been "Too much cheap red wine!"). As was the case with a number of Nirvana songs, the title wasn't used in the song, but stood as an ironic counter-point to the lyric (at the time, no one in the band knew that "Teen Spirit" was a brand of deodorant). For while the title carries a whiff of rebellion, the lyrics, especially in the verses, convey a sense of defeat.

The song had come together in rehearsal. Cobain had the main riff of the chorus, which the group jammed on for a while; Novoselic recalled that either he or Grohl suggested slowing the song down. Cobain then began experimenting with verse melodies (the lyrics would remain unfinished for some time). Originally, the song ran longer as well; a rehearsal take on *With The Lights Out* runs nearly six minutes.

In late April the band headed for LA to record their major label debut, Cobain and Grohl stopping en route in San Francisco to visit Dale Crover. All three, along with Crover's then-girlfriend Debbie Shane, ended up working on a number of songs together in an ad hoc group they called The Retards. One of them, Cobain's "Drain You", would end up on *Nevermind*, the only song the full band hadn't rehearsed before the sessions.

Making Nevermind

On arrival in LA, the group spent a few days at a practice space in North Hollywood. The band and their A&R man, Gary Gersh, had been debating over who would produce the album all spring, with the band holding out for **Butch Vig**. Ultimately the label agreed. "We liked Butch because he brought out the best in us," Novoselic explains. Some of the songs Cobain and Novoselic had previously recorded with Vig would be re-recorded: "In Bloom", "Breed" (previously named "Immodium"), "Lithium" and "Stay Away" (previously "Pay To Play"). They had sent Vig a demo with rough versions of "Teen Spirit", "Come As You Are", "Lounge Act", "On A Plain" and "Something In The Way", and the arrangements were largely worked out already (though, as usual, lyrics had yet to be finalized), so he offered only the occasional suggestion. He was already excited about "Teen Spirit", which hadn't yet been earmarked as a single. And he was equally impressed with Grohl's work (Cobain had already boasted to Vig "We have the best drummer in the world!"). "Krist and Kurt both had their amps cranked," Vig recalls, "and Dave didn't have any mics on his drums. And his drums were louder than their amps. He hit the drums so hard, I was like, holy shit, this guy is really fucking strong!"

Sessions began on 2 May, at **Sound City Studios** in Van Nuys, a suburb of LA (the band lodged at an apartment building nearby, The Oakwood). The studio's glory days had been back in the 1970s, when it hosted acts like Fleetwood Mac (who'd recorded part of their breakthrough smash *Rumours* at the studio) and Tom Petty, as well as Cheap Trick (a favourite of Cobain's). One of Cobain's idols, stuntman Evel Knievel, had also recorded the album *Evel Speaks To The Kids* at Sound City; according to *Heavier Than Heaven*, Cobain stole the master tapes during his stay.

The *Nevermind* cover theme inspired a band promo shoot by the same photographer, Kirk Weddle, in Van Nuys, LA.

As a rule, Vig would arrive first, around noon, the band turning up mid-afternoon and working until around midnight. Recording went fairly quickly, in part because Vig soon learned how much Cobain disliked having to do multiple vocal takes; he'd also frequently sing so hard, his voice would be blown out (before recording his intense vocal for "Territorial Pissings", Cobain warned his producer he was only going to cut one take). As a result, Vig began recording Cobain while he was still warming up, in hopes of catching something he could use. Vig also urged the group to do more overdubbing, in the interest of getting a fuller sound. "In order to get that kind of sound on record you had to use more production work," he explains. "Doubling guitars, using multiple mics on things… just trying to make it sound larger than life 'cause that's how they sounded when they played live."

In retrospect, it's hardly surprising that the Nirvana album that drew so extensively on production techniques the band hadn't used before (and wouldn't use again) would be the record that reached the widest audience. Vig had the responsibility of introducing a cult band to a mainstream public that was largely unfamiliar with them; thus, he was anxious to convey just how powerful the band was live, double-tracking Cobain's vocals and guitar and, on "Come As You Are", Novoselic's bass. Cobain had been reluctant to double-track his vocals, but agreed on hearing that John Lennon had utilized the technique. "I think he thought it was fake," says Vig. "Coming from his punk roots, he wanted everything to be very

au naturale; to record live and leave all the ragged stuff in."

Even the difficulties the band had in the studio paid off in unexpected ways. When the recording of "Lithium" became problematic, the band went into a jam during which Cobain got so worked up he smashed his guitar. Vig had kept the tape rolling throughout, and the jam, later titled "Endless, Nameless", appeared at the end of *Nevermind* as a hidden track. And when a full band arrangement of "Something In The Way" wasn't working out, Cobain played the song on his acoustic for Vig, who realized the quieter setting was just what the song needed. The band considered re-recording "Polly", but decided the version recorded at Smart was good enough. They also recorded "Sappy", "Old Age" and "Verse Chorus Verse", all with scratch vocals, but ultimately decided to not complete them (the latter two would be released on *With The Lights Out*).

Vig also planned to mix the album, and did rough mixes of several songs. Though his mixes have an appealing roughness, after hearing them both Gary Gersh and Nirvana's manager John Silva suggested bringing in someone else; though it was never stated explicitly, it was probably felt that Vig's mixes weren't commercial enough. Gersh provided a list of possible names, among them **Andy Wallace**. When Cobain noted Wallace had worked with Slayer, he said "Get this guy". Mixes were done in around ten days, with Vig and the band making suggestions. Cobain later denounced how *Nevermind* sounded, telling Azerrad "It's closer to a Mötley Crüe record than it is a punk rock record", while Grohl later said the album "had a produced weirdness". But Vig insists that the group was happy with the record at the time, and that Cobain may have been trying to distance himself from *Nevermind*'s success: "As a punk, it's not cool to endorse an album that sells in the millions".

By the time the sessions had finished, the album's original $65,000 budget had doubled, but the cost was still low by major label standards. Nirvana then met with **Robert Fisher**, a designer in Geffen's art department, to work on the album's cover art (even after leaving Geffen to set up his own design studio, Fisher would be the art director for every subsequent Nirvana release on DGC). Fisher had been a fan of the group since the *Bleach* era, and was happy to find Cobain interested enough to make suggestions.

Nevermind's cover was inspired by a TV documentary about giving birth underwater that Cobain and Grohl had seen. Appropriate images from a photo agency had proved prohibitively expensive, so Fisher sent a photographer, **Kirk Weddle**, out to shoot pictures of a few babies swimming. Four-month-old **Spencer Elden** was chosen. Cobain made the further suggestion of adding a fishhook dangling a dollar bill in front of the child, a perfect encapsulation of innocence on the verge of corruption. The label was nervous about using a photo of a naked baby and prepared a cover with Elden's penis airbrushed out, though they ultimately went with the original shot (*Rolling Stone* wouldn't be so bold; their parody of *Nevermind* that ran on the cover of their 28 November 2002 issue featured Bart Simpson sans the potentially offensive appendage). The album's back cover had a photo Cobain had shot of a toy monkey with electrodes strapped to its head in front of one of his collages that meshed together slabs of beef, people burning in hell and, supposedly, diseased vaginas.

Towards the end of the sessions, the band found time to play a show at LA club Jabberjaw. Olympia's **Fitz of Depression** had been scheduled to play, but the club had cancelled, leaving the band in a bind until Cobain suggested Nirvana be added to the bill, at which point the gig was rescheduled. They played most of the songs on *Nevermind*, though the lyrics to "Come As You Are" and "On A Plain" weren't quite finished. "It's called alternative music and it's sweeping the record business by storm!" Novoselic crowed after the first song, little suspecting how in a few months *Nevermind* would end up leading the charge.

A week and a half later they were back on the road properly for an eight-date tour, opening for **Dinosaur Jr.** and **The Jesus Lizard**, taking in Colorado, Utah, Mexico, California, and ending 20 June at Portland's Melody Ballroom. The group then had several weeks off, though they flew to LA occasionally to do promotion for the album. Grohl returned home to Virginia and recorded more solo tracks at Barrett Jones's Laundry Room, after which Jones decided to relocate the studio in Seattle; he and Grohl became roommates.

The Story

On 15 August the group was back in LA to do promotion for *Nevermind*, which was set for release the next month. They did an interview with Loyola Marymount University station **KXLU**, which then had the honour of

Nevermind Triskaidekaphobia, Here's Nirvana

On Friday the 13th,
join Nirvana and DGC Records
for a release party in honor of Nirvana's
DGC debut album **Nevermind**.

Friday, September 13
Re-bar
1114 Howell
Seattle, WA
(206) 233-9873
6:00 PM to 8:00 PM

Edible food, drinks, prizes you might
want to take home, a few surprises,
people to meet, the band to
greet....But nevermind all that, the
important part is the music. Hear
Nevermind in its entirety and loud.

This invitation admits you and a guest
only, and must be presented at the door.
Space is limited. 21 & over with I.D.

DAVID GEFFEN COMPANY
© 1991 The David Geffen Company

being the first radio station to air "Smells Like Teen Spirit" (Boston station WFNX would be the first to play the entire album on air on 29 August). That night an industry showcase had been arranged at the **Roxy**, ostensibly to promote the band to Geffen's staff, but word of mouth had led to a huge demand for tickets. Afterwards, Geffen staffers agreed *Nevermind* would easily match Sonic Youth's sales of *Goo*, which were then just over 100,000 copies.

A landmark video

Flyers had been passed out to the Roxy attendees inviting them to be extras at Nirvana's first video shoot, for "Teen Spirit", on 17 August at GMT Studios. The video was directed by **Sam Bayer**, who would later direct acclaimed videos for Green Day's *American Idiot* album. It was essentially a straightforward performance video, with its setting and execution giving it an additional edge. The set was an unaccountably gloomy-looking high school gymnasium, with kids packed in bleachers and a group of cheerleaders off to the side. After an opening shot of one kid tapping his Converse-shod foot, the camera pans to Nirvana performing the song, as the crowd gets increasingly out of control; by the third chorus, they've leapt out of their seats and surrounded the band, making off with their instruments and crowd surfing amidst the mayhem.

Cobain had wanted the video to be even more anarchic, with the crowd engaging in more pointed destruction; one idea was to have the audience empty their wallets into a big bonfire. He also wanted unattractive cheerleaders, as a jab against the standard beauty queen image. Both of these ideas would have introduced an element of social commentary; instead, it became a more conventionally celebratory display, though the cheerleaders did sport the anarchy "A" symbol on their chests. Adding a surreal element were intercut shots of an elderly janitor, dreamily swaying to the music with his mop, and in a final shot sweeping the floor in front of a bound-and-gagged school principal wearing a dunce's cap. Dissatisfied with Bayer's initial edit, Cobain supervised another edit, which featured a close-up of his face singing "a denial", ending with a smile that he abruptly snaps shut.

European touring

The next day the band flew overseas; aside from the occasional break, they would stay on the road until December. The first jaunt was a European festival tour with Sonic Youth that began with two warm-up dates in Ireland. On 23 August, they made their first appearance at the **Reading Festival**, playing a twelve-song set including just five numbers from *Nevermind*; the high point for Cobain was undoubtedly when the Vaselines' **Eugene Kelly** came onstage to sing "Molly's Lips" with him, photographs of the pair afterwards showing Cobain with a jubilant, somewhat crazed grin. Kelly was in turn impressed by the band's performance: "You knew you were at the centre of something that was going to explode," he later told *Mojo*. At the end of the set, Cobain jumped into

At the 1991 Reading Festival, the Vaselines' Eugene Kelly joined the band onstage to perform their cover of "Molly's Lips".

Grohl's drum kit with such force he dislocated his shoulder. Afterwards, during an interview with Japanese TV, the band took the opportunity to plug another favourite act, Japan's Shonen Knife, whom Cobain called "the best band in the world".

The tour encompassed Belgium, the Netherlands, and several shows in Germany, all filmed by **Dave Markey** for his documentary of the tour, *1991: The Year Punk Broke*. As the band weren't headlining, once their set was done they were free to do what they liked – which in Nirvana's case meant drinking, indulging in food fights, setting off fire extinguishers and trashing their dressing rooms. It was a time when they enjoyed all the perks of rising fame with few of its attendant pressures – exactly what Cobain meant when he told Michael Azerrad a year and a half later that the best time in a band's lifespan was "right before they become really popular".

Nonetheless, when they turned up at the BBC's **Maida Vale studio** on 3 September to record another John Peel session, the band was noticeably tired – "drained, zombified", in the words of the session's producer, Dale Griffin. But the band rallied themselves and recorded three numbers, choosing not to plug their upcoming single, "Teen Spirit".

"Teen Spirit" was released the following week, 9 September in the UK, with the US release the next day. And though the album's street date was a few weeks away, *Nevermind*'s record release party was held on Friday 13 September at hip Seattle club **Re-bar** ("Nevermind Triskaidekaphobia" read the invite – see p.66

– a reference to the superstitious fear of Friday the 13th). The band didn't play, but in usual form, ended up starting a food fight and were momentarily ejected from their own party. The next day "Teen Spirit" debuted on MTV's alternative music programme *120 Minutes*. A more public event, billed as a "Listening Party", was held on 16 September at **Beehive Music & Video** in Seattle. Instead of opting for an acoustic set, the usual practice for in-store performances, the band played a 45-minute electric set, setting up their gear on the store's floor. The free event drew an audience of hundreds, who packed themselves in no more than three feet from the band, though taking care not to bump into the musicians. That wouldn't always be the case on the upcoming tour.

North American Nevermind tour

The North American tour began on 20 September in Toronto, with a show the following night in Montréal; on the day of *Nevermind*'s release, 24 September, the band was in Boston, where Novoselic and Grohl marvelled at the line of kids outside a record store, waiting to buy the album. It entered *Billboard*'s top 200 chart on 12 October at number 144, with "Teen Spirit" hitting the top ten in the Modern Rock Tracks chart (while the Hot 100 Singles chart is based on sales, charts like Modern Rock are based on airplay). The single got a further boost when MTV put the video into their high rotation "Buzz Bin". The record – and the band – was taking off in a fashion that caught everyone off guard. A minimal number of albums had been shipped across the US (the usually cited number is 46,251), meaning until new copies could be manufactured the record was in short supply. Had a larger number been available on release, *Nevermind* would have charted higher much sooner.

Tickets to the shows were in short supply too, as the tour primarily consisted of club dates, and the gigs were packed, many beyond legal capacity. Sometimes the crowds merely added to the excitement, other times they threatened to get out of hand. At the dangerously overcrowded 19 October show at Dallas's **Trees** club, the audience was packed so tightly that

When *Nevermind* came out, Nirvana were still playing clubs and small theatres, venues that were arguably already too small, adding to the crowd's excitement.

The Year Nirvana Broke

fans attempting to crowd surf were dumped back on the stage. When Cobain leapt into the crowd during "Love Buzz" and a bouncer tried to drag him back on stage, Cobain whacked him with his guitar. Back on stage, the bouncer punched Cobain in the head, knocking him to the floor, then began kicking him before he was pulled away. "It was kind of like the Hell's Angels at Altamont," the show's promoter later recalled. The audience erupted and it was several minutes before the show continued. And a reviewer described the October 24 show at Iguana's in Tijuana as "the most violent pop show this critic has ever witnessed".

The next day, the band were back in Los Angeles, where Cobain and Novoselic taped an appearance on MTV's *Headbanger's Ball*, Cobain donning an elaborate yellow ballgown for the occasion. They were in particularly good spirits at that evening's show, a **Rock For Choice** benefit at **The Palace** in Hollywood, with Cobain announcing, "Keep your fucking laws off my sister's body" prior to the band's set. The setting was tailor made for Novoselic to launch into several political rants, at one point urging the crowd, "Be educated and think about the issue, and be educated in general, because that's what the United States needs – and smash your TV set, because that's the opiate!" He later dedicated "Negative Creep" to William Rehnquist, the highly conservative Chief Justice on the United States Supreme Court.

The US leg of the tour concluded on Halloween with a homecoming date at Seattle's **Paramount Theatre**, with Mudhoney and Bikini Kill opening. It was the largest show the band had yet played in Seattle. The setting was austere, with only the band's gear set up in front of a large screen. Two Olympia friends, Ian Dickson and Nikki McClure, added a touch of theatre by go-go dancing on either side of the stage, Dickson wearing a T-shirt reading "Girl", McClure's T-shirt reading "Boy".

There was also a film crew in attendance, which displeased many longtime fans. "I was like, 'Yeah, this is the beginning of the end,'" Charles Peterson, who photographed the show, told Everett True. "It was so unfair to their home audience because it stilted the performance." That doesn't come across in the footage (which was later used in the "Lithium" video and in *Live! Tonight! Sold Out!!*), though Cobain was noticeably reticent, speaking briefly at the beginning of the show, and then at the start of the encore, when he introduced "Rape Me" by explaining, "This song is about hairy, sweaty, macho, redneck men. Who rape." Nor was the end-of-set destruction as extensive, with Grohl's drum kit remaining intact, and Novoselic tossing Cobain's guitar in the air and awkwardly trying to smash it with his bass.

By now, *Nevermind* had gone gold and was about to enter the US top forty. And not only was the band's sudden success a surprise, it was becoming apparent that coping with that success was going to be more difficult than they'd anticipated. A day after *Nevermind*'s release, Cobain had told DGC radio rep Ted Volk he didn't want to do any more radio interviews, stating, "I'm just not interested

When Kurt met Courtney...

When did Kurt Cobain and Courtney Love first meet? In *Come As You Are*, author Michael Azerrad says Portland's Satyricon club in 1989; in *Heavier Than Heaven*, Charles R. Cross agrees it was Satyricon but says the date was 12 February 1990 (and even gives a time, 11pm); in *Nirvana: The True Story*, Everett True says, with typical flamboyancy, that he introduced the two to each other at a Butthole Surfers gig at the Hollywood Palladium in May 1991, and that Cobain later told him "I only ever asked Courtney Love out on a date to impress you." Courtney herself told *Sassy* magazine she first saw Nirvana play in Portland in 1988.

But in the same interview, from January 1992, she also says she met him at a show "about a year or something ago", which Cobain then remembers being a Butthole Surfers concert. So perhaps Love did indeed first see Nirvana at a Portland show in 1989 or 90 (the band didn't play there in 1988), but didn't formally meet him until 1991, when he was in the midst of recording *Nevermind*. All sources do agree, at least, that this was the moment when the two began orbiting around each other. Their paths began crossing more frequently that fall, when Nirvana and Hole ended up playing the occasional show together (indeed, they shared a bill with Dinosaur Jr. soon after the Butthole Surfers gig, at the Hollywood Palladium on 14 June). Finally, on 12 October, following a Nirvana show at Chicago's Cabaret Metro, Love made her way backstage and into Cobain's life for good. Four months later, they were married.

in talking about myself." A week later in Philadelphia, he admitted to Everett True even making music no longer meant as much to him, partly because dealing with the "commercial side" of the business had made him increasingly uncomfortable: "It frustrates me and makes me ashamed to be in rock'n'roll".

Partly the frustration was because much of the increased media coverage was spurred by the album's sales – not the music. Nirvana were also discovering that becoming successful doesn't just mean your audience becomes larger; it also becomes different. They were now playing to audiences that didn't just consist of kids steeped in an alternative rock sensibility, but a mainstream crowd that wasn't necessarily interested in the band beyond hearing its hit song. In Nirvana's first *Rolling Stone* interview Novoselic would admit, "I wish we could have a time machine and go back to two months ago. I'd tell people to get lost." The new motto on the band's T-shirts – "Nirvana: Flower Sniffin, Kitty Pettin, Baby Kissin Corporate Rock Whores" – no longer seemed that funny.

Filming of the Paradiso Amsterdam gig on 25 November 1991 restricted the songs Nirvana were allowed to play, irritating the band and Cobain in particular.

Unknown to his bandmates, one of the ways Cobain had chosen to deal with the growing demands placed upon him was to increase his heroin use. His romantic life had become more complicated too. While in Boston, he'd met singer-songwriter **Mary Lou Lord,** who had then accompanied the band on the road for a few days. After Lord returned to Boston, **Courtney Love,** a musician and actress Cobain had hung out with during the *Nevermind* sessions, showed up backstage at Nirvana's show at Chicago's Cabaret Metro on 12 October and spent the night with Cobain (he met the notorious Cynthia Plaster Caster the same night, infamous for the plaster casts she made of rock stars' genitalia; "You can cast my middle finger because it's representative of how I feel about the music industry," Cobain told her). Love and Cobain next met up at the Rock For Choice show in LA and spent more time together.

Nevermind European tour

The band left for another UK/European tour on 2 November, this time as the headliners. In the UK, *Nevermind* had entered the top forty on 29 September, and the album was now on the verge of going gold. After the first show, in Bristol on 4 November, Cobain was surprised to find Lord waiting for him backstage. He was even more surprised to receive a call from Love the following night demanding to know who this Mary Lou Lord was she'd been

The Story

Nirvana regularly wore T-shirts promoting fellow bands; for the cover of *NME*, Cobain chose Eugene Kelly's new venture.

hearing about. Cobain managed to put Love off, and the next day declined to take Lord on the road with him, still denying he was involved with anyone else. Without directly confronting either woman, he opted to make his feelings clear when Nirvana performed on the late-night television show *The Word* on 8 November, calling Courtney Love "the best fuck in the world".

Cobain's comment unsurprisingly generated headlines, but Nirvana had been making equally provocative statements, albeit only to the UK music press, that were often overlooked. Though not an overtly political band, their interviews revealed a social consciousness not often seen in mainstream rock acts. A 21 September story in *NME* had Novoselic again ranting about the Gulf War ("I was so freaked out and angry that it was so wrong, such a fuckin' lie"), while Cobain bemoaned US immigration regulations that placed undue restrictions on touring artists. *NME*'s 23 November issue, summing up the band's coolness, proclaimed them "The Guns N' Roses It's OK To Like" on their cover (see above). The accompanying story had Cobain saying that men were the ones who needed to be educated about the evils of rape, and Novoselic attacking the apathy of his

fellow Americans: "People are so spoiled. They have VCRs, cheap gasoline and 40 channels and they're not going to rock the boat. Nobody cares that the USA is completely fucking over the Third World".

On 9 November, Nirvana recorded their final BBC radio session, for Mark Goodier's show. The tour then headed off for Germany, Austria and Italy. On arriving in **Ghent**, Belgium, on 23 November, they were joined by *Rolling Stone* reporter Chris Mundy, who interviewed them for the magazine's first story on the band. *Rolling Stone* had only given *Nevermind* a three-star rating in their 28 November issue, but sales were continuing to climb; by the end of the month the album had sold over a million copies in the US and had just landed in the top five, while "Teen Spirit" had topped the Modern Rock Tracks chart (it would finally debut at number forty in the Hot 100 Singles chart in December). These were remarkable statistics for a band that was still largely unknown.

Mundy caught a particularly riotous show in Ghent, the band playing a number of lesser-known songs (the yet-to-be-recorded "Curmudgeon" and "Oh, The Guilt", and the never-recorded "Talk To Me"), and a cover of The Doors' "The End", with Novoselic substituting a crazy monologue about a visit to a waffle house during the song's spoken-word section. During the end-of-show bout of instrument destruction, a chunk of guitar flew into the audience and injured a fan down front, hitting him in the face with such force it dislodged a tooth.

Nirvana's UK TV shows

When Nirvana arrived in the UK on 3 November 1991, both *Nevermind* and "Smells Like Teen Spirit" were selling steadily, and would eventually peak at number seven in their respective charts. But what really brought them to national attention were the three television appearances they made over the next month.

Their 8 November appearance on the Friday-night post-pub show *The Word* was the band's first performance on live TV. Cobain ensured it would be even more memorable by first announcing, "I'd like all of you people in this room to know that Courtney Love, the lead singer of the sensational pop group Hole, is the best fuck in the world", while Novoselic bounced up and down as if he couldn't wait for the song to begin. The band had been asked to play an edited version of "Teen Spirit" but they refused, so the show's closing credits began running over the performance before it was finished, to the group's chagrin. When rebroadcast on *The Best Of The Word*, the end of the song was finally shown, revealing that after singing "A denial" a few times during the last chorus, Cobain then switched to screaming out "Roger Taylor!", the Duran Duran drummer who was about to marry one of *The Word*'s hosts, Amanda de Cadenet.

Next up was a spot on *Top of the Pops*, Britain's longest-running music show. When the band arrived to tape their appearance on 27 November, they were informed they'd be miming to a backing track of "Teen Spirit" with Cobain providing a live lead vocal. The group quickly decided to exploit the situation, and though in the first shot Grohl appeared to be miming adequately, the next showed Cobain's hands strumming nowhere near his guitar strings, a small smirk on his face, while Novoselic appeared to be wrestling with an out of control bass. Prior to the first verse Cobain gave up all pretence of miming, simply gripping the mic with both hands and standing stock still, then singing in a deep bass voice (he later said he was trying to emulate Morrissey), altering the song's lyrics, and appearing at times to fellate the mic. While Nirvana's crew found the performance hysterical, the show's producers were less amused and asked for a second take, but the band demurred. The next night they watched the show air while in Sheffield, Eugene Kelly recalling that Cobain seemed embarrassed, but everyone else congratulated him, saying, "You fucked up the Pops! You got them! Yeah!" Ironically it was perhaps the only time the lyrics of this much-debated song could be clearly understood in live performance.

The band threw another curveball when they appeared live on *Tonight With Jonathan Ross* on 6 December. Cobain didn't show up on set until an hour before recording, and the group did a quick rehearsal of "Lithium". But during the broadcast, they opted instead to perform a frighteningly incendiary version of "Territorial Pissings". It was the type of performance usually followed by a good bout of instrument wrecking, but in this case the band was fairly restrained: Cobain knocked his mic stand over and held his guitar up to an amp to draw out some squalling feedback before dropping it, Novoselic tossed his bass in the air and eventually into Grohl's drum kit, and Grohl knocked over a few more drums as the band exited the stage. Ross recovered nicely from the song switch, drawing a big laugh when he noted Nirvana were available for "playing children's birthday parties and bar mitzvahs".

Later TV performances would be less spontaneous, but in the first flush of fame Nirvana often tried to see how much they could get away with. "I would really love for people to remember Kurt's humour," says soundman Craig Montgomery. "At this time their thinking when they were on stage was, 'What could we do that would be funny?' Anyone who was there knows a Nirvana thing was fun, hilarious and joyous."

Two days later they recorded their final radio show in **Hilversum**, the Netherlands, a joint production between VPRO's *Nozems-a-GoGo* and VARA's *Twee Meter De Lucht In* programmes. By this point in the tour, the strain the band was feeling after months on the road was beginning to show. Jack Endino,

who had been touring Europe with his band **Skin Yard** (who opened for Nirvana on 14 November in Vienna), noticed a change in the band's demeanour when he attended their 25 November show at the Paradiso in **Amsterdam**. The show was being filmed, and the band had been instructed not to play any new songs that

Back in the UK: Cobain coaxing feedback from his guitar at Kilburn's National Ballroom, London, December 1991.

weren't yet copyrighted. Endino recalls their annoyance at being told what they could and couldn't play, and Cobain in particular being irritated by the cameras. "Everybody seemed to be really uneasy and very unhappy," he says. "Like suddenly the success was starting to bother them because people were starting to come at them. Suddenly people wouldn't leave them alone." Cobain's displeasure is most obvious when he performs "Come As You Are", choosing to scream his way through most of the song.

And then it was back to the UK for further dates. As on the previous UK outing, one of the opening acts was Eugene Kelly's new band, **Captain America** (later changed to Eugenius, when Marvel Comics threatened a lawsuit); on occasion Kelly would again join Cobain in singing "Molly's Lips" during Nirvana's set. On 27 November, they taped an appearance for *Top Of The Pops*, where, unlike their radio spots, they were locked into performing "Teen Spirit",

though the band subverted the situation, deliberately miming inaccurately on their instruments while Cobain sang in a deep bass voice. Their final appearance on British television came on 6 December, when they made a live appearance on *Tonight With Jonathan Ross*.

But the stress of touring continued to wear everyone down. Cobain's stomach problem had flared up, as had bronchitis (which he further aggravated by continuing to smoke), Novoselic had been drinking excessively ("A few shows I barely remember playing," he later told Azerrad), and Grohl felt like he was on the verge of a nervous breakdown. So after a final show on 7 December at the TransMusicale Festival in **Rennes**, France, it was decided to cancel the week of remaining dates, allowing for a short break before they were expected back on the road. And though the band's success was already greater than anyone had envisioned, it was about to get even bigger in the months ahead.

Here we are, now entertain us

1992

Here we are, now entertain us
1992

It was in 1992 that Nirvana became world famous, and, in some quarters, infamous. Their whirlwind rise at times threatened to overwhelm the band, not least because Cobain's reaction was a steady retreat into drugs. The band did few shows and even less recording. "That's when everything changed," says Novoselic. "Nothing was the same after the whole fame thing. Things just progressively got worse, like the relationships. But the musical relationship, at least we'd play together and have fun playing. It's like the classic story, once the band makes it big, then everything just gets screwy. Everything went south."

Top of the charts

After a three-week break, Nirvana were back on the road, in Los Angeles on 27 December 1991 for the first stop on a five-day tour. Booked before *Nevermind* had taken off, it had the group back to being an opening band, along with Pearl Jam, for the **Red Hot Chili Peppers**. It was the last time they'd be booked to support a bigger act, though, for on the last night of the tour, 2 January in Salem, Oregon, they were greeted with the news that *Nevermind* would be the number one album in *Billboard*'s 11 January issue, kicking Michael Jackson's *Dangerous* off the top spot. The album would also top the charts in Canada, Ireland, Spain, France, Belgium and Sweden (though oddly, not the UK, where it peaked at number seven). Sales of the album in the US were now over two million. Next, on 8 January came the announcement that *Nevermind* had received a Grammy nomination for Best Alternative Music Album. *Bleach* was also selling to new fans, and would eventually peak at number 89 in the Hot 100, the first Sub Pop album to crack the chart (and eventually the label's biggest seller).

It was in this newly frenzied atmosphere that Nirvana flew to **New York City** for a round of appearances and interviews, including a performance on the TV show *Saturday Night Live*. But at a time when the mood should have

The Story

been celebratory, a time to enjoy the grand payoff after so many years of hard work, there was increasing turmoil behind the scenes due to Cobain's escalating drug use. Love had joined Cobain towards the end of Nirvana's European tour, and the two had been using heroin regularly. They moved in together after

Promotional work and press shoots like this one in Belfast ramped up after *Nevermind* took off.

the tour, and by the time the couple arrived in New York, the rest of the band, and their management were forced to confront the fact that Cobain had a serious drug problem.

The last thing anyone wanted to do was speak about it publicly, but the week the band was in New York, the first article to hint at Cobain's drug use was published, in *BAM* (*Bay Area Magazine*), whose cover story on the band questioned, "Will the Breakthrough Band of 91 Survive 92?" Journalist **Jerry McCulley** had interviewed Nirvana backstage before their 27 December 1991 Los Angeles concert, and described an exhausted Cobain who kept "nodding off" during the interview: "the pinned pupils; sunken cheeks; and scabbed, sallow skin suggest something more serious than mere fatigue." McCulley found his subject thoughtful and articulate, but also captured Cobain's dissatisfaction, quoting him as saying "I hope to destroy my career before it's too late" (his jokier observation, "Hope I die before I turn into Pete Townsend", became the article's second most quoted line). In the magazine's opening editorial, McCulley added, "it just seems to me that, mentally, [Cobain's] not prepared for any of this."

Though heroin (or indeed, any other drug) wasn't mentioned in the article, the implications were obvious, and piqued interest among the press, to whom Cobain's demeanour had been explained as simple exhaustion. On the day of the *Saturday Night Live* show, the band did a photo shoot with Michael Lavine, and Cobain nodded off several times; he later recalled the reaction from his bandmates being "Dirty looks and dead silence." Only Lavine dared to say anything, but Cobain blamed his drug use on his stomach problems. The band spent most of the day at Lavine's, where Cobain prepared his "stage outfit" for the evening, drawing the fish logo from Flipper's *Generic* album on a T-shirt.

On the way to *SNL*, Cobain had the cab pull over so he could throw up, and backstage he spent most of the time sleeping on a sofa. He did rouse himself when one of the show's stars, Victoria Jackson, asked him to speak to her friend **"Weird Al" Yankovic** over the phone, who wanted to ask Cobain if he could do a parody video of "Teen Spirit". Under US copyright law, Yankovic didn't need Nirvana's permission to parody their song, but he'd long made it a practice to request permission out of courtesy. Cobain readily agreed.

"Teen Spirit" was the first song the band performed. Cobain did not look well, keeping his eyes closed most of the time, but the performance was riveting nonetheless. The band pounded out the second song, "Territorial Pissings", in a fury, Cobain spearing a speaker with his guitar and Grohl knocking his drum kit over at the song's conclusion. In a sign of solidarity with other alternative acts, each band member wore a T-shirt of one of their favourite bands; in addition to Cobain's homemade Flipper T-shirt, Grohl wore a Melvins T-shirt, and Novoselic actually changed shirts, wearing a Melvins T-shirt during "Teen Spirit", and an L7 T-shirt during "Territorial Pissings".

At the end of the show, when the cast and guests come out to wave at the audience, Novoselic grabbed Grohl and Cobain and kissed each of them in front of the cameras. It was partly a joke and partly to cheer Cobain up ("I told him, 'It's going to be okay. It's not so bad. Okay?'" Novoselic later explained to Charles Cross); afterwards Grohl attempted to hoist Cobain on his back.

Once the promotional work was over, the band's management began to address Cobain's drug problem, the extent of which they hadn't grasped before (in *Heavier Than Heaven*, Charles Cross asserts that Cobain even OD'd after the *SNL* show). Danny Goldberg later told Carrie Borzillo-Vrenna that between Nirvana's *SNL* appearance and Cobain's death there was "a constant series of discussions and meetings" about Cobain's drug use, though he conceded the focus was more on the fact that Cobain had a drug problem than on any underlying issues. Any treatment plans were complicated by the news that Love was pregnant. A specialist told the couple the baby would be fine if Love stopped using drugs. But instead of entering rehab, the two checked into a hotel for a few days to do their own, private detox.

Pacific Rim tour

Meanwhile, further Nirvana business was pressing. Between 19 and 22 January the group filmed a video for their second single, "Come As You Are", at Cobain's home, Wattles Garden Park in Hollywood, and a hangar at Van Nuys Airport. It was their first time working with director Kevin Kerslake, who would ultimately direct four of the band's videos. Cobain had asked that his face be obscured, as he was tired of being recognized (though by this time it was a case of closing the barn door after the horses had well and truly bolted). Kerslake duly shielded the band behind cascading sheets of water, and drew on other imagery from the song's lyrics (a gun spinning lazily in water) and the *Nevermind* album cover (a baby swimming). And despite his request, Cobain provided a close up himself by kissing the camera at the song's end, before lying face down on the ground.

The next day the band left for a Pacific Rim tour, with the first date 24 January at the Phoenician Club in **Sydney**, followed by a performance at the first Big Day Out festival at Sydney's Hordern Pavilion. Cobain's stomach immediately began giving him problems. He missed an after-party shindig following Nirvana's first show, where the band was presented with record award plaques, and though attributed to illness, journalists began speculating on the real reason for his absence. Subsequently, the show in Brisbane was cut short, and one in Perth cancelled completely. Others were moved to larger venues, as should have happened at a show in Canberra, where police were called in to deal with the hundreds of fans who couldn't gain access to the venue (the Union Bar at Australia National University). The headline on *Select*'s April 1992 cover fittingly described the tour with the headline "At The Brink Of Collapse: Nirvana On The Road". Cobain was eventually taken to a doctor who prescribed physeptone; it was only later that Cobain realized the drug contained methadone. As he noted in his journal, he'd inadvertently become hooked again.

After a show in New Zealand and a press day in Singapore, the tour took in a series of shows in Japan, ending up finally in Honolulu with dates on 21 and 22 February. On 24 February, Kurt Cobain and Courtney Love were married on the beach in front of their hotel, the Hilton Hawaiian Village. But the event was marred by inner band turmoil. Cobain, believing Novoselic's

Photos for Nirvana's first *Rolling Stone* cover story were shot while on tour in Australia and featured another of Cobain's hand-drawn T-shirts; the cover's text used a font not unlike that of Nirvana's familiar logo.

wife, among others, had been gossiping about his and Love's drug use, said she wasn't welcome at the ceremony, so Novoselic himself refused to attend. Grohl was present, as were some crew members. Dylan Carlson, Cobain's friend from Olympia, served as best man and brought Cobain some heroin, which Cobain took before the wedding ("A little teeny bit so I didn't get sick," he told Azerrad).

Spring break

As Novoselic and Grohl returned to Seattle, and Cobain returned to LA, the future of Nirvana was very much in doubt. Further unpleasantness arose when Cobain announced he wanted to change the band's publishing agreement. Songwriting royalties had been distributed equally among the three musicians,

The Story

Grunge hype

Prior to Seattle's ascendancy in the early 1990s, cities like Minneapolis, Minnesota, and Athens, Georgia, were known for having well-regarded alternative music scenes. But Seattle was different, the city's popularity quickly transcending its music and encompassing a presumed "grunge lifestyle".

In this sense, what happened in Seattle had more in common with the "British Invasion" of the early 1960s or San Francisco's Haight-Ashbury scene during the fabled "Summer of Love", which also incorporated fashion trends and other ephemera. So it was with Seattle; while music was key to the scene, much was also made of how people in Seattle behaved: what they drank, what they wore and their dedication to a slacker way of life (shunning acquisitive success in favour of a more laid-back, less stressful, manner of living).

The Northwest's penchant for coffee drinking had already been sent up in David Lynch's TV *noir* series *Twin Peaks*, whose characters often stopped at the show's Double R Diner or Great Northern Hotel for a "damn fine" cup of coffee. Journalists heading to Seattle to cover the grunge scene couldn't help notice the plethora of coffee shops in town (in some neighbourhoods you could walk over a mile and find a coffee shop in each block), headed up by the Starbucks Coffee chain, along with rivals Stewart Brothers Coffee (changed to Seattle's Best Coffee in 1991 and purchased by Starbucks in 2003), Tully's Coffee and hundreds of independently run shops. Since the mid-1980s, Northwest microbreweries had also grown in number; Buddy Bradley, slacker star of Peter Bagge's *Hate* comic (published by Seattle-based Fantagraphics Books) had a penchant for Redhook's Ballard Bitter. These beverages of choice were eventually seen as having an influence on the region's music: "Jolted by java and looped with liquor, no wonder the [Seattle] music sounds like it does," Michael Azerrad

wrote in his *Rolling Stone* story "Grunge City". The *New York Times* made a similar observation when they lauded the region's music as being "inspired and tempered by that city's three principal drugs: espresso, beer and heroin".

Even graphic design played a role in disseminating grungemania. In September 1991 Art Chantry, then art director at *The Rocket*, redesigned the magazine to feature column headings spelled out by a dysfunctional label embosser, improperly aligned and with occasional letters facing the wrong direction. As Seattle bands grew in popularity, designers working for more mainstream outlets appropriated the style, which quickly came to be seen as symbolizing "alternative" culture, turning up in magazines, on posters and record covers (including, oddly enough, Joan Baez's 1992 album *Play Me Backwards*, not quite anyone's idea of a grunge rocker). In its translation to the mainstream, the style was cleaned up, with the letters aligned correctly and all facing the same way. The embossed label style eventually became a typeface, called "Recycle Reverse".

But nothing was more ludicrous than the entirely media-created trend of "grunge fashion". The damp climate of the region led residents to dress in layers for the simple reason of practicality; a flannel shirt worn over a T-shirt could readily be taken on or off depending on the vagaries of the weather. As musicians and artists also preferred to spend more of their money on equipment and supplies, shopping at thrift stores was simply a cheaper way to buy clothes (in addition to being a way to pick up an item that had a more individual flavour than something being sold in bulk at a chain store). Rugged clothing suited for the outdoors, like Doc Marten boots and knit hats, was also favoured. The most unique touch was the baseball cap, which was worn backwards.

The *Boston Globe* may have been the first paper to run a story on the "trend" in February 1992, comparing clothing worn by the homeless and combat boots worn by prisoners of war as capturing the "fashion essence of the typical rock band, epitomized by the group Nirvana". Soon, this "fashion essence" made its way to the catwalk via a Marc Jacobs collection designed for Perry Ellis (featuring plaid shirts made out of sand-washed silk, not flannel), and a *Vogue* magazine spread entitled "Grunge and Glory", featuring models wearing "designer grunge" outfits that cost hundreds of dollars. Even in outlets that strived for greater authenticity, the genuine article wasn't enough; when Scott McCaughey of The Young Fresh Fellows (and later R.E.M.) was tapped by *Rolling Stone* for their fashion spread, shooting in the warehouse at Popllama Records where he sometimes worked, he was asked to take off the shirts he was wearing and to put on the more "fashionable" shirts provided.

Seattlites had the last laugh with "grunge fashion", thanks to Sub Pop employee Megan Jasper, who managed to brilliantly put one over the paper. Asked by a *New York Times* writer to give some examples of "grunge slang", Jasper duly provided a list of completely made-up terms, such as "Cob nobbler" (loser) and "Swingin' on the flippity-flop" (hanging out). The "Lexicon of Grunge: Breaking the Code" ran as a sidebar to Rick Marin's "Grunge: A Success Story" in the 15 November 1992 issue of the paper. Seattle-based C/Z Records later printed up T-shirts featuring two more of Jasper's terms: "Lamestain" (uncool person) and "Harsh Realm" (bummer); the latter was also used as the title of a comic book and the TV series subsequently based on it.

Former music journalist Cameron Crowe made Seattle's music scene the backdrop of his film *Singles*, a romantic comedy revolving around a group of young people who mostly live in the same apartment building. One of the characters, Cliff (played by Matt Dillon), was even in a band, Citizen Dick, one of whose songs, "Touch Me I'm Dick", was a play on Mudhoney's "Touch Me I'm Sick" (members of Pearl Jam played the band's other members). Though some thought the film was created purely to capitalize on grungemania, it had actually been completed by the summer of 1991, with the studio, Warner Bros., initially reluctant to release it, unconvinced of its profitability. Ironically, it was grungemania that then came to the film's rescue, as executives realized that the accompanying soundtrack, which featured contributions from Pearl Jam, Soundgarden, Alice In Chains and Screaming Trees, was sure to be a hit (which it was, reaching number six in *Billboard*). The film was finally released in September 1992. Mudhoney's contribution to the *Singles* soundtrack was an apt summary of the media hype that had descended on Seattle over the past year: "Overblown".

but Cobain now wanted a greater share of the pie, reasoning that most of the musical ideas and all of the lyrics were his. Novoselic and Grohl were agreeable until they realized Cobain wanted the new deal to be applied retroactively. Cobain was insistent he'd break up the band otherwise, and the two musicians eventually gave in, but the incident left a bad taste.

But to the rest of the world, Nirvana were still on a winning streak. An EP, *Hormoaning*, had been released in Australia and Japan to tie with the band's tour. "Come As You Are" was released 2 March in the UK, 3 March in the US, reaching numbers 9 and 32, respectively. In April, "Weird Al" Yankovic's parody of "Teen Spirit", "Smells Like Nirvana", was released on his *Off the Deep End* album, and as a single, whose sleeve pictured Yankovic underwater swimming toward a doughnut on a hook; it reached number 35 in the charts.

The band's first *Rolling Stone* cover story appeared in the magazine's 16 April issue; the cover shot, taken in Australia, had Cobain wearing another hand-drawn T-shirt, reading "Corporate magazines still suck" (see p.81). Written by **Michael Azerrad**, the story was more a profile of Cobain, as the headline revealed: "Inside the Heart and Mind of Kurt Cobain". Cobain had been interviewed at home, lying exhausted in bed, his voice "one or two steps up from a whisper". In addition to relating the band's history, the story also contained several denials from Cobain that he was using heroin, or any other drug, including alcohol.

Despite Cobain's denials, heroin was very much a part of his life. In March he entered a formal rehab programme for the first time, but ended up leaving it early, and was back on the drug again before long. On 7 April the band reconvened in Seattle for a quick recording session at the Laundry Room, cranking out three songs for various upcoming compilations and B-sides. "Return Of The Rat" would appear first on a Wipers tribute album released in June; Nirvana were originally going to contribute "D-7", from the 1990 Peel session, but when there were problems licensing the track, they simply recorded another Wipers song. "Curmudgeon" appeared as a B-side on the "Lithium" single, and "Oh, The Guilt" would appear on a split single with The Jesus Lizard the following year. At some point in April the group also recorded an early instrumental version of "Frances Farmer Will Have Her Revenge on Seattle".

The recording session was the only band activity all spring. Cobain was holed up in LA the rest of the time, occasionally writing songs or painting, but basically turning down any offers that involved leaving the house. He did contact Eugene Kelly during this period, asking him to come to LA to write songs "and maybe join the band". Kelly was recording at the time, and said to get in touch with him later, but he never heard from Cobain again. Meanwhile, Grohl (as "Dale Nixon") teamed up with **Buzz Osborne** to record Osborne's solo EP, *King Buzzo*, at the Laundry Room. For his part, Novoselic became increasingly involved in the anti-censorship movement that was growing in Washington state. The state's governor, Booth Gardner, signed a bill into law that allowed music retailers to be prosecuted for selling "offensive" music to minors. Novoselic spoke at rallies opposed to the bill, which was overturned in November as being unconstitutional.

Nirvana's absence from the music scene led to press reports that Cobain's drug problems were responsible, something then denied by the band's management, who claimed the reason was the singer's ongoing stomach trouble. Among other appearances, the band had been asked to appear at that year's Grammy awards, but couldn't work out the details (they ended up losing Best Alternative Music Album to R.E.M.'s *Out Of Time*). They turned down an offer to tour with Metallica and Guns N' Roses; a wise call, as Nirvana's sensibilities were wildly different from the other two bands. But they also declined to headline a major tour themselves, at the very time *Nevermind*'s sales were peaking.

In other news, a UK band also named Nirvana sued the band for trademark violation. An LA-based band named Nirvana had sued the band the previous year, a case that was settled for $50,000; the UK Nirvana case would be settled for $100,000. (It's also been claimed the UK band Killing Joke sued Nirvana over similarities between their song "Eighties" and "Come As You Are", but the band's bassist Paul Raven says legal action wasn't ever pursued.)

Back to Europe

In mid-June Nirvana headed overseas, to play a series of make-up dates for the shows they'd cancelled the previous December. The tour began 21 June with a show in Dublin. The next night, at King's Hall in **Belfast**, Love rescued a kid who was being roughed up by the bouncers and brought him backstage, where she bought his red-and-black striped sweater for Cobain. Though a *Select* reporter present described Cobain as being unimpressed with Love's entreaties that he'd look "just like Johnny Rotten" in the sweater, it would become an integral part of his later wardrobe, featured in the promo photos for *In Utero* and worn at a number of shows.

The same writer also described Cobain as looking "knackered and ill", though Cobain again denied using heroin, attributing his occasional nodding off to narcolepsy. But the next morning he was sent to the hospital suffering from stomach pains, attributed to a "weeping ulcer" according to one of the band's publicists; Cobain later said it was because he'd forgotten to take his methadone. The next day, the band's management hired two "minders" to keep an eye on Cobain and Love. This infuriated Cobain, who later griped to Azerrad that they "were turning this band into everything it wasn't supposed to be."

Most of the shows were at outdoor venues, and so large scale the band members no longer knew everyone on the crew, adding to the sense of disorientation. They were refraining from playing new material, afraid it would be immediately bootlegged, instead reaching into their catalogue and reviving songs like "Swap Meet" and "Scoff", which they hadn't played in years. Towards the end of the tour, they provided ironic commentary on their situation by opening with a cover of Fang's "The Money Will Roll Right In".

The Story

The tour's final dates were in Spain. Prior to the band's show in Madrid, Love began to experience contractions and was sent to a local hospital. It was determined she was in no immediate danger, but the band cancelled their last date in San Sebastian and returned to the US. Cobain and Love got home to find that a broken pipe had flooded the bathroom in their apartment, destroying journals and instruments that had been stored in the bathtub for "safekeeping". They decided to move, choosing a house on a bluff in North Hollywood that had been used as the home of Elliott Gould's detective character in Robert Altman's *The Long Goodbye*.

Nevermind's third single, "Lithium", was released 20 July in the UK, 21 July in the US. The cover art was by Cobain, the front depicting dolls from his collection, the rear a shot of a skeleton lying on a bed of flowers. Inside was a sonogram of Cobain and Love's child, literally *in utero*, along with the more useful printing of the words to all the songs on *Nevermind*. The single made it to number 11 in the UK, and to 64 in the US (though it reached numbers 16 and 25 in *Billboard*'s Mainstream and Modern Rock charts respectively). In contrast to their previous videos, "Lithium" was quite basic. There being no time to shoot – or interest in shooting – fresh material, Kevin Kerslake simply assembled a compilation of live footage.

Frances Bean arrives

In August Cobain agreed to go back to rehab and was soon joined by his wife at Cedars-Sinai Medical Center in Los Angeles. On 18 August Love gave birth to a girl, named **Frances Bean Cobain** ("Frances" in honour of the Vaselines' Frances McKee, "Bean" because Cobain thought she had resembled a bean in her sonogram). Cobain was at Love's side, though he passed out during the delivery. While the press release noted that the baby was perfectly healthy, news reports continued to suggest otherwise, beginning with a 23 August *Los Angeles Times* story reporting that leaked medical records claimed to show that Love had been administered prenatal vitamins and methadone when she entered the hospital, just one of a number of articles that speculated on the extent of the couple's purported drug use (Love later sued the hospital and her former doctor over the leaked records; the case was settled out of court). Keith Cameron, who had accompanied the band on the Spanish leg of their recent tour, turned in a story that ran in *NME*'s 29 August issue, which focused on the drug rumours (which Cobain again denied) and what he perceived as friction in the entourage about Love's presence. The story was entitled "Love Will Tear Us Apart".

But far more damaging – and more widely read – was **Lynn Hirschberg**'s profile of Love that ran in the September issue of *Vanity Fair*, published mid-August. Love was described as a "charismatic opportunist" who was sowing discord in the Nirvana camp, and dominating a weak Cobain who "looks as if he might break". Even worse was a quote from Love that seemed to say she'd taken heroin after knowing she was pregnant, coupled with anonymous quotes from "insiders" who claimed to be worried about the health of the unborn child. In a country where reproductive rights are a divisive issue, Hirschberg's story was bound to cause controversy, but neither Love nor Cobain could have imagined the furore that would follow.

On reading an advance copy of *Vanity Fair*, the couple immediately released a statement insisting that the story contained "many inaccuracies, distortions, and generally gives a false picture of both of us", and "unequivocally" denying Love had used heroin after knowing she was pregnant. Nevertheless, two days after Frances was born, a social worker from California's Department of Social Services arrived at the hospital, a copy of *Vanity Fair* in hand, to launch an investigation. As a result, the couple were initially denied custody of Frances, who remained in the hospital for "observation" when Love checked out on 21 August. At a court hearing on 24 August, the couple was again denied full custody, and only allowed to be with Frances in the presence of a guardian; Cobain was also ordered back into rehab. Given the fractured relationships Cobain and Love had with their own parents, it was agreed that Love's half-sister, Jamie Rodriguez, would be the designated guardian, and she was duly flown to LA and installed in the same apartment building Nirvana had lived in while recording *Nevermind*.

Cobain was alternately thrilled and frightened by his new status as a father ("I was so fucking scared," he told Azerrad), but also spiralling into depression over this new crisis. At one point, he told Azerrad, the couple considered killing themselves. Love went into greater detail in *Rolling Stone*, saying Cobain had snuck out of the hospital and returned with a gun, which she ultimately turned over to bandmate Eric Erlandson (asked later about the incident, Erlandson said "I can't remember").

The general public remained largely unaware of the couple's custody issues; when shows planned for Portland and Seattle on 22 and 23 August were postponed, the reasons given were Frances's imminent birth and Cobain's suffering

As headliners at Reading 1992 (see p.88), Nirvana proved beyond doubt they weren't about to split up.

from what was referred to as "a chronic stomach ailment". But the media continued to speculate about drug use. *Entertainment Weekly* ran an article about the rising use of heroin in the rock scene in general, and the Seattle scene in particular. Tabloid *The Globe* ran a story headlined "Rock Star's Baby Born A Junkie", illustrated with a gruesome photograph of a newborn undergoing withdrawal; only in the caption was it made clear that the baby wasn't Frances.

Reading revival

It was against this backdrop of incessant speculation and innuendo that Nirvana returned to Britain to headline the **Reading Festival** on 30 August. Speculation was rampant that the band either wouldn't play or that the gig would be their last show. As a slap back at the rumourmongers, Cobain had donned a hospital gown and blonde wig, planning to have Everett True push him onstage in a wheelchair. When the musicians did stroll onstage, which was bare except for their gear and a riser with Grohl's drum kit, the crowd roared with anticipation. "You're gonna make it, man," Novoselic said into Cobain's mic as he was being wheeled up to it. The two shook hands, and Novoselic announced to the crowd, "With the support of his friends and family, he's gonna make it!" Cobain slowly stood and took hold of his microphone, shakily sang the first line of "The Rose", theme song from the film of the same name, then collapsed onto the stage. As the crowd again cheered, Cobain got

to his feet, took up his guitar, and the band tore into "Breed".

Nirvana were in the odd position of being a world-renowned act that nonetheless had to prove themselves all over again. They came through with flying colours, playing a 25-song set that ranged from their earliest material ("Spank Thru", "Love Buzz") to numbers they had yet to record ("tourette's", "All Apologies"). They even played a snatch of Boston's "More Than A Feeling" before launching into "Smells Like Teen Spirit", highlighting the similarities in the main riffs of the two songs, and threw in "The Money Will Roll Right In" for good measure. Cobain dedicated "All Apologies" to his wife and daughter, and asked the crowd to shout out "Courtney, we love you" in a show of support. The crowd spontaneously sang along with "Lithium", spurring audiences at subsequent shows to follow suit.

The end-of-set destruction, following "Territorial Pissings", was almost leisurely. Novoselic got behind Grohl's kit and pounded away, as Grohl carried sections of the kit to different corners of the stage, later picking up a cymbal and hurling it at the drums he'd placed on speaker stacks. For his part, Cobain drew howls of feedback from his guitar, finally coming to the front of the stage and playing part of "The Star-Spangled Banner". Afterwards, he handed the guitar to the audience, whose members could be seen fiercely clutching the instrument from all sides, struggling for ownership of it, as Cobain walked offstage.

The Story

Nirvana vs. Guns N' Roses

After Reading, Cobain returned to his court-ordered rehab. Band business continued regardless; Nirvana were next scheduled to appear at the **MTV Video Music Awards** on 9 September at UCLA's Pauley Pavilion. Inevitably, another controversy arose, when at the rehearsal on 8 August the band announced they wanted to perform the as yet unrecorded "Rape Me". MTV's executives expected the band to do "Smells Like Teen Spirit" and became increasingly heavy-handed in their demands that Nirvana play ball. When the company's threats to drop Nirvana from the show, stop playing their videos and even stop playing videos by any other act managed by Gold Mountain didn't meet with any success,

A fresh-faced Cobain demonstrates his camaraderie with most other rock bands at the MTV Video Awards in September 1992, posing here with Red Hot Chili Peppers' Flea.

they threatened to fire Amy Finnerty, one of Nirvana's longtime champions at the network. Nirvana finally caved, though the network did agree they didn't have to play "Teen Spirit". The group opted for "Lithium", to MTV's relief – at least it was a hit song.

Yet more drama broke out backstage during the show between Nirvana and **Guns N' Roses**. Axl Rose, Guns' lead singer, had initially been a fan of the group, even wearing a Nirvana baseball cap in Guns' "Don't Cry" video. But Guns N' Roses represented a kind of corporate-sanctioned rebellion that flew in the face of everything Nirvana prided themselves on standing for. Cobain had no hesitation expressing his disgust for the band, dismissing them as "really talentless people, and they write crap music". Rose took such insults to heart, and had verbally attacked Cobain and Love during a concert in Orlando, Florida, the previous week, calling Cobain "a fucking junkie with a junkie wife. And if the baby's born deformed, I think they both oughta go to prison." By the time of the concert, of course, Frances had been born and was perfectly healthy.

So when Rose and his entourage walked by Cobain and Love, who were sitting with their baby and other friends, Love couldn't resist teasing him, calling out, "Hey Axl, will you be the godfather of our child?" Rose duly went for the bait and stalked over to the couple, jabbing his finger at Cobain as he ranted about Love's behaviour, finally shouting, "You better shut your bitch up, or I'm taking you to the pavement!" Cobain neatly defused the situation by turning to Love and deadpanning,

"Shut up, bitch!" Everyone laughed, and Rose stormed off. Later Guns' bassist Duff McKagan confronted Novoselic and tried unsuccessfully to goad him into a fight.

For the performance itself, Cobain momentarily set MTV staff into panic mode by playing the opening line of "Rape Me", before shifting into "Lithium", as Novoselic stood to attention beside him, giving a mock salute. Fresh-faced, with a new short haircut, Cobain looked younger than his 25 years, and the picture of health compared with his last appearance on US television, the *SNL* show back in January. The rest of the performance passed without incident, MTV even allowing a little stage-diving. At the song's conclusion, Novoselic threw his bass into the air only to have it smack him in the head; as he staggered offstage, Cobain rammed his guitar into a speaker stack and Grohl ran to the microphone to shout, "Hi Axl! Hi Axl! Where's Axl?"

When the band won the award for Best Alternative Music Video (for "Teen Spirit"), a Michael Jackson impersonator, introducing himself as the "King of Grunge", accepted on their behalf, a joke that mystified everyone (it was meant to be a reference to the fact that *Nevermind* had pushed Jackson from the top spot in the charts). When it was announced that Nirvana had won the Best New Artist award, the band all trooped out to the podium together. Cobain's acceptance speech was brief. "I'd like to thank my family and our record label and our true fans," he began, his voice then trailing off. Prompted by Novoselic, he added, "You know, it's really hard to believe every-

```
SC0911  1A      15  10    COMP
$   0.00  AISLE 24 MF        0.00
N 60770      MONQUI PRESENTS
1A        -*-  NIRVANA  -*-
PP   5x          PLUS
15  10      SPECIAL GUESTS
TB02101  SEATTLE CENTER COLISEUM
C11SEP2  FRI SEPT 11, 1992 8:00PM
```

thing you read," and flashed a winning smile. Driving the point home, Novoselic cracked, "Remember Joseph Goebbels!" in reference to the Third Reich's notorious minister of propaganda. "Teen Spirit" had also been nominated for two other awards, Video of the Year (it lost to Van Halen's "Right Now") and Viewer's Choice (lost to Red Hot Chili Peppers' "Under the Bridge"). "Weird Al" Yankovic's "Smells Like Nirvana" had been nominated for Best Male Video, but lost to Eric Clapton's "Tears in Heaven".

The next day the band headed up to the Pacific Northwest to play the rescheduled Portland and Seattle gigs. The **Portland Meadows Racetrack** date was a benefit for the "No On 9" campaign, opposing ballot measure 9 that would have eliminated civil rights protections on the basis of sexual orientation. Unsurprisingly, the group was chattier than usual during the show. "Did you know that I'm gay?" Cobain said at the show's beginning. "Then I got married to a hermaphrodite. But if someone tried to take away my gay rights I would have been really mad, because I really like to buttfuck!" Later, Novoselic took a typically more serious line,

saying, "Thanks a lot for coming out supporting the No On 9 campaign, we can't have all this fascism going on." One attendee, referencing the MTV fracas, held up a sign reading "Kurt U shoulda kicked Axl's ass".

The show at the **Seattle Center Coliseum** the next night was also a benefit, for the Washington Music Industry Coalition, an anti-censorship organization. To Cobain's surprise, his father, whom he hadn't spoken to for more than a year, turned up backstage along with Kurt's half-brother, Chad. It was an awkward and uncomfortable reunion, especially as Cobain's mother and sister were also backstage. His parents sniped at each other, causing Cobain to shout at his father, after which his mother and sister left the room. Cobain then calmed down and even signed an autograph for Chad. But though Don had urged Kurt to keep in touch, it was the last time father and son would see each other.

Nirvana faced a sell-out crowd of 16,000, the biggest show they would ever do in Seattle. "Wow, you know, I saw Sammy Hagar in here about ten years ago!" Cobain said when he came on stage. "And Krist was booted out of here about a year ago!" Grohl added, referring to a Neil Young/Sonic Youth show where Novoselic had been ejected from the backstage area for being too inebriated. "Oh yeah, you're banned for life from here!" said Cobain, inadvertently providing the title for a future bootleg of the show (*Banned For Life*). Both shows stuck largely to the *Nevermind* material, though they also featured "Rape Me", the song MTV had not let them play.

Back to the clubs

Less than a month after the arena shows, Nirvana made an unexpected return to their club roots when they appeared as the surprise opening act for **Mudhoney** at two local shows, 3 October at the Sam Carver Gymnasium at Western Washington University, **Bellingham**, and 4 October at Seattle's **Crocodile Café** (Cobain had earlier made a guest appearance at a Mudhoney show in Castaic, California, late September). At both dates the group chose not to play their hit songs, instead pulling out early numbers like "Beeswax" and "Pen Cap Chew", which they hadn't performed since 1988; "Talk To Me", a song they never recorded; and a number of songs that would appear on *In Utero*. In Bellingham, Cobain and Novoselic gave their instruments to two kids in the audience at the set's conclusion and let them destroy the gear. The next night, word of Nirvana's appearance had leaked out, resulting in a line down the block. The atmosphere inside was one of excited anticipation; since the success of *Nevermind*, no one had expected the band to play such a small-scale show again.

The relaxed atmosphere of the Washington shows, where Cobain had ended up joining Mudhoney on guitar for a few songs, couldn't have contrasted more with the band's next gig, in **Buenos Aires**, Argentina, on 30 October. It was one of the band's biggest shows, in front of a sold-out crowd of 50,000. In the spirit of promoting their favourite bands, Nirvana had also invited Portland's **Calamity Jane** to open; the all-female group had appeared with Nirvana in Portland the previous month, and Cobain had known guitarist Gilly Ann Hanner since his Olympia days (Nirvana played Hanner's birthday party in 1988). Unfortunately, the male-dominated crowd wasn't at all receptive to the band's music, and screamed obscenities while pelting them with dirt and spit until they left the stage after three songs (the traumatized band broke up soon after).

Cobain was furious. "It was the largest display of sexism I've ever seen at once," he later told Azerrad, and his anger was apparent in Nirvana's subsequent performance. He refused to play "Teen Spirit", though he teased the crowd by playing the opening bars a few times. For "Come As You Are", he shouted "Hey!" during the first verse instead of singing the lyrics. After "Polly", Cobain abruptly told Grohl, "Do a drum solo. This is our encore," and walked off the stage, leaving Grohl and Novoselic to fend for themselves. But he was eventually persuaded to return and the band played another eight songs.

As the band's last show of the year, it perhaps typified a year that had seen its share of unexpected highs and lows. And now that they'd established to the rest of the world they weren't about to break up, it was time to move on to the next item on their agenda: recording a new album.

Third album: a difficult conception
1992–93

Third album: a difficult conception
1992–93

It's never easy following up a multi-million-selling release, and the recording of *In Utero* would be fraught with tension from beginning to end. This was due in part to the fact that every move Nirvana made was now scrutinized, building minor events into major dramas. DGC were hopeful that Nirvana's next album would be similar in style to *Nevermind*, an approach in which the band couldn't be less interested. More important was the growing schism within the band. Gone were the days of intense rehearsal, constant touring (Nirvana would perform only 35 shows in 1992, the fewest in a year since 1988) and just spending time together. For most of the year the band members weren't even living in the same state; when they did get together, they would often be confronted by some new crisis.

In Utero demos

It was in this desultory atmosphere that Nirvana entered the studio on 25 October to record demos for their next album, working with Jack Endino at Reciprocal Studios, now renamed **Word of Mouth**. Endino found the sessions very different from the previous occasions he'd worked with the group, starting with the first day, when Cobain didn't arrive for hours. "I remember asking, 'Is this normal? Why is he so late?'" Endino recalls. "And whoever it was just sort of shrugging and going, 'You get used to this

when you're dealing with Kurt.'" It was the first sign of an underlying discontent. When Cobain finally did show up, the atmosphere remained strained, and little was accomplished; the sessions ended early when a terminally ill teenager and his family came by, in a visit coordinated by the Make-A-Wish foundation.

The next day was just as tense, but more productive, with the band recording instrumental versions of "Dumb", "Pennyroyal Tea", "Radio Friendly Unit Shifter" and "tourette's" (all of which actually had lyrics) and "Frances Farmer Will Have Her Revenge

Cobain proving the doubters wrong at the Reading Festival, 1992 (see p.88).

The Story

On Seattle". Only "Rape Me" was recorded with lyrics, and the additional, disturbing element of Frances Bean's cries, recorded as she sat on her father's lap. This night, the session ended with the arrival of the police, who'd been summoned due to a complaint about the noise of Grohl's drumming.

The session's atmosphere, coupled with the assumption that DGC wanted the band to make another *Nevermind*, convinced Endino that he wouldn't be interested in working on the album proper. "At no point did I put myself forward and say, 'Hey you guys, can I do your record?'" he says. "It really would have been an unpleasant hot seat sort of situation to try to follow up *Nevermind*. Frankly, after just seeing how the band was interacting – they were obviously not getting along, there was all this weird vibe in the air – it was really nothing whatsoever like the band that I had worked with."

Endino wrote the name "S. Ritchie" on the session tape boxes at the band's request (being a reference to the real name of Sex Pistol Sid Vicious – John Simon Ritchie). But when he asked the band if they were interested in a follow-up session, he received a noncommittal response. "They were sort of like, 'Well, we'll come back and do the vocals later, we don't have time to do it right now,'" he says. But not only did no one call to set up another session, no one even called to pick up the tapes. "I was baffled," says Endino. "That's when I concluded that nobody was really in control."

Dealing with the media

It was at this time that yet another controversy erupted, around a biography that two British journalists, **Victoria Clarke** and **Britt Collins**, were writing on the group. Led to believe that the book was going to be an unflattering exposé, Cobain and Love left threatening messages on Clarke's answering machine. On 26 October, Clarke, who had been staying in Seattle, filed a complaint with the Seattle Police Department, then fled to LA.

Nirvana's management initially denied any threatening calls had been made, but Cobain and Love later admitted to making them, predictably resulting in further headlines. Talking with Michael Azerrad a few months later, Cobain was still very angry about the incident, and unrepentant about his own threats of retaliation ("I'm a firm believer in revenge"), though a few weeks later he had, in Azerrad's words, "simmered down" ("I just wanted to seem as extreme and irrational as possible to scare them," he said). Clarke and Collins continued work on the book, and submitted a copy of the manuscript to the band the following year for their inspection; at the time of writing it remains unpublished.

The idea of an unauthorized book may have provoked them, but Cobain and Love had already done some interviews regarding the controversies in their personal lives. On 21 September 1992, the *Los Angeles Times* published a piece in which Cobain had insisted to writer Robert Hilburn that his drug use had ended. He conceded he had "dabbled" with heroin, but that his habit had only lasted three weeks; he also pointed to his ongoing stomach problems as part of his reason for doing drugs. Now, he enthused, "Holding my baby is the best drug in the world." On the day of Nirvana's surprise show at the Crocodile Café on 4 October, Love did an interview with the author of this book, which appeared in the November issue of *The Rocket*; she also did an interview with UK style magazine *The Face*.

And the couple did two joint interviews, one with Jonathan Poneman for *Spin*'s December issue, in which Nirvana were also lauded as Artist of the Year. One of the piece's pictures showed Cobain holding Frances, with Love standing next to him, pulling up her shirt to reveal the words "Family Values" scrawled on her stomach – a catchphrase from that year's US presidential election. In the UK, **Everett True** wrote a two-part story for *Melody Maker* entitled, perhaps in an answer to Keith Cameron's story in *NME*, "All You Need Is Love". The article, later published in the book *The Nirvana Companion* as well as his own book, *Nirvana: The True Story*, allowed the couple to expound at length on their vilification in the media, revealing yet again Cobain's feelings of persecution: "It's impossible to be subversive in the commercial world because they'll crucify you for it," he said. Gold Mountain also approached **Michael Azerrad** about writing Nirvana's biography, part of the rationale being that a band-endorsed account would help counter the controversy that was swamping the group.

"In Bloom" and Incesticide

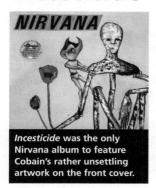

Incesticide was the only Nirvana album to feature Cobain's rather unsettling artwork on the front cover.

A fourth single, "In Bloom", was pulled from *Nevermind* and released overseas on 30 November. Though some fans felt the album was being over-milked for singles, the track nonetheless reached number 28 in the UK, and received enough US airplay to make number five on the Mainstream Rock Tracks chart. Cobain had an ambitious idea for the video, involving a little girl born into a Ku Klux Klan family (a few drawings of ideas for the video appear in his *Journals*). But the idea was scrapped for a more satiric one, a parody of 1960s television variety shows, complete with a conventionally square host (Doug Llewelyn of TV's *The People's Court*), who hails the band as "thoroughly nice and decent fellows".

The video was shot the evening of 15 October at Sunset Stage in Hollywood. Two versions were made, one with the group wearing identical striped jackets and ties (Grohl donning a blonde wig, Cobain with slicked-down hair and glasses), miming to the song, and a second where the group wore dresses, made few attempts to mime properly,

and spent most of the song twirling around the set before tearing it down. The original plan was to release the suits version first, then release one combining the suits and dresses version. But the suits/dresses version ended up being released first, which, though suitably anarchic for Nirvana's sensibilities, diluted the TV parody joke.

And though it might have seemed too early for an "odds and sods" compilation, demand for Nirvana product was such that Sub Pop and DGC joined forces on *Incesticide*, a fifteen-track collection released 14 December in the UK, 15 December in the US. Most of the songs had been released by Sub Pop or on other compilations, but alongside them were six previously unreleased tracks. The cover (pictured, left) featured one of Cobain's paintings: a skeleton sitting staring gloomily into space, while a child figure with a smashed doll's head tugs on its arm. Cobain's liner notes also drew comment. As well as name-checking over twenty other artists, he lambasted critics of Love and the couple's marriage, then implored any misogynists, racists and homophobes that might be reading to "Leave us the fuck alone! Don't come to our shows and don't buy our records". On a more conciliatory note, he offered this assessment of

Featuring a Cobain portrait set against a pink background, the *Advocate* cover was photographed by Charles Peterson.

Nirvana's career: "I'll be the first to admit that we're the 90's version of Cheap Trick or The Knack but the last to admit that it hasn't been rewarding." The notes were signed "Kurdt (the blond one)." The album reached number 39 in the US, number 14 in the UK.

In perhaps another attempt to goad the homophobes Cobain feared might be in Nirvana's audience, he arranged an interview with *The Advocate*, America's best-known gay and lesbian magazine, which appeared as a cover story in the 9 February 1993 issue. Journalist Kevin Allman wrote approvingly of the band's pro-gay stance, and the piece was notable in that it was exceedingly rare at the time for a major rock star to give an interview to a national gay magazine. The interview primarily discussed social issues (Cobain claiming he was "gay in spirit"), the misperceptions of the Cobain/Love relationship (Cobain admitting his embarrassment at the recent "fluff pieces" they'd had to do), and, to his label's embarrassment, included plenty of Guns N' Roses bashing.

Nirvana in Brazil

Nirvana's first gigs of 1993 were two large concerts in Brazil as part of the Hollywood Rock Festival, sponsored by the eponymous Brazilian cigarette company. The first date, on 16 January in **São Paulo**, degenerated into a lacklustre performance Novoselic later described as a "mental breakdown". Novoselic eventually became so frustrated he threw his bass at Cobain and stalked offstage, only to be forced back on, as the band had to play at least 45 minutes in order to get paid. They jammed on a number of covers, including "We Will Rock You", "Rio", "Kids In America" and, appropriately, "Should I Stay Or Should I Go". The audience was unimpressed. At one point, Earnie Bailey, the band's guitar tech rolled a canteloupe onstage; Cobain picked it up and smashed it into his guitar.

The next show, on 23 January in **Rio de Janeiro**, was better, though it still had its own odd moments, beginning with an off-key instrumental rendition of "L'amour est un oiseau rebelle" (the first major aria sung by the title character in the opera *Carmen*), which had been performed occasionally at other shows. "Scentless Apprentice" spiralled off into a lengthy jam, with Cobain eventually climbing down to the TV cameras in front of the stage, caressing each lens gently before spitting onto it, a gesture designed to show anger or sarcasm – or both. For the encore, he donned a black slip and crown (with Grohl sporting a black bra), finally crawling offstage on his hands and knees, appearing to be totally exhausted.

In between the two shows, from 19 to 21 January, the band entered BMG's **Ariola Discos Ltda. studios** in Rio to record more demos. Unlike the previous October's session at Word of Mouth, new songs were recorded, all of them with vocals, including early versions of "Heart-Shaped Box" (then titled "Heart-Shaped Coffin"), "Scentless Apprentice", "Milk It" and "Very Ape" – all of which would appear on *In Utero*, plus "Moist Vagina" and "I Hate Myself And Want To Die" (which would turn

The Story

up on a B-side and compilation, respectively). These early versions weren't very different from the final released versions, the musical arrangements in particular largely identical. The most substantial changes were lyrically: on "Heart-Shaped Box", for example, Cobain had only written one verse, which is repeated three times in the demo. The band also recorded extended improvised jams, with no initial plan to release them. "Gallons Of Rubbing Alcohol Flow Through The Strip", a track that meandered on for over seven minutes, did end up as a "hidden" track on the European edition of *In Utero*, as "Endless, Nameless" had on *Nevermind*. Another jam, belatedly entitled "The Other Improv", would appear on *With The Lights Out*.

The group also recorded a cover of "Seasons In The Sun" with everyone swapping instruments: Cobain played drums, Novoselic played guitar and Grohl played bass. In contrast to the downbeat sound of "Seasons", Grohl recorded a lively track based on "Onward Into Countless Battles" by Swedish heavy metal group Unleashed, demonstrating his multifaceted skills by playing all the instruments. Instead of doing a straight cover, Grohl altered the lyrics to a single word – "Meat!" – hence its provisional titles, "Meat" and "Dave's Meat Song" (Grohl and Cobain recorded jokey, high-pitched voiceovers, listing different types of meat). Cobain and Love, together with Hole's new drummer Patti Schemel, also worked on material, including an early version of "Miss World" that was later released on the Hole compilation *My Body, The Hand Grenade*.

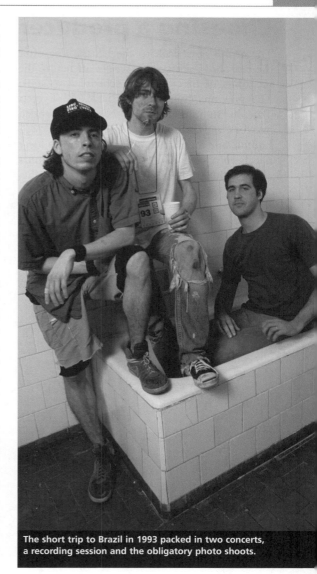

The short trip to Brazil in 1993 packed in two concerts, a recording session and the obligatory photo shoots.

Choosing a producer

The group flew back to the US the day after the Rio show, with a few weeks off before the recording of *In Utero* was scheduled to start. The previous June, Cobain had told Everett True in an interview that Nirvana intended to work on their new album first using Jack Endino, and then **Steve Albini**. Neither producer had been contacted at that point, but rumours about Albini's involvement began circulating,

Maverick producer Steve Albini: Nirvana's first choice for recording their third studio album.

particularly in the British music press, to the point that Albini sent out a letter denying he was involved. Ironically, Nirvana's management then contacted him about working on the album. It was, he later recalled, "the first of many little micro-controversies" that would swirl around the album before, during, and after its creation.

Cobain had been considering working with Albini even before Nirvana signed to DGC. Not only was he familiar with Albini's own bands (including Big Black and the provocatively named Rapeman), he was also a fan of his work as a producer, particularly his records with the Pixies, and Pixies–Throwing Muses spinoff the Breeders. Like Endino, Albini eschewed the "Producer" title in favour of "Recorded By". Nor was he impressed by major label businessmen, denouncing them as "bigwig music industry scum". Nirvana would definitely regain some indie credibility by working with such an iconoclast.

Not that the band's management or label were happy about Nirvana's choice of producer. But Albini's fee was modest – a flat $100,000, with no "points", or royalties, from the record (while other producers regarded a share of royalties as standard, Albini considered the practice immoral). Neither was the designated studio, **Pachyderm Studios**, outside of Cannon Falls, Minnesota, noted for its extravagance – recording costs would total just $24,000. It was hoped, too, that the studio's remote location would remove any outside distractions.

Albini had recently recorded PJ Harvey's *Rid Of Me* at Pachyderm and sent Cobain an advance copy to give him an idea of what the studio sounded like. He also talked with Cobain and Grohl before the sessions to get a sense of what they wanted to accomplish. All the band members were in agreement that they wanted to get away from the piece-meal approach of *Nevermind*, which suited Albini, who preferred "recording the band as a band, rather than trying to build things out of components". He'd been sent a cassette of the songs the band had worked on in Rio, which he felt illustrated their desire to make a "conceptual break" with the more conventional approach taken on *Nevermind*. Albini's one stipulation was that he wanted to deal with the band directly, and not anyone from their management or label – to which the band agreed.

Recording In Utero

Booked in as "The Simon Ritchie Bluegrass Ensemble", the band arrived in Minnesota, and recording began on 13 February. Working quickly, they laid down basic tracks for sixteen songs in just four days. Both band and producer found the sessions, in Novoselic's words, "pretty simple, straight ahead", which was unsurprising, given they'd already recorded demos of all the songs except "Serve The Servants" (though Cobain had made a home demo of it). In addition to the two formal demo sessions, the band had also clearly been rehearsing; one tape that survives from such a rehearsal captures the song "Scentless Apprentice" in the process of being created

(it later appeared on *With The Lights Out*. Only four songs required more than one take, though interestingly three of those were older songs: "Rape Me", "Pennyroyal Tea" and "All Apologies", the fourth being "Heart-Shaped Box", which had multiple takes. Most of the songs from the recording session would be released, if not on the album, then on compilations and B-sides, including Grohl's song "Marigold", recorded 15 February. Unreleased would be a short instrumental ("Dave Solo") on which Grohl played all the instruments, and a group jam called "Lullaby", featuring a swirling organ.

After the basic takes were done, Cobain added additional guitar parts to the songs and his vocals. "A lot of it was sort of mood singing," Albini recalls. "He wanted to get a certain style or certain personality across without having a specific set of words." There was little studio trickery, such as making a composite vocal performance from different takes, as had been the case on *Nevermind*. "*Nevermind* was polished; every mistake was taken out of it," Grohl later told Dutch magazine *Oor*. "With *In Utero* we meant to produce an honest group album again." Mixing was done over the course of five days, and was also, according to Albini, a straightforward process.

The only note of discord during the sessions came in the second week, when Courtney Love arrived with Frances, though the specifics have never been discussed beyond Azerrad's mentioning a dispute between Love and Grohl over some undisclosed matter. But

Verse Chorus Verse and Sappy

For some years, there was confusion among Nirvana fans about the songs "Verse Chorus Verse" and "Sappy". A track called "Verse Chorus Verse" appeared on the *No Alternative* compilation in 1993. But it was later discovered that a song called "Verse Chorus Verse" had been recorded during the *Nevermind* sessions, and producer Butch Vig said the track was most certainly not the "Verse Chorus Verse" that was on *No Alternative*.

In fact, the song on *No Alternative* was originally called "Sappy". Nirvana began playing it on their first European tour in 1989, and first recorded it in the studio on 2–3 January 1990. Endino, who produced the session, recalls it as being "the first time I knew that Kurt was fallible, because everything he'd done had been brilliant to me up to then. And then there was this song which just didn't seem that interesting." Undeterred, the band recorded it three more times: with Butch Vig in April 1990 at Smart Studios, with Vig again during the

Nevermind sessions, and with Steve Albini during the *In Utero* sessions (the version that appears on *No Alternative*). The song was dropped from the set list after 1990, but reappeared for a few shows on the band's final tour.

"Verse Chorus Verse" was first performed during the summer of 1990. But though the band demoed the song before the *Nevermind* sessions, and subsequently recorded two versions with guide vocals (one of which appears on *With The Lights Out*), they almost immediately lost interest in it, and never performed it live again.

Perhaps not wanting to let anything go to waste, the song's title was eventually recycled. Cobain's *Journals* reveal he had already decided to give "Sappy" the name "Verse Chorus Verse" in a proposed track listing for *In Utero*. But on *Sliver: The Best Of The Box* (and on the collector's circuit), the title "Sappy" is used, while "Verse Chorus Verse" refers to the original song with that name.

overall, the participants recall the sessions as a good time, with personal baggage left at the door and the band being remarkably productive as a result. There was also time to relax; one night everyone went to Minneapolis to see local noise band the Cows, and on another occasion there was a visit to the Mall of America, the largest shopping mall in the US, in the Minneapolis suburb of Bloomington. The sessions were completed by 26 February, with everyone in high spirits, celebrating by smoking cigars and indulging in a bizarre ritual: each person lit their pants on fire, passed the flames to the next person's

pant leg, then doused their own with beer to prevent serious burns.

The band toyed with different running orders for the album; Novoselic recalled it taking two weeks to find an order they were satisfied with. One early version started with "Rape Me", but it was decided that the song's opening was too close to that of "Teen Spirit", so it was changed to avoid immediate comparisons to *Nevermind*. Novoselic suggested moving "Scentless Apprentice" to the opening slot, but the final choice was "Serve The Servants", a track that had its own caustic commentary on the band's success. "I Hate Myself And

Want To Die" and "Sappy" were considered for inclusion but eventually dropped. "I Hate Myself…" was also a contender for the album's title, a phrase that cropped up frequently in Cobain's *Journals*.

The trouble with mixing

Though everyone initially professed happiness with the final product, as the weeks passed misgivings began to set in. The band's management and label felt the recordings were too raw, and Cobain later revealed that Gary Gersh hadn't liked the songwriting, telling *Melody Maker*, "Having your A&R say that is kind of like having your father or stepfather telling you to take out the trash." When the band was asked to make changes, they resisted at first, but after repeated listenings, concluded that the vocals and bass weren't prominent enough in the mix. Eventually, Cobain and Novoselic each phoned Albini, Cobain telling him they wanted to remix the entire album. Despite their protests, Albini suspected they were being pressured by their label to make changes. In any case, he told Cobain he didn't feel he could improve on the original mix, but gave him the go-ahead if the band wanted to do a remix themselves.

In May, **Scott Litt** was enlisted to remix "All Apologies" and "Heart-Shaped Box" at Seattle's Bad Animals studio. To the latter track Cobain added an acoustic guitar part and backing vocals, while Litt removed an effect that Novoselic felt had ruined the guitar solo. "Pennyroyal Tea" was also remixed but for some reason not included on the album. The album was then sent off for mastering by **Bob Ludwig** at Gateway Mastering in Portland, Maine.

By this time, the conflict surrounding the album's production had hit the press, inevitably becoming yet another Nirvana controversy. On 19 April the *Chicago Tribune* published the story "Record Label Finds Little Bliss in Nirvana's Latest" by Greg Kot, in which he claimed a "source close to the band" deemed the album "unreleasable". Albini was quoted as saying, "I have no faith this record will be released", a comment disputed by Geffen representative Bryn Bridenthal, though she conceded the album's release had been pushed back due to a "hangup with mixing and mastering". Manager John Silva was given the last word: "If the band says the record's ready, then it's ready. But as of now, there is no Nirvana record to release."

The story that Nirvana were being forced to kowtow to their label, losing their alternative edge, was quickly picked up by other outlets, including the *Village Voice*, *Newsweek* and *Entertainment Weekly*. In response, the band sent a letter to *Newsweek* refuting the magazine's story, and had the text of the letter printed as a full-page ad in *Billboard*. They also issued a press release denying there had been any pressure from the label to make changes. In future interviews, the band stuck to the line that while their label and management were initially unhappy with the record, the band members eventually became dissatisfied with the mix of their own accord.

Cobain dreamed up a scenario that would allow him a pre-emptive strike at his critics: releasing the Albini mix on vinyl, cassette and 8-track, then releasing the post-Albini version a month later on CD. Instead, the Ludwig-mastered version was the only official release, and Albini's mix was relegated to the collector's circuit (though it's also said to be on some vinyl versions of the album). Albini wasn't pleased with the final record, explaining "The dynamic range was narrowed, the stereo width was narrowed, there was a lot of mid-range boost EQ added, and the overall sound quality was softened. And the bass response was compromised to make it sound more consistent on radio and home speakers. But the way I would describe it in non-technical terms is that they fucked it up."

To the vast majority of the record-buying public, all of this was of little importance. That it blew up into a situation where the band's entire future seemed to be at stake (as on *Select*'s July 1993 cover, which asked "Nirvana: What's Gone Wrong?") was yet another demonstration of how being a popular rock band was a more complicated position to be in than one might realize. On the other hand, the rampant speculation did help make Nirvana's second major label release the most anticipated album of the year.

Now I'm bored and old
1993

Now I'm bored and old
1993

With the new album not scheduled to be released until the fall, when a coinciding tour would promote it, the members of Nirvana lay low for the next few months. To the outside world, Nirvana remained the most exciting rock band to come along in years, and there was much speculation in the music press as to what their next album would sound like. But the band members continued growing apart; when not working together, they saw each other infrequently.

Down time

In March, Cobain and Love moved into a rental house in Seattle's Sand Point neighbourhood; that same month they were finally awarded full custody of Frances. Nirvana then shot a belated video for *Incesticide*, using the song "Sliver". Directed by **Kevin Kerslake**, it was filmed in the garage of Cobain's house, with Cobain wearing the Johnny Rotten sweater Love had bought him from a fan at Nirvana's Belfast show in June 1992, while Frances Bean also made a cameo appearance. That spring Cobain also began work with Kerslake on an extended video, which would eventually become *Live! Tonight! Sold Out!!*

Apart from the videos, there was little band business over the next six months, Nirvana playing just three shows and doing no recording. The first of the gigs, on 9 April in San Francisco, was organized by Novoselic as a benefit for the **Tresnjevka Women's Group**, an organization based in Zagreb, Croatia, which had set up the country's first hotline for battered women, and was now setting up a shelter for the thousands of women who had been raped during the Bosnian War. Novoselic had been following closely the events as Yugoslavia broke up, and wrote an article about the conflict for *Spin*'s May 1993 issue, reverting to the Croatian spelling of his first name, Krist. "An epic tragedy is happening in Europe and nobody's doing anything about it," Novoselic told the *San Francisco Chronicle*. "I don't have the ability to launch an invasion or an air strike. A benefit to raise money and awareness is the most I can do."

It was the first large-scale show the band had played in the US since the Seattle show the previous September, and they turned in a strong set that spanned their entire catalogue, from the first single to seven songs that would appear on *In Utero*. Infused with energy, Cobain climbed a speaker stack next to Grohl's drums during the closing number, "Endless, Nameless", and plunged straight into the kit while Grohl was still playing.

Drug problems

Though the show seemed to indicate that Nirvana were as vital a band as ever, over the course of the spring Cobain retreated

Cobain wearing his "Johnny Rotten" jumper at the Roseland Ballroom show in July 1993, the night of his overdose.

fully into heroin use. According to *Heavier Than Heaven*, Cobain had "as many as a dozen" overdoses over the course of 1993. On 1 June, Love staged an intervention at the couple's home; Cobain's response was to take a red felt-tip pen and write "None of you will ever know my intentions" on the wall (asked about the message by a journalist from *Details*, Cobain refused to elaborate, saying only "Guess we won't be getting the deposit back on the house"). On 4 June, a fight erupted over Cobain's drug use and Love ended up calling the police. In domestic violence cases in Washington state, the police are required to make an arrest, and both Cobain and Love argued over who should have this dubious honour. Cobain won, but was undoubtedly less pleased when the police confiscated his three guns along with several rounds of ammunition. He was released after a few hours, and the charges later dropped.

News of the arrest broke on 1 July, the same day **Hole** were doing a show at Seattle's Off Ramp. The couple played down the arrest as a quarrel that had got out of hand, Love making several joking references to it during her set. Afterwards, the *NME*'s **Brian Willis** approached Love for an interview; she invited the writer home, and gave him an unexpected coup – an advance listen to *In Utero*. Willis was just the first of many to note that the album was clearly influenced by everything that had happened to Cobain since the release of *Nevermind*, from his unanticipated fame, his marriage and the birth of his daughter, to his drug use and gradual withdrawal from the

world. In future articles, Cobain, typically, would disparage the notion that the album's songs reflected his personal life.

Willis's write-up appeared in the 24 July issue of the paper, by which time the band had reconvened in New York City. There they spent the week doing interviews to promote *In Utero* and played a show on 23 July at the **Roseland Ballroom**. Since Cobain had publicly admitted his drug use the previous year, the topic invariably came up in every interview, but he generally insisted it had been a short dalliance that was now over. Another, more disturbing, theme had begun to surface in his interviews, though it wasn't pointed out until after his death: repeated, casual references to suicide, beginning with Everett True's interview with the couple the previous December, when Cobain, commenting on the media harassment he'd endured, said, "I want to kill myself half the time". When it was learned that *In Utero*'s first proposed title had been "I Hate Myself And Want To Die", Cobain had shrugged it off as black humour, the likes of which appeared in such headlines as *Q*'s "Heroin, Paranoia, Hatred, Death... Things Are Looking Up For Nirvana" in September 1993.

What was unknown by the public at the time was that Cobain had overdosed during the afternoon of 23 July, before the Roseland gig. Love had found him passed out on the floor of their hotel room; her screams brought the couple's nanny, Cali DeWitt, running, and the two managed to revive him. Perhaps the close call led to his being more open; when he talked about his heroin use in an interview with

The Story

The Face's **Amy Raphael** after the show that night, he admitted, "I still have problems with it. This year I've fucked up a few times", later adding "I couldn't fool myself or anyone else that I won't do it again; I'll always be a junkie." Cobain, Raphael concluded, "will never find an inner peace. Especially while he's a rock star. He will always be leaning on the self-destruct button in a way that's become almost masochistic."

The Roseland show featured most of the tracks from *In Utero*, and saw the band working with two new members. **Lori Goldston**, a member of Seattle's Black Cat Orchestra, had been brought in to add cello to five songs, and **"Big" John Duncan**, a former member of the Exploited who also served as one of Nirvana's guitar techs, played second guitar on four songs. Duncan wouldn't perform with the group again, but they would soon add a second guitarist permanently to the line-up, to both give the band a fuller sound and enable Cobain to focus more on his vocals.

Two weeks after the Roseland show, on 6 August, Nirvana played their final show as a trio. The occasion was a benefit for the **Mia Zapata Investigative Fund**: Zapata, lead singer for Seattle band The Gits, had been murdered on 7 July and the crime remained unsolved at the time (her killer was charged and convicted a decade later). The show was originally going to be headlined by Tad, but the promoter managed to secure Nirvana as a last-minute headliner. The venue was the **King Theater**, a former movie house, and though Nirvana's presence had been confirmed in a radio announcement, people still wondered whether they would truly show up. The tension and rising anticipation were palpable following Tad's set, as Nirvana's gear began to be set up. Though Novoselic later recalled the show as being somewhat ragged, the audience was ecstatic, someone even shrieking out "We did it!" at the end. The set included some numbers from *In Utero*, a few covers, including Led Zeppelin's "No Quarter" and a dirgeful version of "Seasons In The Sun", but none of the band's big hits.

The Heart-Shaped Box video

Nirvana's next order of business was shooting a video for *In Utero*'s first single, "Heart-Shaped Box". Cobain had been discussing ideas for the video with Kevin Kerslake, but in the end opted to use Dutch photographer and filmmaker **Anton Corbijn**. Corbijn had first worked with the group when he shot promotional photos for DGC and pictures for *Details*' November 1993 cover story on the band. Cobain asked Corbijn to send him some of his video work, and soon after Corbijn was hired to do Nirvana's video.

Corbijn had initially hesitated because Cobain had sent him such a detailed treatment that he felt there would be no room for his own ideas. But he eventually agreed, and found Cobain willing to collaborate after all. The video has the strongest – and most disturbing – imagery of any the group made. The main set was a field of red poppies with a large cross in the middle, next to a group of gnarled trees with human

The band and Frances Bean Cobain, accepting the MTV Video Award for "In Bloom" with the video's director, Kevin Kerslake, in September 1993.

foetuses hanging from their limbs. An old man is seen in many sequences, lying in a hospital bed, later hanging on the cross, alternately wearing a Santa Claus hat and a miter; Cobain had originally wanted William Burroughs for the part. A little girl romps through the fields dressed in a Ku Klux Klan outfit. Corbijn's ideas added to the surrealism: using fake birds and butterflies (Cobain had wanted to use real ones), designing a transparent "organ suit" that a fat woman wears, and having the old man climb up on the cross using a ladder. The band had wanted to shoot in Technicolor, but the process was no longer used in the US. Corbijn devised another

method of achieving a colour-saturated look, shooting in colour, transferring the film to black and white, then having it colour-tinted by hand.

The first edit of the video used, at Love's suggestion, a long shot of Cobain singing the song's final verse; but Corbijn felt the shot went on too long, and produced another version using different shots during the final verse, including the eerie image of Cobain lying in the poppy field, eyes closed, mist rising around him. Cobain was happy with Corbijn's work, telling MTV "That video has come closer to what I've seen in my mind, what I've envisioned, than any other video."

On 2 September, Nirvana attended MTV's **Video Music Awards** show at the Universal Amphitheatre, now the Gibson Amphitheatre, in Universal City, California. The band didn't perform, but did win Best Alternative Video for their previous video, "In Bloom". Kerslake, in the audience, was invited to join the band on stage as they accepted their award. No one mentioned the "Heart-Shaped Box" video, though, which Kerslake would later file suit over, alleging that several of his ideas had been used without authorization. The case was settled out of court.

Later that week, on 8 September, Love and Cobain performed together at a **Rock Against Rape** show in aid of LA-based First Strike Rape Prevention, which took place at **Club Lingerie** in Hollywood. Love was joined onstage by Cobain at the end of her set, introducing him as "My husband, Yoko". The duo played two songs, "Pennyroyal Tea", with Love singing lead and Cobain providing harmony during the verse, and "Where Did You Sleep Last Night", with Cobain taking the lead. Though the two frequently talked about playing together at home, it was the only time the public would see them perform together.

Radio Friendly Unit Shifting

"Heart-Shaped Box" was released overseas on 30 August and reached number five in the UK charts. There was no official US release; it was simply issued to US radio, and topped the

In Utero's original back cover, designed by Cobain; a revised version, minus the foetuses, was produced in order to sell the album in two major US chains.

Modern Rock Tracks chart, reaching number four in Mainstream Rock Tracks. *In Utero* soon followed, released in the UK on 14 September, in the US on 21 September. It topped the charts in both, while reaching the top ten in eight other countries.

In Utero's US sales were hampered by the fact that two major chains, Wal-Mart and Kmart, initially refused to carry the album, supposedly due to lack of consumer interest. In fact, it was later reported that both retailers objected to the album's artwork. Cobain had been involved in designing the cover art for both *In Utero* and its singles, and was even credited on *In Utero* for "Art Direction and Design", along with Robert Fisher. The front cover depicted a **Transparent Anatomical Mannikin** (TAM), taken from a postcard Cobain had; he added wings to "make it just a little bit more special", Fisher later explained. The back cover had a collage designed by Cobain, featuring foetus models lying on a bed of orchids, bones and internal organs; the photo was later "tweaked" by Fisher, bathing everything in an orange glow.

The imagery aptly reflected an album whose songs were replete with references to birth, babies, abortion, excretions and other bodily functions. But the Wal-Mart and Kmart chains specifically objected to the foetuses, which they felt might cause offence; they also objected to the title of "Rape Me". With more album sales generated through discount chains than record stores, having an album banned by these two retailers would seriously impact Nirvana's bottom line.

The band agreed to change the back cover for the chains, and a section of the collage that didn't have foetuses in it was enlarged for the rear image; "Rape Me" was retitled "Waif Me" (Cobain had originally suggested "Sexually Assault Me"). The new version of the album (which also featured Scott Litt's remix of "Pennyroyal Tea") was released on 29 March 1994. The band's willingness to compromise reignited the by now tiresome debate about their "selling out". It's still unclear if the band was pressured by their label to make the change or not. **Carrie Borzillo-Vrenna**'s *Nirvana: The Day By Day Eyewitness Chronicle* quotes Danny Goldberg as saying there was no pressure, while quoting Bill Bennett, then Geffen's General Manager, as saying, "I think the record company really

Pat Smear joined the band as second guitarist on their final US tour.

just pressured them. Left to their own devices, they never would have done it." For his part, Cobain simply explained that in small towns Wal-Marts and Kmarts were often the only places where kids could buy records.

The last US tour

On 25 September, the band made their second appearance on *Saturday Night Live*. The performance marked the debut of **Pat Smear** on second guitar. Smear, born Georg Ruthenberg on 5 August 1959, had previously been a member of LA punk bank the Germs and had subsequently played with various other acts (including Nina Hagen and 45 Grave), also releasing his own solo albums. He was working at a record store when he got a call from

Cobain asking him to join the band. Though he'd never seen the group perform, Smear was a fan of Nirvana and readily agreed.

Smear's easygoing personality helped defuse some of the tensions within the band. On Nirvana's *SNL* appearance he's clearly having a great time, bouncing all over the stage more than any other band member. Though the band's performance lacked the frisson of their first *SNL* appearance, they nonetheless turned in solid performances of "Heart-Shaped Box" and "Rape Me".

The US tour began just over three weeks later, on 18 October in **Phoenix**, Arizona, and would continue, with breaks, into the first week of January. The shows opened with the pile-driving rhythms of "Radio Friendly Unit Shifter", and went on to feature most of the songs from *In Utero*, aside from "tourette's" (which after the 23 July 1993 show wasn't played live again), and "Frances Farmer" and "Very Ape", both of which made infrequent appearances until later in the tour and in the 1994 set lists. It was Nirvana's only full-length arena tour, and they had an elaborate set to match, featuring two winged reproductions of the TAM model (in numerous pictures taken on the tour, when Cobain was positioned in front of the TAM model, it looked like he had wings) and spooky-looking trees, echoing the feel of the "Heart-Shaped Box" video.

The tour got off to a slow start (the first show was panned by *USA Today*), but soon hit its stride. Cobain chose some of his favourite groups as opening acts, including **Mudhoney**, **Half Japanese** and the Breeders. Some saw evidence of a growing rift in the band in their use of two tour buses, with Cobain and Smear on one, and Novoselic and Grohl on the other, but for the most part the atmosphere was positive, especially when Frances joined the tour for short stretches. On Halloween, the group even celebrated by dressing up: Cobain in an outlandish Barney dinosaur costume, Smear as Slash from Guns N' Roses, Grohl as a mummy, and Novoselic in white face makeup with a black "PC" (for politically correct) on his forehead, parodying a stunt by TV star Ted Danson, then dating Whoopi Goldberg, who'd worn black face makeup at a function.

While in Kansas, Cobain was taken to meet one of his literary idols, **William Burroughs**, who lived in the town of Lawrence. Though the two had collaborated on a record released on T/K Records the previous summer (which had Burroughs reading the short story "The 'Priest' They Called Him" to Cobain's guitar accompaniment), they had recorded their parts separately.

While the band was on tour, a few more songs from the *In Utero* sessions came out. Two previously unreleased tracks appeared on compilations, "Sappy", retitled "Verse Chorus Verse" on *No Alternative*, and "I Hate Myself and Want To Die" on *The Beavis and Butthead Experience*. "All Apologies" was also released as a single overseas, to radio in America, backed with another unreleased track from the *In Utero* sessions, "Moist Vagina", tastefully renamed "MV". The single reached number 32 in the UK, and topped the Modern Rock Tracks chart in the US. Despite being on the road,

Cobain had found time to give Robert Fisher a suggestion for the single's artwork, telling him to use "something with seahorses".

On 18 October **Michael Azerrad**'s biography, *Come As You Are: The Story Of Nirvana*, was published. Though Azerrad had the band's cooperation, along with access to their family and friends, he later stressed that the book wasn't "authorized" in the sense of the band, or their management, having any control over what went in it. "The first time I discussed the book with Kurt, I told him flat out that I didn't want the book to be authorized," Azerrad explained to nirvanaclub.com. "He knew exactly what I meant and replied – and this is a verbatim quotation – 'No way, that would be too Guns N' Roses.'" Though not shying away from the controversial aspects of the band's career, the book did lean toward more positive interpretations of events, describing the band's morale as currently being "at an all-time high". And, as he'd been doing in most interviews since late 1992, Cobain maintained that his drug use was behind him. Nonetheless, the book's original edition ended on something of a down note, with Cobain forecasting that sales of *In Utero* wouldn't match those of *Nevermind*, gloomily concluding, "I'm going to have to get a job in ten years".

Cobain also spoke to Azerrad, and other interviewers, about his desire to break out of the Nirvana formula: "That kind of classic rock and roll verse-chorus-verse, mid-tempo pop song is getting real boring," he told Azerrad. He talked of pushing the ideas in "Milk It" and "Scentless Apprentice" to a new

extreme, but he also talked of going in the other direction, in search of a quieter, more acoustic sound. Lori Goldston remembered Cobain talking about using an oboe in their future work, noting, "That's an instrument you hear even less in pop music than a cello!" He soon had the chance to explore this route when Nirvana was invited to appear on MTV's *Unplugged* programme.

MTV Part 1: softer

The show, which had bands forsaking their electric guitars for acoustic instruments, had debuted on MTV on 26 November 1989. Producer **Alex Coletti** had previously worked with Nirvana, when the group had taped a live set for MTV in January 1992, and he'd noted Cobain's interest in how the set was designed. So when Nirvana agreed to do *Unplugged*, he asked Cobain how he thought the set should look. Cobain's request that there be plenty of flowers (he specified star lilies) was in keeping with their use on the covers for *In Utero* and the "Heart-Shaped Box" single, and the candelabras and plush, heavy drapes gave a warm, autumnal feel that's apparent in every picture of the event. But Cobain's ideas made Coletti think of something else. "You mean like a funeral?" Coletti asked. "Yeah," Cobain replied.

Predictably, there was consternation on MTV's part over the band's set

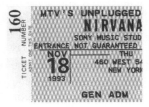

list. Instead of simply taking their biggest hits and performing them acoustically, Nirvana wanted to do something more interesting. They practised some songs from *Meat Puppets II* for the show, and as the Meat Puppets were an opening act on part of Nirvana's tour, they were invited to participate (to MTV's further dismay,

the network hoping for better-known guests). Nor were the band planning to play any of their big hits, feeling they wouldn't translate well to an acoustic setting. A set list from a rehearsal includes some songs that weren't used: "Molly's Lips", Grohl's "Marigold", and the never released "Old Age". John Silva suggested

For *MTV Unplugged*, Nirvana played their set straight through with no retakes, their performance intensified by the intimate atmosphere.

The Story

some other numbers, including "Heart-Shaped Box" and "Sliver", and less obvious choices like "Rape Me" and "Verse Chorus Verse". In the end, the band opted for songs that were acoustically driven ("About A Girl", "Dumb"), songs that would adapt well to the acoustic format ("Come As You Are", "On A Plain"), and an unusually high number of covers – six, including three Meat Puppets songs.

But though rehearsals were held 16 and 17 November, then on the set itself on 18 November to check camera angles, there was never a full dress rehearsal, which left all the musicians nervous. Grohl also had problems playing the drums quietly enough and grew increasingly frustrated by Cobain's constant requests to play with a lighter touch. Coletti presented Grohl with a pair of brushes, and a pair of Pro-Mark Hot Rod drumsticks, which were actually sizzle sticks – a type of stick specially designed to hit a percussion instrument with less force than a solid stick – and these did the trick. In fact, the show wasn't going to be entirely "unplugged", as Cobain put his guitar through a Fender Twin Reverb amp and effects boxes, though Coletti tried to hide the fact by placing a box around the amp to make it look like a monitor.

Every available seat was taken during the taping at **Sony Music Studios** in New York. The casual atmosphere – far from keeping the band hidden until the show began, Grohl strolled around the set with a beer in his hand – belied the sense of anticipation underneath. The show began on a slightly petulant note, when Cobain said, "This is off our first album.

Most people don't own it," by way of introducing the first song, "About A Girl", with audience applause coming in after a few bars.

Unlike many *Unplugged* tapings, there were no second takes. The band simply played straight through, though they took the time to discuss song choices between numbers, even soliciting requests from the audience (though declining to play any of them). Lori Goldston assumed some songs would be performed again. "It's really hard to tell how things are turning out when you're playing," she says. "At the time I thought everybody was too nervous to play very well and it was a little stiff. I was totally wrong. It sounds a little bit like we're just playing in somebody's living room. Which is I think ideal." The show concluded with a stunning rendition of "Where Did You Sleep Last Night".

MTV part 2: louder

A few weeks later they were back before MTV's cameras again for the filming of a special New Year's Eve show, *Live and Loud*, which was shot on 13 December in Seattle and aired on 31 December (though it would end at 11.30, making way for a Janet Jackson special to see in 1994). The venue was an odd one: **Pier 48**, then used as a ferry terminal for cruise ships to Victoria, BC. It was cold during rehearsals, and everyone huddled in their trailers when not needed on stage. After rehearsing, each member of the band was interviewed for MTV's programme *Past, Present And Future*, a summary of the band's history. But when the author of this book asked Novoselic that day how the band dealt with their increasing involvement with the "corporate" side of the industry, his answer had a dark tone. "We're dancing with the devil," he said. "There's no denying it. We always have been, since the day we signed that contract. Not the contract with Geffen, but the contract at the crossroads. There's just no denying it."

The show was strong, though unfortunately the MTV audience only saw a portion of it, as the set was edited down to ten songs, and further broken up with commercials and embarrassing introductions by Flea and Anthony Kiedis from

Cobain was frequently photographed in front of a winged TAM model; at the *MTV Live & Loud* show, he'd later decapitate one with his guitar.

the Red Hot Chili Peppers, dressed up as female groupies. Following "Blew", a fan bellowed out "MTV sucks!" Cobain, in the middle of tuning his guitar, stopped, went to his mic, and asked, "Then why are you here?" The MTV broadcast also only featured an excerpt of the end-of-set destruction, which went on for longer than usual, the band starting their jam quietly, building to a raging swirl of sound, then taking it back down before raging once again. As fans began frantically crowd surfing and trying to reach the stage, Cobain waved them forward encouragingly, even attempting to haul a fan up, only to be defeated by the bouncers, who were struggling to hold the fans back. After decapitating one of the winged TAM stage props with his guitar, Cobain then threw it down and began clapping along with the crowd, a maniacal look in his eyes.

On the night MTV aired *Live and Loud*, Nirvana were performing their final show of the year, in **Oakland**, California. In a spirit of camaraderie, nanny Cali DeWitt invited members of various local bands to hang out backstage (including **Green Day**, whose major label debut *Dookie* would explode with *Nevermind*-like force the following year). At midnight, comedian **Bob Goldthwait**, one of the tour's opening acts, descended from the venue's ceiling as "Baby New Year" (some accounts said he wore a diaper, but Goldthwait insisted he was naked, save for a hat). It was a light moment that gave no indication of the tragedy that would soon overtake the band.

Into the black

1994

Into the black
1994

On the outside, it appeared that things were going well for Nirvana. *In Utero* had entered the charts at number one; *Unplugged* had aired on MTV on 16 December to great acclaim; and the band were in negotiation to headline that summer's Lollapalooza festival. But Cobain's inner struggles were still plaguing him. He attempted to deal with his heroin addiction over the Christmas holidays by going through another "hotel detox" at the Canyon Ranch Spa, near Tucson, Arizona, but to no avail. His reluctance to go on another lengthy tour, in the face of opposition from everyone – his bandmates, label, management and his wife – didn't bode well for the upcoming European dates. Something had to give.

In Bob's Bunker

Nirvana's final American shows were, appropriately, in **Seattle** on 7 and 8 January 1994.

This backstage pass from 1994 used an image that first appeared printed on the CD of *In Utero*.

The group was in an expansive mood on both nights, repeatedly thanking friends and making song dedications. On 7 January, Cobain deadpanned "This song made Seattle the most liveable city in America" before they played "Teen Spirit"; on 8 January, he thanked Bruce Pavitt and Jonathan Poneman prior to playing "School". The last words spoken that night came from Novoselic, who for some reason was inspired to quote Hamlet: "To be or not to be, that is the question!"

On the last weekend of January, Nirvana entered a recording studio for the final time. Though Cobain had told *Rolling Stone*'s David Fricke during an interview on 25 October 1993, that he'd written no new songs, the band had worked on new material during soundchecks, and had even played a rough version of one song on 23 October 1993, mistakenly called "Autopilot" or "On The Mountain" by those who misheard Grohl's introduction (he was actually announcing "All Apologies", which had been the next song on the set list). The song would become the cornerstone of their last session. The musicians had talked about doing a quick session before the European tour, and Grohl suggested they use a studio he'd learned was in his neighbourhood in what was then unincorporated Seattle (since incorporated into the city of Shoreline): **Robert Lang Studios**.

Grohl and Novoselic dropped by the studio in December 1993, and were suitably impressed by the space: the studio's main room, with its 24-foot-high ceiling, had essentially been carved out of a hillside. Lang's home rested on top, giving the place the look of a fortress (Novoselic jokingly dubbed the place "Bob's Bunker"). The band hoped the session might be as fruitful as the 1992 Laundry Room session, when they'd cranked out three songs in one day. The studio was booked for 28–30 January 1994, and **Adam Kasper** (who would go on to work with Grohl's Foo Fighters) was enlisted as producer.

Novoselic and Grohl duly arrived in the afternoon of 28 January, and when Cobain didn't show up, passed the time recording their own material. Some were noise jams given self-explanatory titles like "Thrash Tune" or "Dave With Echoplex" (Grohl jamming to the sounds coming out of a theramin plugged into an Echoplex tape machine). "Chris w/acoustic" was an instrumental with a country feel, not too dissimilar to the Nirvana instrumental bootleggers call "Black And White Blues". A number of songs would later turn up in Grohl's subsequent projects: "Exhausted", "Big Me" and "Butterflies" were all re-recorded in October 1994 at Lang's (the first two appearing on *Foo Fighters*, the third never officially released); "Dave Acoustic + Vocal" became "February Stars" on *The Colour

Perched on a hillside in greater Seattle, Robert Lang Studios hosted the band's last recording session.

and the Shape*, and "New Wave Groove" turned up in "Bill Hill Theme" and "Final Miracle" on the soundtrack of *Touch*, the Paul Schrader film that Grohl would score.

The two had time to record a number of songs, as Cobain didn't show up until the afternoon of 30 January – nor had he brought his own equipment. Fortunately, the band's guitar tech, Earnie Bailey, had a Univox guitar he was reworking for Cobain out in his car, so Cobain was soon set up. There was no discussion about Cobain's tardiness; everyone simply wanted to get to work. The band began with a twenty-minute jam that used the main riff of "Verse Chorus Verse", and then began working on "You Know You're Right", at that point written on the tracking sheets simply as "Kurt's Tune #1".

Cobain's Jag-Stang

In 1993, Kurt Cobain began designing a custom guitar that would combine elements of two Fender guitars: the Mustang (which he often cited as his favourite guitar) and the Jaguar. He met with Fender's master builder, Larry Brooks, and Mark Wittenberg, Director of Artist Relations, to relay his idea, illustrating what he meant by pasting pictures of a Mustang and Jaguar together (further illustrations can be seen in his *Journals*). He also sent Brooks a Mustang guitar neck he especially liked to be copied. Brooks created a prototype, and, after receiving further feedback from Cobain, made a final version. The hybrid guitar essentially had the Mustang's neck and upper body and a Jaguar's lower body, a mix that led to its being named the "Jag-Stang".

Cobain had specified two colours for the instrument, Sonic Blue and Fiesta Red. The Sonic Blue guitar was the first one he received, and the guitar was subsequently used on the European *In Utero* tour and made at least one appearance on the US leg, at Dallas; the Fiesta Red guitar was about to be sent to Cobain at the time of his death. After Cobain's death, an agreement was made to mass produce the guitar; though Cobain would probably have suggested further modifications (his guitar tech, Earnie Bailey, noted that Cobain had the pickups and bridge changed on his Sonic Blue), no further changes were made. The guitar was first issued in 1995, and discontinued in 2001; it was later reissued from 2003 to 2006. There are no differences between the two editions, though some of the first editions may have a "Designed by Kurt Cobain" sticker. More information can be found at jag-stang.com.

Courtney Love later gave Cobain's Sonic Blue Jag-Stang to Peter Buck of R.E.M.; he can be seen playing it in the video for "What's The Frequency, Kenneth?"

It only took seven takes for the song to come together, more evidence that once personal difficulties were set aside, the band were quite capable of working well together. On take three, Cobain added the chiming sounds at the song's opening, created by playing the section of strings on his guitar located between the bridge and the tailpiece. After a dinner break at a nearby pizza joint, the band cut a punchy three-and-a-half-minute instrumental, and Cobain quickly laid down his vocal on "Kurt's

Tune #1". Nirvana's final recording session was over, although "Kurt's Tune" wouldn't be released for another eight years.

Back to Europe

Three days later, the band were on their way to Europe. Their first appearance was on the French TV show *Nulle Part Ailleurs*, on 4 February 1994, filmed at **Canal+ Studios** in Paris. Echoing their 1960s-era look in the "In

Bloom" video, the group dressed identically, wearing black straight-legged trousers, white shirts, black vests and skinny black ties. Clad in what Cobain dubbed their "Knack outfits", the group ended up looking not unlike The Beatles or Rolling Stones circa 1963–64, even executing Beatlesque bows after each song.

They gave a powerful performance of "Rape Me" and "Pennyroyal Tea" from the new album; called back for an encore, they played "Drain You". Cobain's guitar had been giving him problems throughout the recording, and cut out completely during the last song's instrumental bridge, so he unstrapped it and let it

The show in Modena, Italy, was one of the band's last live gigs.

The Story

drop to the floor. The audience was then treated to the rare sight of Cobain singing without his guitar, his frustration expressed in a mighty scream as the lead-in to the final verse.

The tour proper began on 6 February in **Portugal**, with one change in the line-up: **Melora Creager**, from the band Rasputin, was now on cello. There were again two tour buses, the Cobain/Smear coach designated the "smoking bus", with Novoselic and Grohl on the other, non-smoking bus. As the tour progressed through Spain and back to France, Creager noticed Cobain becoming increasingly withdrawn. At after show meet-and-greets, while the others mingled, Cobain would lie on a couch elsewhere until it was time to leave. "What I thought was weird was that people acted like nothing was wrong," Creager recalled about the reaction to Cobain's behaviour. "I felt like, 'Excuse me, this guy is miserable.'"

He became increasingly miserable as the tour progressed, from France to Switzerland to Italy. Despite being ill with a sore throat, he continued using drugs (Steve Diggle, of opening act the **Buzzcocks**, recalled there being plenty of cocaine on the "smoking bus"), having a London doctor write prescriptions for narcotics, which were sent to him by courier if he couldn't obtain them any other way. He missed Love, who wasn't on the tour as Novoselic and Grohl's partners were, as she was working on promoting her upcoming album, *Live Through This*, and when they did talk, most of their phone calls ended in fights.

The band's last photo session, held in Paris with photographer **Youri Lenquette**, produced a series of disturbing pictures. Cobain posed with a handgun in several shots, mostly smiling, though in one, where he aims the gun directly at the camera, he looks deadly serious. Another is even more chilling: as Grohl and Novoselic sit smiling on either side of him, Cobain points a rifle in his mouth while glaring defiantly at the camera.

Cobain's change in demeanour was also apparent in the band's next, and final, TV appearance, on 23 February on the programme *Tunnel*, filmed at Rai's TV studio in **Rome**. The band performed in front of a tunnel, with fireworks spitting out of the walls intermittently throughout the first song, "Serve The Servants". While Novoselic and Smear bounce around with good humour, Cobain's expression evinces a deep weariness. At one point, Novoselic moves toward Cobain and cuts some rock star poses with his bass, to no response.

Things didn't improve between songs, when an actor trying to look like the height of "grunge fashion" (wearing a Nirvana T-shirt and long-sleeved flannel shirt) stumbles onto the set and jabbers away at the band in Italian, until shooed away by the show's female host. Novoselic plays along, but again, there's no reaction from Cobain. Melora Creager joined the group on cello for "Dumb", which featured an even more listless performance from Cobain, though at least this matched the mood of the song.

Two days later, Cobain told Novoselic he wanted to cancel the tour, blaming his stomach troubles. Novoselic could tell there was something else bothering him, but Cobain offered no further insight. Told there would be financial penalties if they cancelled, the tour continued. On 27 February, the band played in **Ljubljana, Slovenia**, and Novoselic, who had relatives in the audience, addressed the crowd in Croatian.

The last show

The group arrived in **Munich**, Germany, on 28 February; two shows were scheduled at Terminal 1 on 1 and 2 March, with a show on 3 March in Offenbach, after which there would be a week's break. Cobain phoned **Art Cobain**, a cousin back in Aberdeen whom he hadn't spoken to in years, complaining about the pressures he was facing. Art listened sympathetically and invited Kurt to an upcoming family reunion. Just before the tour began, Cobain had unexpectedly reached out to another relative, phoning his father, ostensibly to discuss the health of his grandmother and Don's mother, Iris, who had been in a Seattle hospital recently with heart disease. Increasingly estranged from those in his immediate circle, Cobain seemed to be reaching out in an attempt to make a meaningful connection with someone.

His relationship with Love remained troubled. Prior to the 1 March show, he phoned her and the two got into another fight. Hanging up, he then called the couple's lawyer, **Rosemary Carroll**, and announced he wanted a divorce. The Melvins had now joined the tour as an opening act, and after their set Cobain went in their dressing room and complained to Buzz Osborne, mentioning not only getting a

divorce, but also wanting to break up Nirvana and fire their management.

But Nirvana's set betrayed few signs of this tension. The group began with a loose cover of The Cars' "My Best Friend's Girl", one of the first songs Cobain had learned to play, which degenerated into Novoselic singing a brief snatch of the same band's "Moving In Stereo" before blasting into the usual opening number, "Radio Friendly Unit Shifter". Shows on the European leg mostly ran between eighty and ninety minutes, and the Munich show was no different. There was a momentary disruption when the power went out during "Come As You Are", but after a few minutes the power was restored and the show continued. Though Cobain's voice was noticeably raw, it nonetheless held up relatively well through the 24-song set (though threatening to go off the rails towards the end, on more raucous numbers like "School" and "Lounge Act").

The show's oddest moment came after "Lithium", when Novoselic remarked, "We're not playing the Munich Enormodome tonight because our careers are on the wane. We're on the way out. Grunge is dead, Nirvana's over. So we haven't come up with a new shtick yet, some kind of new image. Our next record's going to be a hip hop record!" It was delivered in Novoselic's usual jocular fashion, and would probably not be much remembered if it hadn't been made at Nirvana's last show, though you can't help wondering what provoked it. Cobain made few comments, though he did take the trouble to mention "About A Girl" was from *Bleach*, a distinction he rarely pointed out

The Story

about other songs on the album. The last song of the night was "Heart-Shaped Box".

As soon as the show had ended, Cobain told the band's booking agent he wanted the remaining shows cancelled. He saw a doctor the next day, who diagnosed him as having laryngitis and bronchitis, then flew to Rome with Pat Smear, where Love and Frances planned to join them. Novoselic and his wife returned to Seattle. Grohl remained in Germany to work on a video for the film *Backbeat*, a biopic of the early years of The Beatles; Grohl played alongside the likes of Sonic Youth's **Thurston Moore** and R.E.M.'s **Mike Mills** in the alternative supergroup that provided the soundtrack for the film.

Near-fatal overdose

Cobain and Smear checked into Rome's posh **Hotel Excelsior**, and Cobain bought gifts and flowers for Love, which he set up in their room as a surprise. Love arrived on 3 March, but was too tired to celebrate and soon went to bed. She awoke some hours later to find her husband unconscious on the floor, fully dressed, with blood coming out of his nose. He'd earlier sent a bellboy out to fill a prescription for Rohypnol, generally prescribed for serious insomnia. After Love went to sleep, he was said to have taken a massive number of pills (as many as sixty, according to some accounts), washing them down with champagne. An ambulance was summoned, and at Umberto I Polyclinic Hospital, Cobain's stomach was pumped. He remained in a coma for twenty

hours; on regaining consciousness, he was transferred to Rome's **American Hospital**.

CNN mistakenly reported that Cobain had died, and for a while Novoselic, Grohl, and people at Geffen and Gold Mountain thought he had as well, due to a phone call a woman claiming to be Love had placed to David Geffen's office. He hadn't, but it had been a close call. When Love found him, Cobain had a three-page note in his hand, stating his intentions. "Dr Baker [a counsellor he'd consulted at the Canyon Ranch Spa] says that, like Hamlet, I have to choose between life and death. I'm choosing death," he wrote, going on to complain about the constant touring, and his belief that his wife didn't love him. Despite speaking of divorce a few days before, he now wrote, "I'd rather die than go through another divorce." Clearly, memories of his parents' divorce still stung.

Publicly, the incident was explained as an inadvertent overdose, the result of an incautious mixture of sleeping pills and alcohol. The doctor who treated Cobain, Dr Osvaldo Galletta, painted a picture of a man on the way to recovery, playing with his daughter at the hospital. "I had hope for him," Galletta said later. "His wife also behaved quite normally. She left a thank-you note." But the *NME* caught the underlying feeling more accurately than they knew in their cover story on the overdose, asking "Nirvana: Is This the End?" With eerie prescience, they illustrated the story with the Youri Lenquette photo showing Cobain pointing the rifle in his mouth, asking, "Will we ever see Nirvana again?"

More fatefully, perhaps, many of those close to Cobain, including Novoselic, Grohl and Dylan

Carlson, weren't told the Rome incident was a suicide attempt. And so Cobain was discharged from the hospital on 8 March, returned to Seattle on 12 March, and was essentially left to his own devices. According to *Heavier Than Heaven*, Cobain and Love got into a fight the night they arrived back home (they had moved into a three-storey luxury home in Seattle's exclusive Madrona neighbourhood in January); someone called 911 from the house and hung up before saying anything, but police responded to the call nonetheless. The couple assured the police their fight was now under control, "and with Love and Cobain's assurances they'd work things out, I left the residence," wrote Officer Levandowski in his report.

At this point, the remaining dates on Nirvana's European tour hadn't been cancelled, just rescheduled, and it was still assumed the group would headline Lollapalooza that summer.

The "greenhouse" over the garage at Cobain and Love's Seattle home.

But Cobain was uninterested in fulfilling these commitments, and in response to his wife's demand that he not do drugs at their home, he simply left the house and spent his days getting high in cheap motels. He also hung out at the apartment of one of Cali DeWitt's girlfriends, telling them, "You guys are my only friends." But he was at home on 18 March, when yet another fight led Love to call 911, after Cobain had locked himself in a room. When the police arrived, Love claimed Cobain had threatened to kill himself, which he denied. Love eventually conceded he hadn't made such a statement, but that she'd been concerned when he locked himself in a room with a number of guns. Due to the "volatile situation" (in the words of the police report), the police confiscated four guns and a bottle of Klonopin (an anti-seizure/anti-anxiety drug), and detained Cobain for further questioning, though he was eventually released without charge.

In desperation, an intervention was scheduled for 21 March, but Novoselic felt that it wouldn't help and told Cobain about it, putting an end to the plan before it had started. Novoselic had tried to reach out to his old friend after tracking him down in one of the cheap hotels he'd been staying at, inviting him to visit his farm in southwest Washington. Instead, Cobain got Novoselic to unwittingly drive him to his drug dealer's neighbourhood on the pretext of going to a nearby Jack In The Box fast-food restaurant. When Novoselic realized what was happening, the two got into a fierce argument and Cobain ended up running from the car.

On 25 March, Cobain came downstairs to find a rescheduled intervention awaiting him. One by one, Love, John Silva, Danny Goldberg and Janet Billig from Gold Mountain, Gary Gersh and Mark Kates from DGC and Pat Smear confronted Cobain about his drug use. But Cobain, who had just taken heroin with Carlson (who he mistakenly thought was also in on the intervention) threw everyone's pleas back in their faces, accusing them of hypocrisy. Love said she was flying to LA to undergo rehab herself, and Cobain was urged to join her, but he refused. It was the last time Love would see her husband alive. After she left, Cobain retreated downstairs with Smear and Eric Erlandson for a jam session, with Cobain on drums, Smear on guitar and Erlandson on bass. Along with a song Cobain had recently written, later named "Do Re Mi", the ad hoc group is also said to have jammed on The Clash's "Should I Stay Or Should I Go", among others. Cobain then went to one of his dealers and expressed his feelings of isolation: "Where are my friends when I need them? Why are my friends against me?"

With Love now gone, Cobain continued to do drugs unimpeded; indeed, he was now shooting up so incautiously dealers were hesitant to sell to him, afraid he would OD (he had survived at least two more ODs since returning from Rome). His mother and sister came up from Aberdeen to try and persuade him to seek treatment on 26 March, and he again refused. Still, over the next few days, he talked to a psychiatrist on the phone, as well as lawyer Rosemary

Carroll, and finally agreed to undergo treatment in LA. But when Novoselic drove him to Sea-Tac Airport on 29 March, he balked, trying to jump from the car and later fighting with Novoselic in the terminal before running off. Highly distressed by their parting, Novoselic soon headed back to the isolated farm he'd previously asked Cobain to visit with him.

The next day, Cobain again agreed to go to rehab, and plans were made for him to fly to LA. Prior to leaving, he and Carlson went to **Stan Baker's Sports** store in Seattle's Lake City neighbourhood. Cobain explained he wanted a gun "for protection", and as the police had recently confiscated his other guns, he wanted Carlson to make the purchase in his name. Cobain chose a Remington M-11 20-gauge shotgun, giving Carlson the money to buy both the gun and a box of shells. Carlson offered to keep the gun for him, but Cobain insisted he wanted to take it home. But he mistakenly took the shells with him when he left for his flight, turning them over to his limo driver on arrival at the airport.

He was met at LAX by Pat Smear and Gold Mountain's **Michael Meisel**, who took him to Exodus Recovery Center in **Marina Del Ray**. One of the first people he encountered there was **Gibby Haynes** of the Butthole Surfers, who had headlined one of Nirvana's early shows in 1988 and had just been an opening act for Nirvana in January. A nanny brought Frances to visit Cobain in rehab during the next two days; Love was undergoing a more private "hotel detox" at the Peninsula Hotel in Beverly Hills. On Friday, 1 April, the two spoke for the last time on the phone. According to Love, Cobain's final comments had an ominous ring. "No matter what happens, I want you to know that you made a really good album," he told her, referring to *Live Through This*, due for release on 12 April. Puzzled, Love asked what he meant. "Just remember, no matter what, I love you," Cobain replied, and then hung up.

Leaving rehab

Shortly before 7.30pm that evening, Cobain telephoned Meisel, only to find he was out. He then went to the Center's rear patio and scaled the wall, disappearing into the night. On learning Cobain had left the Center, Love immediately began tracking down local dealers in hopes of finding him. But Cobain had apparently gone straight to the airport, where he booked a return flight to Seattle on Delta Airlines, departing at 10.20pm. His neighbour in row two turned out to be **Duff McKagan** from Guns N' Roses; ironically, a member of a band Cobain had consistently bad-mouthed would be one of the last people to see him alive. But the conversation was friendly, with Cobain even admitting he'd left rehab. McKagan, who'd had his own problems with drugs, became increasingly concerned about Cobain's state of mind. On arriving at Sea-Tac at 1am, McKagan was picked up by a friend, and they decided to invite Cobain to hang out at McKagan's home. But before they could ask, Cobain had already departed in the car he'd arranged to take him home. Later that morning, he took a cab to Seattle Guns and bought a new box of shotgun shells.

Other sightings of Cobain over the next few days are uncertain. Though no longer Frances's nanny, Cali DeWitt had been staying at the Cobain house with one of his girlfriends, **Jessica Hopper**. At some point, both recalled seeing Cobain, who appeared calm and not like someone on the run or trying to hide, in their room, probably on 2 April; Hopper later told Everett True she thought the date was 4 or 5 April. They both told him to call Love, and Cobain attempted to contact her at her hotel, but couldn't get through, having forgotten the code word to reach her room. DeWitt and Hopper would later hear someone moving around the house they assumed was Cobain, but having been told by Love they should keep to their room, they didn't investigate further. There was another sighting of him on 3 April (Easter Sunday) at a local restaurant.

In the meantime, Love, still in LA, continued in her efforts to locate him. She cancelled his credit cards, thinking this would force him to emerge from hiding and help to track his movements (she'd tried this tactic the previous month, when Cobain had disappeared for a few days). On 3 April she hired a private investigator, and on 4 April she filed a Missing Persons Report with the Seattle police (claiming to be Kurt's mother). She also attempted to continue with promotion for her upcoming album (which was already garnering positive reviews), doing an interview on 4 April with Robert Hilburn of the *Los Angeles Times* that was published on 10 April. Hilburn noted her obvious distress, writing, "For once, the woman known for her biting sarcasm and savage wit in marathon interviews is speechless. For all her cockiness, she now seems frightened and fragile." She was also scheduled to do an interview with the author of this book for *The Rocket* magazine in the late afternoon of 5 April. Told Love was not available, I left a message with the hotel. Eric Erlandson returned the call soon after, explained that Love was ill, and he would try to get her to call me by Wednesday. The call never came.

"Peace, love, empathy"

When did Kurt Cobain decide to kill himself? On returning from Rome, no immediate provisions were made for his care, and he sought no treatment himself, going right back to doing drugs. It's unknown what he discussed with the counsellors he spoke with during his final month, but one of the last, **Nial Stimson** at the Exodus Center, described him as "totally in denial" that he had a drug problem (neither Stimson, nor any of the other counsellors Cobain spoke to during this period had been told that the Rome incident was a suicide attempt). His resistance to entering rehab, and the fact he arranged for the purchase of a shotgun before leaving for LA on 30 March, suggests that his mind was to some degree already made up – as does the fact that on returning to Seattle one of his first actions was going out to buy another box of shotgun shells.

At some point during the week of 3 April, Kurt made his decision. He took the shotgun and shells, towels, a cigar box containing heroin, syringes and other drug paraphernalia, a pack of Camel Light cigarettes and a can of Barq's root beer up to the "greenhouse", a 19- by 23-foot room above the property's detached garage, about 15 feet from the main house. He had written a suicide note in red ink on the back of a paper placemat, and planted this in a tray filled with potting soil, sticking the pen through the note to fix it to the dirt.

The note was addressed to "Boddah", an imaginary childhood friend, and revisited many of the themes that had come up in interviews over the past year, and, indeed, ever since *Nevermind* had made him famous. Chief among them was his lack of interest in both music and his own career, and the guilt he felt in cheating his audience by not "pretending as if I'm having 100 percent fun" (the previous October, he'd told David Fricke "I can't pretend to have a good time playing [Teen Spirit]", and in December, while watching a TV concert of Pete Townsend, he'd remarked to Michael Azerrad, "His music isn't even that good anymore but he's still so passionate about it. I wish I still felt that way"). In the note he expressed his frustration at not being able to enjoy his success, but also wrote of his love for his wife and daughter, and the conflict he felt in feeling too much for people while at the same time having become "hateful towards all humans in general" since childhood. After concluding "It's better to burn out than to fade away", he signed the note "peace, love, empathy. Kurt

Cobain", then added a postscript to his wife and daughter, closing with "I love you". He then injected himself with heroin, took up his shotgun, and shot himself in the head. Though his death certificate listed the date of death as 5 April, the coroner said the margin of error could be up to 24 hours.

Though only those in Cobain's inner circle knew he was missing, the outside world was becoming increasingly aware that something was amiss in the Nirvana camp. A *Los Angeles Times* story on 6 April finally confirmed that the remaining dates on the band's European tour had been cancelled, and that they were pulling out of Lollapalooza, due to concerns over Cobain's health. The story also noted there were rumours the band had broken up, though **Janet Billig**, along with "others close to Nirvana caution[ed] that the breakup should not be considered permanent: 'They've been on the verge of breaking up forever and this doesn't sound more serious than the other 43,000 times,' said one source close to the band." In a *Billboard* article that didn't run until 16 April, Billig denied the *Los Angeles Times* report that Nirvana had broken up, but did admit, "We don't know when they're going to tour again."

Also on 6 April, **Tom Grant**, the private investigator Love had hired, flew up to Seattle. He'd subcontracted a surveillance team in Seattle on the previous Sunday, but no one had seen Cobain. After the Missing Persons Report had been filed, Seattle police also sent patrol cars to check out the Cobain residence, though Captain Brent Wingstrand noted, "I thought he may not have been truly a missing person but a person who didn't want to be found." There were several charge attempts made on Cobain's credit card, but as the card had been cancelled, the bank had stopped recording exactly where the charges were attempted, effectively making Cobain even harder to trace.

Grant met up with Dylan Carlson late Wednesday, and the two went to some of Cobain's regular haunts, also searching his house, but not the garage. On Thursday 7 April the two attempted to visit a house Cobain and Love owned in **Carnation**, a small town around thirty miles away, but got lost and returned to Seattle. At some point during the week, Eric Erlandson flew to Seattle from LA to aid in the search. Jessica Hopper had flown home to Minneapolis on 5 April, and Cali DeWitt had left the house, finding the atmosphere too foreboding. But he returned on 7 April with friends to search the property again, leaving at 4pm when a cab arrived to take him to the airport for his flight to LA. By then, Love had been arrested at her hotel for possession of a "controlled substance" – a packet that was later determined to be nothing more than "good luck ashes" in a Hindu charm. On receiving bail, Love checked into the Exodus clinic her husband had left nearly a week before.

On Friday 8 April electrician **Gary Smith**, of Veca Electric, arrived at the Cobain house to install a burglar alarm system. Climbing the stairs outside of the garage, he looked through the window of the greenhouse and saw what he initially thought was a mannequin lying on the floor. He then noticed blood coming out of the right ear and a shotgun lying across the body. He called the police, and then Veca; an unnamed person at the company then called local rock radio station KXRX with the news, saying, "You guys are going to owe me some pretty good Pink Floyd tickets for this."

Aftermath

1994–

The Story

Aftermath
1994–

Cobain's death sent shock waves through the music industry, as the first instance of a major artist killing himself while seemingly at the peak of his career. The pain was felt most keenly in Seattle, where friends and fans struggled to come to terms with the tragedy; meanwhile, reporters descended en masse, trying to get comments from anybody who had even the most tenuous connection to Cobain or Nirvana.

Breaking the news

On learning from police that a body had indeed been found, at 9.30am KXRX broadcast the first report that an unidentified male in his twenties had been found dead at Kurt Cobain's home. By 10am, other stations had picked up the story, and by noon there were unoffi-

Crowds gathered at the Seattle wake in honour of Cobain.

cial confirmations that the body was Kurt's. The headline in that evening's *Seattle Times* read "Nirvana's Cobain Dead", even as the story acknowledged there had been no official confirmation. In fact, the King County Medical Examiner's Office had made an official positive identification at 12.20pm, matching Cobain's fingerprints with those on file after his June 1993 arrest.

Kurt's mother, **Wendy O'Connor**, told Aberdeen's *Daily World* she learned about her son's death from someone who called her after hearing it on the radio. Cobain's sister Kim also heard the news via KXRX; on calling the station, she was told to contact the police. O'Connor made a very brief statement to the press, one quote in particular being immediately reported around the world: "'Now he's gone and joined that stupid club,' she said, referring to the early deaths of such rock stars as Jimi Hendrix and Jim Morrison. 'I told him not to join that stupid club.'"

Don Cobain also heard the news of his son's death over the radio, while Kurt's grandparents Leland and Iris found out about it from television. The couple's lawyer, Rosemary Carroll, broke the news to Courtney Love: walking into Love's room at the Exodus clinic, she simply looked at her until Love broke the silence by asking "How?" Love and Frances then flew straight to Seattle.

Both Seattle's Police Department and Fire Department had responded to the 911 call, and Fire Department officers gained entry to the greenhouse by breaking the glass in the French doors at the west end of the room. Coincidentally, the first police officer on the scene was **Von Levandowski**, who'd been to the house just a few weeks earlier in response to Love's 911 call. Although early accounts reported that Cobain had left his wallet open with his driver's licence exposed, presumably to help identify him, the police report states it was Levandowski who opened the wallet. Homicide detectives arrived shortly after 10am; at 11am, personnel from the King County Medical Examiner's Office arrived, including **Dr Nikolas Hartshorne**, who as a medical student had promoted one of Nirvana's Seattle shows in 1988.

As the news continued to spread, fans and the media descended on Cobain's home. The house was immediately adjacent to **Viretta Park**, which provided space for the gathering crowd. A stairway that led to the upper part of the park also led to the street behind the house, offering a view of the rear of the property. It was from this angle that *Seattle Times* photographer **Tom Reese** shot a picture of Kurt's body lying on the floor, viewed through the open French doors. Cobain's right leg and foot, wearing a Converse One-Star sneaker, are visible, as are his right forearm and fist. Two policemen are also in shot, as is the cigar box that contained Cobain's drug paraphernalia and various personal effects. The picture ran on the front page of the *Seattle Times* 9 April edition, under the headline "Kurt Cobain's Troubled Last Days". Unsurprisingly, it drew some criticism, but in an editorial published on 17 April, executive editor **Michael Francher** explained the rationale for publishing the picture. As the story was still developing, the *Times* used a different picture for the 8 April edition, a wide-angle shot of the house and garage, with a police officer standing in the greenhouse's open French door, minutes before the windows were covered by drapes. But the picture of Cobain's body, Francher argued, established "an essential reality about Cobain's death. Our concern was that Cobain's suicide would be romanticized by some – suicide, the ultimate high. As one editor said, the photo showed, 'This wasn't cool, it was death and that's the result of suicide.'" Reese's picture later won an award from the Society of Professional Journalists in the regional News Photography category. The *Times*' rival, the *Seattle Post-Intelligencer*, used a less provocative shot of Cobain's covered body being carried out on a stretcher.

Both Geffen Records and Gold Mountain issued statements. "We are all devastated by the unbelievable tragedy of Kurt Cobain's death," read Geffen's. "The world has lost a great

The Story

Kurt Cobain was murdered?

Whenever a well-known person dies unexpectedly, particularly if they're young, there are rumours of foul play. So it should come as no surprise that Kurt Cobain's death has provoked its share of controversy.

The one fact everyone agrees on is that Cobain was found dead in his home in Seattle on the morning of 8 April 1994. But just about everything else concerning that event has been subject to dispute. One of the first to question the official verdict of death by a self-inflicted shotgun wound was Tom Grant, the private investigator Courtney Love had hired to track down Cobain after he left the Exodus Recovery Center in California. Since then, websites, TV shows, books and films have discussed a conspiracy surrounding Cobain's death. Following are the main points of contention.

The suicide note

Some argue that because Cobain's note doesn't explicitly mention taking his life, it isn't a true "suicide note". Others have said that the note's final lines (stating that Cobain's daughter's life "will be so much happier without me") look like they're written in a different hand, and were added to make the note look more "suicidal". But not all suicide notes do make clear references to the writer's death. Experts in programmes like *Dateline NBC* have been divided over whether the final lines were written by someone else or not (Charles Cross's *Heavier Than Heaven* suggests the final lines were written when the note was placed on an uneven surface, accounting for the variation in writing styles).

The shotgun

No legible prints were found on the shotgun, the shells, the suicide note or the pen that wrote the note, which some call suspicious (other accounts have inaccurately stated that no prints were found on the gun at all). Again, experts have been divided, with some saying that the lack of legible prints on the items is not unusual.

The amount of heroin

Cobain was said to have had 1.52 milligrams per litre of morphine in his bloodstream at the time of his death (heroin breaks down into morphine in the body). Some have said a person with that much of the drug in their system would be severely incapacitated and unable to kill themselves with a gun. But then again, other

artist and we've lost a great friend – it leaves a huge void in our hearts. Obviously Kurt will be missed by all." "The intensity and creativity of Kurt's music and his thoughts will always be treasured," said Gold Mountain's. "Kurt's art has transcended beyond the popular to speak to millions around the world. Painfully, Kurt's passions and feelings about his fame overwhelmed him. We will miss him, his music and his friendship deeply." That was as close

as anyone got to an official statement from Novoselic and Grohl. Reporters had also been calling Sub Pop's offices, only to receive a terse "No comment."

So for a time, news organizations wanting quotes had to rely on fans, radio station DJs, record store employees, and people who'd had a passing acquaintance with Cobain, or were thought to (Charlie Campbell of Sub Pop band Pond told Michael Azerrad, "Some woman experts have said a person with a high tolerance of the drug could indeed have committed such an act. The figure of 1.52 may not even be accurate; though it is said to be from the official toxicology report, the figure has never been officially confirmed.

None of which would definitively point towards murder in any case – though that hasn't stopped others from wading into the breach, creating a cottage industry of conspiracy theories. Nick Broomfield's 1998 documentary *Kurt & Courtney*, which brought the story out of the realm of music magazines and into the mainstream, let some of the theorists have their say, including Grant, Hank Harrison (Love's father), and Eldon "El Duce" Hoke, lead singer and drummer with The Mentors, all of whom pointed the finger at Courtney Love. Hoke went one further and claimed Love had offered him $50,000 to "whack" Cobain (though in his interview with Broomfield he seems a little uncertain as to where Cobain actually lived). The tabloid TV programme *Hard Copy* paid for a polygraph test that Hoke passed, but there was no further investigation, nor was any corroborating evidence for Hoke's story ever offered. But theorists had a field day

when, a month after his interview with Broomfield, the longtime alcoholic died after being hit by a train.

The belief that Love was involved (for reasons of financial gain) is actually one of the milder theories; others spin Byzantine webs that implicate drug dealers, record company/management executives, government officials and CIA "mind control" experiments. In *Love & Death*, authors Max Wallace and Ian Halperin (whose first book on the conspiracy theories was *Who Killed Kurt Cobain?*) encounter a friend of Hoke's who implies he was also involved, leaving the writers uncertain as to his motives. But no fresh, credible evidence has ever been brought forward. The Seattle Police Department has declined to even consider reopening the case. Nikolas Hartshorne, the Medical Examiner who performed the autopsy, consistently maintained in numerous interviews that Cobain's death was due to suicide (Hartshorne died in a BASE jumping accident in 2002).

Of course, there's always the possibility Cobain isn't dead after all. In early January 2004, when police arrested a man in Aberdeen on an outstanding warrant, he insisted to police officers "You got the wrong guy! I'm Kurt Cobain!"

from some magazine called me up and I didn't even know the guy"). It didn't take long for cynicism to set in. "Welcome to checkbook journalism," the *Seattle Times* wryly observed on 10 April, noting the number of news reporters that were now in town. In addition to local media, reporters from *Inside Edition*, *Hard Copy*, *Rolling Stone*, *The Village Voice*, *People*, *Entertainment Weekly*, *Newsweek*, *Details*, *First Person* (an NBC news magazine

show), *Billboard* and *MTV* were among those in town. One TV show offered electrician Gary Smith $1500 for exclusive rights to his story; he turned them down, concerned that he'd be seen as "a profiteer". On 9 April, the *New York Times* featured a front-page story about Cobain; within hours, the story was printed on T-shirts that were sold on the streets of Manhattan.

By coincidence, Sub Pop's anniversary party had been scheduled for 9 April at the Crocodile

Café. The label briefly considered cancelling, but reasoned that as it was an invite-only event, unwanted media could easily be kept out. Reporters nonetheless hovered outside, offering attendees $100 for their invitations. At one point during the evening, which saw performances from Velocity Girl, Pond and Sunny Day Real Estate, Bruce Pavitt told the crowd, "We should remember and celebrate the positive things about Kurt Cobain." And in fact the mood that night was not as downbeat as might have been expected; it was a bittersweet wake to be sure, but provided Seattle's music community with a place to gather and share their feelings and memories. On the same evening, a public vigil was held at Aberdeen's **Morrison Riverfront Park**, drawing around 300 attendees.

Seattle vigil

Seattle's public wake, organized by local radio stations KXRX, KISW and KNDD, was held the following day at 5pm, at the Seattle Center's **Flag Plaza**. Crowd estimates ranged between 5000 and 10,000, with many people bearing signs and candles. Carrie Borzillo-Vrenna, a *Billboard* editor who'd flown in to attend Sub Pop's party, covered the public vigil and noted the bizarre informality of some of those in attendance, describing the scene as a "mini-Lollapalooza". Kids played hacky sack, one brought his pet iguana, another sported a homemade T-shirt reading "Kurt died for your sins", while others passed out flyers for their bands: "a seemingly inappropriate time to be a self-promoter," she noted.

The official speeches were brief: **Reverend Stephen Towles** and a representative from the local Crisis Clinic spoke, and a local poet read a short piece. One of the DJs read a letter from **Larry Smith**, Cobain's uncle by marriage, which shared some anecdotes about a youthful Cobain: on a fishing trip, screaming his head off as he stood by the river, "trying to thicken my vocal cords"; a fight with a bully with Cobain merely giving "the appropriate hand

Devastated fans paying tribute at the public wake in Seattle.

gesture" every time the bully knocked him down; heading up a small group of children romping around a backyard. "I guess you could say he was the Pied Piper of compassion," Smith concluded in a commentary that captured an aspect of Cobain's character missing from other accounts, which focused on his years of fame or his drug use.

The most dramatic moments came when a taped message from Love was played. "I don't know what to say. I feel the same way you guys do," she began, going on to read Cobain's suicide note, breaking in with her own comments, as if having a last, desperate argument with her husband. On calling his inability to pretend he was having fun his "worst crime", Love responded, "No, Kurt, the worst crime I can think of is for you to just continue being a rock star when you fuckin' hated it. Just fuckin' stop!" After reading the note she denounced "That 80s 'tough love' bullshit... It doesn't work. I should have let him, we all should have let him have his numbness. We should have let him have the thing that made him feel better, that made his stomach feel better." Her intensity was such that even members of the media openly wept. A message from Novoselic was also played, this one shorter and more low-key, "We remember Kurt for what he was: caring, generous and sweet. Let's keep the music with us; we'll always have it, forever."

When the speeches were over, kids descended into the fountain behind the Plaza, dancing, tossing Frisbees and singing along to the Nirvana songs that played over the PA system.

When the music was turned off and security tried to get the crowd to disperse, the kids refused, setting their flannel shirts on fire and shouting, "Fuck you! Fuck you!" defiantly.

While the vigil at the Seattle Center was going on, a private service was held not far away at the **Unity Church of Truth**, overseen by Reverend Towles after his speech at the public wake. Guitar tech Earnie Bailey had prepared a tape of songs, including The Beatles' "In My Life" and a Vaselines number. "A suicide is no different than having our finger in a vise," Towles said after reading the 23rd Psalm. "The pain becomes so great that we can't bear it any longer." Love read from the suicide note, and quoted the Book of Job; Dylan Carlson read from Buddhist literature. Novoselic, Bruce Pavitt and Danny Goldberg also spoke about Cobain. The front page of the 11 April *Seattle Post-Intelligencer* carried a picture of a shattered-looking Novoselic and Grohl arriving for the service with their partners. Afterwards, Love turned up at the public vigil at the Seattle Center, passing out some of Cobain's clothing to the mourners who remained, and showing them the suicide note.

Sadly, the division exhibited among the band members when they'd split into two camps on the road remained; following the service, there were two different wakes, one at Cobain's house, and one at Novoselic's. As Everett True (who attended the wake at Cobain's home) noted in *Nirvana: The True Story*, the politics around the band "didn't die away for one second upon Kurt's suicide, only intensified." Love made plaster casts of Cobain's hands and clipped some of his hair, then had his body cremated.

Hole's album was released as scheduled on 12 April, though its title, *Live Through This*, now seemed grimly ironic. "How's that for sick?" Love said to the *Post-Intelligencer*'s Gene Stout in a short interview before the private service. "I'm tough and I can take anything. But I can't take this... I listened to too many people. I'm only going to listen to my gut for the rest of my life. It's all my fault." A tour which had been planned to follow the album's release was now cancelled.

"Call me insensitive, but... "

With the news element of the story largely over after the weekend, it was now left to the media to pass judgement on the event, with a clear generation gap emerging. **Andy Rooney**, a commentator on the news magazine show *60 Minutes*, drew ire for his editorial on Cobain, shown on 17 April. After admitting he'd never heard of Cobain, Nirvana or "grunge rock" before reading Cobain's

The underside of the bridge over the Wishkah has become something of a graffiti shrine to Cobain and is often the first place fans head in Aberdeen.

obituary, he went on to mock the mourning fans, and critiqued the music he admitted he'd never heard, making the strange assertion, "No one's art is better than the person who creates it. If Kurt Cobain applied the same brain to his music that he applied to his drug-infested life, it's reasonable to think that his music may not have made much sense either."

This rather callous attitude was echoed even in Seattle, by the *Seattle Times*' **Erik Lacitis**, in a 12 April column entitled "Rock Star's Anguish Hard to Understand": "Call me insensitive, but I can think of plenty more things to get anguished about than traveling the world, pretending you're having 100 percent fun on stage in front of crowds of adoring fans." What seemed to especially irritate critics like Lacitis and Rooney was that Cobain hadn't faced any "real problems", as they perceived them – as Rooney had put it, "What would all these young people be doing if they had real problems like a Depression, World War II, or Vietnam?" Ironically, Cobain had made a similar observation himself to Azerrad: "I'm a product of a fucking spoiled America. Think of how much worse my family life could be if I grew up in another country, in a depression. So many worse things than a divorce." Rooney later admitted, "Perhaps I was unfair," and noted that he'd received "more than 10,000 angry letters from viewers under thirty years old".

Cobain's lifestyle also provoked controversy among those trying to decide how best to honour him. In Aberdeen, **Randi Hubbard**, a former truck driver, sculpted a 600-pound, five-foot-six statue of Cobain out of concrete, seated

and playing the guitar, with a tear running down his cheek; she titled it "All Apologies". She'd hoped it would be displayed for a few months in Morrison Riverfront Park, and the Aberdeen City Council initially agreed. But there followed a storm of protest from local residents who felt it might glorify the life of a self-confessed drug addict. Another potential site, Zelasko Park, was scratched because veterans thought it was too close to a statue of a World War I soldier. Cobain's grandfather, Leland, was unhappy about the town's attitude. "This is exactly the reason Kurt left Aberdeen in the first place," he told the *Seattle Times*. "They can't accept anything new."

But even Novoselic was uncomfortable with the idea of a statue. "Kurt would hate the idea of a statue," he said in a letter faxed to Aberdeen's *Daily World*. "When Kurt is put on a pedestal, it leaves him exposed to attack, be it from the 'self-appointed judges' who harshly condemn the junkie outcast, the well-meaning misguided fans whose idolatry is proof that they never understood what Nirvana was all about, or just from pigeon droppings fouling up the likeness of a man who talked about the real things people should understand." He said he'd go as far as to knock the statue down ("To let it stand would signal the defeat of all that we tried to make happen") and suggested that establishing a youth centre in Cobain's memory would be more appropriate. In the end, Hubbard left the statue in a corner of her husband's store, Hubb's Muffler Shop.

Another factor that had discomfited Aberdeen residents was the media deluge that swamped their town after Cobain's death. Reporters in search of what led to Cobain's unhappiness, the *Daily World* complained, all too often portrayed Aberdeen as "Sort of like *Deliverance* with logs". It hadn't helped that Cobain was seen as someone who all too readily ran down his home town in interviews.

Novoselic went to some lengths to correct what he saw as a misperception of his bandmate. When the **Hoquiam** City Council held a public hearing on 25 April about whether the town should host the Lollapalooza festival, Novoselic attended to speak in support of the festival, and about Cobain's feelings for his home town. The city council was divided over the festival: proponents pointed out the money it would bring to the local economy, while those opposed expressed concerns over parking, possible drug use by the attendees and its bringing "the wrong element" to town. The manager of Aberdeen's Safeway was quoted by the *Daily World* as saying, "The alternative music isn't really, I don't know how to say it, isn't really wholesome."

Novoselic was the last to speak at the hearing. "First I'd like to clear something up," he said. "There's this perception that Kurt Cobain hated Aberdeen. That made a really good media story, but wasn't true… We've been all around the world and there's a little bit of Aberdeen everywhere". But though the city council voted to continue negotiations with the promoters, concerns over the influx of people – its potential 25,000 attendees would outnumber Hoquiam's own population two to one – meant the festival was ultimately held elsewhere.

Meanwhile, detectives had been investigating Cobain's death, clocking up over 200 hours on the case. A definitive chronology of his activities after 2 April was never established, nor was it ever determined who tried to use his cancelled credit cards on 6 and 8 April. These unanswered questions led to the rise of various conspiracy theories. It was said the autopsy had revealed the level of heroin in Cobain's bloodstream to be 1.52 milligrams per litre. But the figure was never officially confirmed; the autopsy results were released to Cobain's family, and, in accordance with Washington State law, were not made public. Nor, to date, have they ever been.

Two live releases

In the wake of Cobain's sudden death, sales of Nirvana records had jumped; in the week after his death, *In Utero* went from number 72 to number 27 in the charts, *Nevermind* went from 167 to 56, *Incesticide* re-entered the charts at 47, and *Bleach* sales more than quadrupled. But DGC was leery of being seen as cashing in on the tragedy. The Scott Litt remix of "Pennyroyal Tea" had been planned as a third UK/European single, but it was pulled after Cobain's death, and all available copies recalled and destroyed (one of the B-sides had been "I Hate Myself And Want To Die"). Some copies and promos escaped destruction and have gone on to be highly sought after collectables.

DGC did go ahead with July's release of *DGC Rarities Vol. 1*, a compilation that featured "Pay To Play" (the early version of "Stay Away") from the Smart sessions, as it had been scheduled well before Cobain's death. But there were plans to honour Nirvana's live legacy, and on 23 August it was announced that a double album set, *Verse Chorus Verse*, would be released that fall, one album featuring live material from 1989 to 1994, and the other featuring the band's *Unplugged* performance, matching the band's "loud" and "soft" sides. But Novoselic and Grohl became overwhelmed by emotion during the process of mixing, and so the live compilation portion was scrapped. Instead, *MTV Unplugged In New York* was released as a single album on 1 November (the album entered the US charts at number one, and topped the charts in six other countries, including the UK). But a "loud" release nonetheless followed, when the feature-length video Cobain had been working on with Kevin Kerslake, *Live! Tonight! Sold Out!!* was released on 15 November.

Given the unceasing media attention that had at times threatened to engulf the band over the previous three years, having two releases that brought the focus back to where it should've been, on the strength of the band's music and the power of the band's performance, was the most fitting tribute of all.

The legend begins

For Love, Novoselic and Grohl, life went on. Nirvana – and particularly Cobain – passed into legend. Cobain appeared on the cover of nearly every major music magazine; even *Newsweek*, which had a previously planned cover story on suicide for its 18 April issue, quickly adopted a picture of Cobain for the cover. Numerous books appeared, mostly quick cash-ins, exceptions being an updated version of Azerrad's *Come As You Are*, and *Cobain*, which compiled *Rolling Stone*'s many articles on the group. A copy of Cobain's suicide note even appeared on a T-shirt. Sadly, a rash of "copycat" suicides, said to have been inspired by Cobain's action, also occurred.

Cobain's house in Seattle became a shrine, with visitors hanging out in the adjacent park, writing graffiti on the park benches. Love eventually had the garage/greenhouse torn down in an effort to stop fans from coming by the house ("It's become bigger than the Space Needle," she told the *Seattle Post-Intelligencer*), but they continued to arrive, in part because they had nowhere else to go. Love had buried some of Cobain's ashes among the roots of a willow tree at the Seattle home; others were consecrated at a Buddhist monastery in **Ithaca**, New York. But there was no public grave site. Love had hoped to inter some in Seattle's Calvary Catholic Cemetery, but couldn't meet their demands for $140,000 a year in security costs. Seattle's Lake View Cemetery also declined to take Cobain's ashes, finding the traffic of fans visiting the gravesites of martial arts legend Bruce Lee and his son, Brandon, enough to deal with. On 31 May 1999, more ashes were scattered in a creek behind the house Cobain's mother was then living in, just outside Olympia. By then, Love was no longer living in Seattle (she'd moved

The Story

to LA in 1997), but fans continued making pilgrimages to Viretta Park, particularly on the anniversary of Cobain's death.

On 8 September 1994 "Heart-Shaped Box" won two awards at the MTV Video Music Awards, for Best Alternative Video and Best Art Direction. A subdued-looking Novoselic, Grohl and Pat Smear went onstage to accept the first award, with Grohl saying "It'd be silly to say that it doesn't feel like there's something missing. And I think about Kurt every day. And I'd like to thank everyone for paying attention to our band." Novoselic was equally sombre on introducing a short film tribute to Cobain, compiled by **Dave Markey**. "This last April we all lost a good friend," he said. "And we'd like for you to watch this presentation and remember the life of Kurt Cobain." Markey's poignant film mixed home footage of a young Cobain (seen in one shot in the front yard of his childhood home, leaping into the air with his guitar) with Nirvana performance footage, some of which Markey himself had shot in 1991, along with some in-jokes: there was a shot of a plate of macaroni and cheese, one of Cobain's favourite foods, and several "Visible Man" models. The film concluded with a disturbing image of Cobain collapsing onstage at Reading in 1992, followed by an abrupt cut to black, tempered by an "epilogue" of sorts, showing Cobain waving to the crowd after Nirvana's Reading performance in 1991.

Novoselic and Grohl never considered continuing as Nirvana without Cobain, and by 1995 they each had new bands. Nor were any Nirvana records immediately forthcoming,

the first year since 1988 that the band released no new recordings. In 1996, a live version of "Radio Friendly Unit Shifter" from a February 1994 date appeared on the compilation *Home Alive: The Art of Self Defense*. A higher profile release was *From The Muddy Banks Of The Wishkah*, the live record that had originally been planned as part of a double album set with *Unplugged*. The album, released in October 1996, drew on shows from 1989 to 1994, and entered the US charts at number one; it also topped the Australian charts and reached number three in the UK. The same year saw *Unplugged* win a Grammy for Best Alternative Music Album. Then there was another lull in record releases until 1999, when Nirvana's *Saturday Night Live* performance of "Rape Me" appeared on *Saturday Night Live: 25 Years Of Musical Performances, Vol. 2*.

But although Nirvana were no longer an active force on the music scene, their presence continued to be felt. Cover stories would invariably appear on anniversaries of Cobain's death or the release of *Nevermind* and *In Utero*. In the increasing number of Top 50/100/500 songs/albums/band lists that threatened to take over entertainment magazines and television progamming, "Smells Like Teen Spirit", *Nevermind* and/or Nirvana could be counted on to appear near the top. Cobain made the cover of *Spin*'s tenth and fifteenth anniversary issues, as well as sharing the cover of their "90 Greatest Albums of the 90s" issue (along with Beck, Trent Reznor and Lauryn Hill); in 1999, a *Rolling Stone* cover named Cobain "Artist of the Decade".

With The Lights Out

For the series 'Rock Shrines' BBC TV are filming a short documentary about Kurt Cobain through the eyes of his fans. If you'd like to share your thoughts with us on camera, just turn up at the park next to 171 Lake Washington Blvd between 10-7.

Or contact: Kate/Jamie on 44 7120 598008

In 1998 Love, Novoselic and Grohl began work on a box set that would provide an overview of Nirvana's career. But relations amongst the three had often been fraught over the years, and in 2001 Love filed an injunction to stop the set's release. A protracted legal scuffle followed, with hurtful allegations made on both sides. It was unfortunate timing, as the box had been scheduled for release in the fall of 2001, to tie in with the tenth anniversary of *Nevermind*'s release. Now all fans were left with were commemorative articles about the album in music magazines, along with the publication of Charles Cross's *Heavier Than Heaven*, the first major biography of Cobain.

Among the issues disputed was how to handle the release of the last complete song Nirvana had recorded, now called "You Know You're Right" (when Hole had performed the song during the band's 1995 appearance on MTV's *Unplugged*, it was called "You Got No Right" and featured different lyrics). Novoselic and Grohl had wanted to include the song in the box set, but Love felt it would be better showcased on its own. In anticipation of a settlement, the song was mixed during the summer of 2001. But negotiations on its release then stalled.

Brief clips of the song were featured on the US TV show *Access Hollywood* in 2001, and more were leaked online the following year. In September, word came that a settlement was close to being reached. But before it could be officially announced, "You Know You're Right" leaked in its entirety online on 21 September. It was rapidly disseminated, and played on radio stations around the world, despite cease and desist orders from the band's label. On 30 September, a press release stated that Love, Novoselic and Grohl had finally resolved their differences and that a compilation album, box set and rarities album were due to be released.

First came the compilation, a "Best Of" collection simply entitled *Nirvana*. The cover was simple as well: a plain black design with the Nirvana logo in silver placed squarely in the middle. Originally scheduled for release in November, the leak of "You Know You're Right" meant it was brought forward a month. The album reached number three in the US and UK, and topped the charts in Australia and Austria. "You Know You're Right" was not officially released as a single, but was sent to radio, topping the Mainstream Rock and Modern Rock charts. Another Nirvana-related release came with the publication of some of Cobain's private writings, in *Journals*, published in November 2002, which topped the *New York Times* non-fiction bestseller list. By the year's end, *Mojo* was proclaiming Cobain "The Year's Biggest Star"; *Q* went further on their October 2002 cover, heralding Nirvana as "The Most Important Band In The World".

Kurt Cobain Memorial Committee

On 29 February 2004, an article by three Aberdeen High School teenagers ran in Aberdeen's *Daily World* asking why there was no official Kurt Cobain memorial anywhere in town. It was a reasonable question to ask on the eve of the tenth anniversary of Cobain's death, but Aberdeen has long had an uneasy relationship with its famous son. Cobain had denigrated Aberdeen in numerous interviews, an attitude the media was only too happy to seize upon in the wake of his death, which understandably caused some resentment from the town's residents. There was also the feeling that a memorial would "glorify" the life of a self-confessed drug user who had committed suicide. Indeed, in June of 2004, the Hoquiam City Council vetoed a proposed mayoral proclamation honouring Cobain for precisely these reasons, with council member Tom Plumb asking, "What kind of message is this sending to my kids?"

But the article struck a chord with the *Daily World*'s Jeff Burlingame. As the paper's Arts & Entertainment editor, he was regularly contacted by other media outlets about Nirvana, and had himself been asked why there was no public memorial in town, as fans continued to arrive from around the world to walk in Cobain's footsteps. In response, Burlingame, who had met Cobain as a teenager through a mutual friend and while hanging out at Melvins' practices in the 1980s, soon teamed up with Aberdeen City Council member Paul Fritts (who'd been thinking along the same lines) to form the Kurt Cobain Memorial Committee (others on the original eight-member committee included Cobain's grandfather Leland, and the three Aberdeen High students who'd written the newspaper story). "Our city has failed to acknowledge somebody that basically influenced an entire generation of people," Fritts told the *Daily World*. "Thousands were affected by Kurt Cobain's music and the words he wrote. You don't have to agree with him or what he did, but you have to acknowledge his impact."

The Committee held a public meeting in Aberdeen to solicit ideas, and by the following year, their first endeavour was unveiled: the original "Welcome To Aberdeen" sign at the town's east entrance was replaced by a new version, with the phrase "Come As You Are" added below. It was a suitable compromise for a place trying to figure out how best to honour an individual whose lifestyle made some uncomfortable. "In the beginning stages for the project, we knew we would have to approach the Aberdeen City Council for approval," Burlingame explains. "Among our earliest ideas were things like 'Welcome to Aberdeen: Birthplace of Kurt Cobain'. But, because we assumed we would meet with some strong resistance – which, surprisingly, turned out to be a false assumption – we needed a phrase that had dual meanings. The Nirvana fan will recognize 'Come As You Are' for the amazing Nirvana song it is. The non-Nirvana fan will read the sign and hopefully say, 'Here's a city that welcomes me'. And Aberdeen is pretty much, partially by necessity, that way. You can go into the fanciest restaurant in town and see people in business suits dining with loggers in flannel. For me, that's about as 'Come As You Are' as you can get."

But though the way was now clear for the box set's release, work on it would not recommence until the summer of 2004. In its final version, the box featured 65 songs over 3 CDs, along with a DVD. Though some tracks had been available (in varying quality) on the collector's circuit, over

The Committee also plans to establish a Kurt Cobain Memorial Park and a youth centre in the area. "For generations, the city's youth have said there's nothing for them to do in Aberdeen," says Burlingame. "That's especially true for kids like Kurt, those who are more interested in non-mainstream artistic ventures than high school sports or pep band. Our youth centre will provide a place for Kurt-like kids to hang out and participate in those types of activities. The park will give the countless Nirvana fans that come into town a centralized place to gather. Many now aimlessly wander Aberdeen's streets looking for something Kurt touched, some place he spent time. They tend to migrate under the bridge they believe he slept under, although it's doubtful he did (see box, p.000). One feature we will incorporate into our park is a graffiti wall, upon which fans can scribble messages to Kurt in as big and bold of a way as they'd like."

Funds are being raised for these projects through events like the "Lounge Acts" benefit concerts. The first concert was held on 15 September 2007 in Hoquiam, featuring a number of regional bands, and it's hoped that the concert will become an annual event. The Committee's website, kurtcobainmemorial.org, also sells T-shirts, mugs and other items with a picture of the "Come As You Are" sign. The Committee also has a MySpace page at myspace.com/kurtmemorial.

In addition to Cobain's grandfather, his mother and bandmate Krist Novoselic have expressed support for the Committee's efforts, which helps to offset the

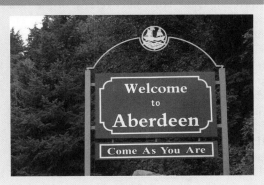

occasional complaints. "The experience of fighting for projects in the name of Kurt Cobain has been frustrating, humbling and rewarding," Burlingame admits. "I've been challenged by countless people who don't believe 'a junkie' should be honoured. I've received death threats from anonymous people via email." But he also adds that residents of Aberdeen, Hoquiam and other outlying areas have generally been "extremely supportive". "I know what we're doing is the right thing to do," he says. "I'm proud to have known Kurt Cobain. I'm proud to be from the same city he was from. And now I'm proud of what our committee is doing to honour him. We believe Kurt Cobain should be honoured in his home town of Aberdeen. We've begun to do that, and we're working hard to continue to do so. I think most have come to realize we're not honouring 'a junkie', but rather a brilliant artist who changed the course of music history. And that's something to be proud of."

a third had evaded even the wiliest bootlegger. The DVD also offered some unseen material, such as a rehearsal from 1988, as the band prepared to record *Bleach*; a song from Dan Peters' sole date with the band; and the recording of "Seasons In The Sun" in January 1993.

There had been a surge in media coverage at the tenth anniversary of Cobain's death in April 2004; the November release of the box set, entitled *With The Lights Out*, gave the media something more positive to focus on. First week sales in the US were 105,760 copies, a record for a box set and it performed better in the charts than most box sets, reaching the top twenty in the US. The following year, *Sliver: The Best Of The Box* was released, and included three songs that hadn't appeared in the box set, including the first official release of a song from the Fecal Matter demo ("Spank Thru"). The CD reached number 21 in the US, number 56 in the UK. No new Nirvana material has been released since, though *Live! Tonight! Sold Out!!* and *Unplugged* came out on DVD in 2006 and 2007, respectively.

"New licensing opportunities"

In April 2006, it was announced that Love was selling 25 percent of her stake of Nirvana's publishing to Primary Wave Music Publishing (founded by **Larry Mestel**, formerly CEO/General Manager of Virgin Records), in a deal estimated to be worth over $50 million. Love had inherited Cobain's share of Nirvana's publishing rights on his death; now she planned to explore new licensing opportunities for Nirvana's music via her partnership with Primary Wave. In a press statement, Love assured fans, "We are going to remain very tasteful and true to the spirit of Nirvana while taking the music to places it has never been before." Mestel later told *Forbes* magazine, "You will never see Kurt Cobain's music in a fast-food hamburger advertisement – that won't ever happen. We're looking at things that relate to cutting-edge technologies, products that are green and eco-friendly, products that Kurt would have liked to have his music represented by." The deal was responsible for making Cobain that year's top earning "dead celebrity".

Since the deal with Primary Wave, the first officially sanctioned remix of a Nirvana song, "Lounge Act" (remixed by DJ Z-Trip), has appeared in the videogame *skate*; other songs have been featured in the "virtual band" videogame *Rock Band*. With album sales now in steady decline, exposure through film, TV and other outlets is seen as an effective way to reach new listeners, particularly younger generations.

And there's certainly room for future Nirvana releases: a comprehensive set of all the radio sessions or non-album tracks, for example. Enough stray ends remain in the vaults to allow for expanded releases of Nirvana's three albums. The market for official live recordings has barely been scratched. Judging by the collection of Cobain's home demos seen on the cover of *Sliver*, there's the good possibility of a solo Cobain release as well. In the meantime, both Novoselic and Grohl have continued their own careers, working on a variety of projects, musical and otherwise.

Learning to fly:
the solo years

Learning to fly: the solo years

Cobain's death brought Nirvana to a sudden and unexpected halt. Neither Novoselic nor Grohl gave any extensive interviews to the media at the time, and both later said they wondered if they wanted to continue as musicians. But they soon realized the therapeutic value of playing music, and within a year each was playing in his own band, eager to carve out their own musical identity.

Foo Fighters lift off

In May 1994, Novoselic and Grohl returned to Robert Lang Studios to play on two tracks of **Mike Watt**'s *Ball-Hog or Tugboat?* album, which was released the following year. On 12 July they joined the **Stinky Puffs**, formed by Simon Timony, then the stepson of Jad Fair from the band Half Japanese, when they played the opening night of the Yo Yo a Go Go festival in **Olympia**, their first performance together since Cobain's death; the four-song set was released the next year on the Stinky Puffs' album *A Little Tiny Smelly Bit of…* Since then, the two men have performed together on other occasions, but have primarily pursued different musical paths.

Grohl soon found himself fielding offers to join other bands, and played drums with **Tom Petty and The Heartbreakers** when the band appeared on *Saturday Night Live* on 19 November 1994. He was asked to join the group on a permanent basis, but declined, wanting to helm his own project. By that time he had already laid down the groundwork for his next venture, having returned to Robert Lang Studios in October 1994 to work on the recordings that would ultimately comprise the first **Foo Fighters** record. Drawing on the stockpile of songs he'd written over the years, he recorded fifteen tracks, providing all the vocals and, aside from a guitar line on "X-Static" by Afghan Whigs' **Greg Dulli**, playing all the instruments himself. He also co-produced alongside **Barrett Jones**.

Grohl had intended the recordings to serve as a demo, but considered releasing them under an assumed name. Then two songs were transmitted on Pearl Jam's *Self-Pollution Radio* broadcast on 8 January 1995 (singer **Eddie Vedder** being among those who'd received a copy of the demo from Grohl), and word began to leak out. Major labels became interested, and Grohl ultimately signed with Capitol, where Nirvana's A&R rep, Gary Gersh, was then president. As part of the deal, Grohl set up his own label, Roswell Records, named for the alleged alien crash site in New Mexico.

Grohl had no desire to be a solo artist and so his next move was to form a band. He approached Novoselic, but neither wanted their next project to be compared to Nirvana. Nirvana's touring guitarist, Pat Smear, expressed an interest in joining, and Grohl also recruited **Nate Mendel** and **William Goldsmith**, who'd most recently been playing in Seattle band Sunny Day Real Estate, to play bass and drums, respectively; Grohl would front the group on guitar. He carried the extraterrestrial theme of his record label over into the name of his band, calling it Foo Fighters, a term used by Allied pilots in World War II for aerial phenomena of unknown origin – UFOs.

Foo Fighters' first show is said to have been at a private party in Seattle on 30 November 1994, which was in keeping with Grohl's desire to start the group off on a small scale. Beginning in March 1995, the band played shows at small clubs around the US (including many of the same venues Nirvana had once played), then signed on as a support act with Mike Watt's tour, Grohl also playing drums in Watt's group after Foo Fighters had finished their set. On 22 July, Foo Fighters shared the bill with Novoselic's new group, **Sweet 75**, at a fundraiser for Novoselic's political action committee, JAMPAC, at the Kitsap County Fairgrounds in Bremerton, Washington, and on 26 August Grohl returned to the Reading Festival, where his insistence on playing a secondary stage led to overflow crowds.

The band's self-titled debut album – simply a remixed version of Grohl's original demo – had been released the previous month. Its

Foos 1996 line-up: Pat Smear, William Goldsmith, Nate Mendel and Dave Grohl.

cover, shot by Grohl's wife, continued the sci-fi theme, showing an XZ-38 Disintegrator Pistol, as used in the Buck Rogers serials, against a greenish background (bizarrely, some people thought the depiction of a gun was meant as a reference to Cobain's suicide). The public proved receptive to Grohl's engaging pop/punk, with the album reaching number 23 in the US and number 3 in the UK. The singles also performed well (though in the US, they were generally only released to radio, meaning they appeared only in charts determined by airplay, like Modern Rock). The video for "Big Me" won an MTV Award for Best Group Video. A parody of commercials for Mentos candy, renamed "Footos" in the video, it was an early indication of the fun the band would have with the format (it also led to the group being pelted with Mentos when they played). The album was also nominated for Best Alternative Rock Album, though Grohl ended up losing to himself – the award was given to Nirvana's *Unplugged*.

Foo Fighters continued their relentless touring through July 1996, though they did squeeze in a date at Robert Lang's to record a cover of Gary Numan's "Down In The Park" for *The X-Files* TV show soundtrack, *Songs in the Key of X* (Grohl and his wife also made a cameo appearance in an episode). Following the tour, Grohl took up an offer to score a film, Paul Schrader's *Touch*. **Louise Post** of Veruca Salt also contributed to the soundtrack, co-writing the "Touch" theme with Grohl and duetting with him on "Saints In Love"; the two soon became romantically involved, marking the end of Grohl's marriage.

Line-up changes

A split was on the horizon in Foo Fighters as well. In November the band began working on their second album, initially at **Bear Creek Studios** in Woodinville, outside Seattle. The sessions broke for Christmas (though Grohl managed to fit in a reunion show with Scream on 28 December), during which time producer **Gil Norton** (then best known for his work with the Pixies) told Grohl he felt the drums could be improved. Grohl agreed, and redid most of them himself (Goldsmith's work remains on "Doll" and "Up In Arms"). When Goldsmith heard what had happened, he quit. Work on the album was completed at Grand Master

Records in LA, which is where Grohl had relocated following the split from his wife.

The album was released in May 1997 as *The Colour And The Shape* and, like the band's debut album, peaked at number three in the UK and number ten in the US (though the singles all did better in the US than the UK). With another heavy slate of touring scheduled, the band enlisted **Taylor Hawkins**, who'd previously been in Alanis Morrissette's touring band, as their new drummer. He immediately fit right in, gamely jumping into drag in the "Everlong" video. But the line-up was again in flux as Pat Smear announced he was leaving, having grown tired of touring, when they played the MTV Video Music Awards on 4 September. Grohl then brought in **Franz Stahl**, his fellow bandmate in Scream, and the band remained on the road right through to August 1998, playing North America, the UK, Europe, Japan, Australia and New Zealand. Notable dates included opening for the **Rolling Stones** in October 1997, and **Ozzfest** in June 1998.

After a break, the band began work on their next album, and it soon became apparent that Stahl's musical sensibilities didn't mesh with the rest of the group. Grohl sadly let him go ("He was one of my oldest friends and we wanted it to work out so badly, but it didn't"), and decided to work on the album as a trio with Mendel and Hawkins. Grohl had by now tired of the superficiality of LA, and moved back to **Virginia** (living a mile from his old high school), building a studio in his basement (dubbed **Studio 606**), where the new album would be recorded. The band was also momentarily without a label:

The Story

Gary Gersh had left Capitol, and a clause in their contract allowed them to leave the label if Nirvana's old A&R man did.

Instead of immediately signing with another label, the band opted to concentrate on recording their album. This sense of newfound freedom was reflected in the album's title, *There Is Nothing Left To Lose*, recorded between March and June, with **Adam Kasper** co-producing with the band. Released in November 1999 on the band's new label, RCA, the album brought the group another top ten success in the US and UK, with the first single, the ebullient "Learn To Fly", becoming the first Foos track to top the US Modern Rock chart. Another single, "Next Year", was later used as the theme song for the US TV series *Ed*.

Even before the album was released, the band was back on the road, beginning with a 3 November date at the Troubadour in Hollywood, debuting their new guitarist, **Chris Shiflett**, who'd most recently played with No Use For A Name. Typically, the band spent much of the following year on the road. On 21 February 2001, Grohl accepted his first post-Nirvana Grammy, when *There Is Nothing Left To Lose* won Best Rock Album (the "Learn to Fly" video, which had the band playing a variety of characters – male and female – on a commercial airliner, also won an award for Best Short Form Music Video). Another high point came on 19 March, when Grohl and Hawkins proudly inducted one of their favourite acts, **Queen**, into the Rock and Roll Hall of Fame, and joined **Brian May** and **Roger Taylor** onstage in performing "Tie Your Mother Down".

A few months later, it seemed that history was going to repeat itself. Foos had just started playing the festival circuit overseas, when on 20 August Hawkins overdosed on painkillers and fell into a coma. Hawkins had been over-indulging in drugs and alcohol for some time, to the point where he hadn't even played drums on every track of *There Is Nothing Left To Lose*. Now matters were far more serious. Grohl was naturally distraught, having been through a similar situation with Nirvana. Thankfully, Hawkins pulled through, and, heeding the wake-up call, entered rehab.

Time out for Queens

However, coming back together wouldn't be so easy for the band. They recorded several songs for the next album, but Grohl felt they didn't have the necessary "spark", and the material was scrapped. After playing two shows in support of the Winter Olympics in **Salt Lake City** in February 2002, Foos then went on hiatus, with each member pursuing various side projects. Grohl took up with hard rockers **Queens of the Stone Age**, drumming on their 2002 *Songs for the Deaf* album. When it was announced he was planning on touring with the band that summer, his fellow Foos worried that their group was on the verge of breaking up.

But his stint with Queens of the Stone Age (which Grohl described as "liberating") had made Grohl realize how much he liked playing in Foo Fighters as well, and work on the band's fourth album recommenced in May. The record was put together in piecemeal fashion, with Grohl and Hawkins working together, and Shiflett and Mendel adding their parts later when Grohl went on the road with QotSA. It was, Shiflet admitted, "a weird, broken-up way of making a record". Brian May also made a guest appearance on "Tired of You" (he'd guested with the band when they recorded a cover of Pink Floyd's "Have A Cigar" on the *Mission: Impossible 2* soundtrack). The album was co-produced by the band, Adam Kasper and Nick Raskulinecz.

One By One, released in October 2002, was a big success, debuting at number one in the UK (before it was knocked off by the *Nirvana* compilation), reaching number three in the US, and going on to win the Grammy for Best Rock Album; its first single, "All My Life", won the Grammy for Best Hard Rock Song. Ironically, in spite of its acclaim, Grohl confessed to never liking the album much, later telling *Rolling Stone*, "Four of the songs were good, and the other seven I never played again in my life."

Foo Fighters accepting one of their numerous Grammy awards, in 2004.

Back to LA

Grohl eventually moved back to LA, and on 2 August 2003, married **Jordyn Blum**, a former MTV producer; ever the workaholic, he was working on songs with Hawkins on the morning of his wedding. The couple had a daughter, Violet Maye, in 2006. Studio 606 was relocated to LA as well, along with Grohl's mother and sister, for whom he bought homes in the neighbourhood, though the band wouldn't release a new album until 2005. The rest of 2003 was spent on the road (and saw the release of the first live Foos DVD, *Everywhere But Home*); in contrast, 2004 saw them play just fifteen times, the fewest since the group began. Most of the dates came in the fall, when Grohl appeared at numerous rallies for Democratic presidential candidate **Senator John Kerry**, both on his own and with the band; at a 19 October rally in Las Vegas, he was joined onstage by Krist Novoselic, though they didn't play together. The Republican candidate, George W. Bush, was evidently unaware of Grohl's political leanings when he chose "Times Like These" from *One By One* to play at his rallies, an experience Grohl later memorably described as "like being raped in the ass".

Kerry's defeat was a disappointment, but the experience of campaigning for him inspired much of Foo Fighters' next album, *In Your Honor*: playing for audiences of veterans and blue-collar workers "all coming together for an honourable reason" made Grohl want to create an album that gave "a sense of hope and release and faith". It was the band's first double album, one disc being hard rock, the other a showcase for their so far unexplored acoustic side. The acoustic disc featured a re-recording of "Friend Of A Friend", which had appeared on a solo tape Grohl had released in 1992, and a song on which Hawkins sang lead, "Cold Day in the Sun". Several guests also made an appearance on the acoustic disc, including **John Paul Jones**, **Josh Homme** and **Norah Jones**.

The album was released in June 2005, with a special release party held at the Walker Air Force base in **Roswell**, New Mexico. It just missed the top spot in the US and UK charts, peaking at number two in both countries (though it did top the charts in Sweden, Finland, Australia and New Zealand), though "Best Of You" and "DOA" gave the band two more number ones in the Modern Rock charts. The album also received five Grammy nominations, but, for a change, there were no wins.

Following the usual pattern, the album's release was followed by continual touring that was extensive even by Foos' standards; for the next three years, there were only six months when the band didn't play a show. Some of the band's biggest and most notable performances during this period were in the UK, including a concert in London's **Hyde Park** in June 2006 that drew 85,000 people, and a much acclaimed appearance at the **Live Earth** concert at Wembley Stadium on 7 July 2007.

During the fall of 2006, they took the quieter side they'd unveiled on *In Your Honor* to the stage, playing a short series of acoustic shows in North America. Grohl, more used to running around an arena stage "screaming my balls off", confessed to being nervous about the gigs. "I

didn't know if it was going to be any good or not," he told *Metal Hammer*. "But we started the first show with 'Razor' and at the end of the song, the audience stood up and gave us a standing ovation and I was like 'Holy shit! This is cool!'" Three shows on the tour were recorded and released as the live album *Skin And Bones* in November 2006 (followed by a DVD of the entire show the same month). Pat Smear also returned to the Foos line-up for these shows, and would play on the group's next album.

In between touring, the band recorded their sixth album, *Echoes, Silence, Patience & Grace* with Gil Norton co-producing, which was released in September 2007. The album topped the charts in the UK, Canada, Australia and New Zealand but yet again failed to do so in the US, peaking at number three (though "The Pretender" topped the Modern Rock and Mainstream Rock charts). Among the songs was "Ballad of the Beaconsfield Miners", an instrumental tribute to two men who had been trapped when a mine in Beaconsfield, Australia, had collapsed in 2005; in order to keep their spirits up while rescuers were digging a hole, the miners had asked for an iPod with Foo Fighters tunes to be sent down to them. The album went on to win a Grammy for Best Rock Album, "The Pretender" winning Best Hard Rock Performance.

For Grohl, a longtime Led Zeppelin admirer, the highlight of Foo Fighters' 2008 shows undoubtedly came when **Jimmy Page** and John Paul Jones came onstage during the second of the band's two sold-out shows at Wembley Stadium in June, to perform "Rock 'n' Roll" and

The Story

The Story

"Ramble On". "Where do you go after playing two nights at Wembley?" Grohl wondered aloud in an interview, before providing the answer: "I guess you go and make another record and you keep playing shows, same as always." But there are indications that Foo Fighters may slow down the pace in the future. All members of the group are now fathers, and Grohl has said in numerous interviews he plans to cut back on touring in order to spend more time with his family. It's doubtful that he'll cut back on work, however, for in addition to Foo Fighters, he's also been involved with innumerable side projects over the years. Grohl's usually sunny disposition has seen him labelled "the nicest man in rock"; he may argue that one, but he can't dispute the fact that his post-Nirvana career has him in the running for being "the hardest-working man in rock".

Sweet 75

Krist Novoselic's post-Nirvana career has been a mix of music and political activities. His first post-Nirvana band got its start at his 29th birthday party in May 1994. As part of the entertainment, his wife hired a Venezuelan street singer, **Yva Las Vegas**, to perform. She and Novoselic hit it off, and he suggested producing an album for her. But the two musicians ended up playing together as they worked on the project, and after writing a song, "Oral Health", decided to form a band instead. Las Vegas handled vocals, and swapped guitar and bass duties with Novoselic on different songs. The two enlisted a drummer, **Bobby Lurie**, and called themselves Sweet 75 (a line from a poem by Theodore Roethke, referring to a payment he'd received). The band played their first show in March 1995 in Seattle.

Sweet 75 played sporadic dates over the next few years, and recorded demos with Jack Endino, but they didn't release an album until 1997; by then, Lurie had been replaced by **Bill Rieflin**, formerly with Ministry and an early Seattle art-punk band, The Blackouts. The self-titled album was produced by **Paul Fox** (who'd worked with XTC and the Sugarcubes) and

Foo Fighters playing a secret acoustic set at the V Festival in the UK, 2007.

The Story

also featured guest appearances by **Peter Buck** and **Herb Alpert**. "We're just gonna go out there and dive into the commercial world and see how bad it burns us," Novoselic said at the time, and unfortunately he found out all too soon. The album received a decidedly cool reception, and the subsequent drummer changes (Rieflin left after the album's release, replaced by **Adam Wade**, who was then replaced by **Gina Mainwal**) made it hard for the band to build momentum. Sweet 75 sputtered on, but finally came to a halt in 2000.

During this time, Novoselic had also been flexing his political muscles. In 1995 he founded a now-disbanded political action committee, JAMPAC (Joint Artists and Music Promotions Political Action Committee); among other causes, the group worked to overturn regulations that restricted the staging of all-ages shows in Seattle, and fought against so-called "Erotic Music" legislation (laws that would have banned the sale of albums deemed "unsuitable for minors") in the state of Washington. It was not uncommon to see Novoselic speaking before the Seattle City Council, at events like Hempfest (which advocated the legalization of marijuana), and, increasingly, at meetings promoting his interest in electoral reform. He also made appearances as part of the Spitfire tour (a "package tour" of musicians, actors and activists debating current issues), and executive produced AMPT Radio, a syndicated political radio show.

His music and political interests merged in The **No WTO Combo**, a group that was formed to perform at the World Trade Organization conference in Seattle in December

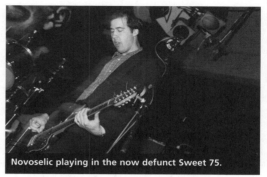

Novoselic playing in the now defunct Sweet 75.

1999. The group also included Gina Mainwal on drums, Soundgarden's **Kim Thayil** on guitar and Dead Kennedys lead singer **Jello Biafra**. Their performance was originally scheduled for 30 November, but was delayed till the next night due to the rioting that had broken out in the city during the conference. The show was also taped, and released on Biafra's Alternative Tentacles label the following year as *Live From The Battle In Seattle*.

Novoselic pursued other musical avenues as well, such as the ambient art-rock band **Sunshine Cake** (which he called a "hobby band"), which also included Bill Rieflin, **Roderick Romero** from Sky Cries Mary and jazz musician **Jeff Grienke**. He also made occasional one-off appearances, often little noticed in the media: in August 1994 he played in a makeshift group at the Garlic Festival in Arlington, Washington, along with Earnie Bailey (and, as a surprise guest, Eddie Vedder, who came onstage to sing "I Am The Walrus"); joined Foo Fighters on stage when the band played Seattle in August 1997 and December 1999; and played benefits

The Story

with the likes of K Records' co-founder **Calvin Johnson**, and former Jimi Hendrix drummer **Buddy Miles**.

Eyes Adrift

In 2001, Novoselic finally founded a new band. A Seattle show by the Meat Puppets' **Curt Kirkwood**, then working as a solo artist, had provided inspiration. After the show, Novoselic and Kirkwood got talking and decided to join forces. Kirkwood also roped in **Bud Gaugh** (from Sublime) and the three musicians decamped to Austin. The following year, the group, called **Eyes Adrift**, released a self-titled album. But though the album fit neatly into the alt-country genre, reception was again mixed, and the group disbanded in 2003. Novoselic issued a statement about the band's demise on their website in July, which also noted his intention to quit the music industry, though he stressed, "I haven't quit music, I've just quit the business."

Novoselic had long toyed with the idea of running for office, and after Eyes Adrift broke up, he considered running for Lieutenant

Governor of Washington state in 2004. But he opted instead to write a book about politics, *Of Grunge And Government: Let's Fix This Broken Democracy!*, published September 2004 by RDV Books/Akashic Books. Novoselic also remarried the same year (having divorced his first wife in 2000), marrying textile artist **Darbury Stenderu**.

In 2006, Novoselic became more actively involved in music once again, joining a reformed Flipper on bass, playing with the band until September 2008 (see pp.18–19).

Nirvana's future

Cobain's death would seem to preclude the possibility of any kind of a Nirvana reunion (though a bizarre rumour circulated online claiming Nirvana would reform at Sub Pop's July 2008 twentieth anniversary shows, with Courtney Love replacing Cobain on vocals). Both Novoselic and Grohl have been outspoken in their opposition to creating a "new" recording by adding music to a Cobain demo à la The Beatles' "Free As A Bird").

Nirvana remains an important chapter in both men's lives, but they've also moved on. They've also always expressed interest in taking on new challenges: Grohl has said he'd like to score another film, Novoselic hasn't ruled out running for public office. And though there may be no future Nirvana shows or new recordings, the impact of the band's legacy ensures that their records will never go out of print. And there's certainly plenty of officially unreleased Nirvana material in the archives that fans can hope will eventually see the light of day.

EYES ADRIFT

Krist Novoselic (Nirvana)
Curt Kirkwood (Meat Puppets)
Bud Gaugh (Sublime)

Live Performance and Signing
Easy Street

5 PM on October 31st

Come celebrate the release of
their debut album!

See them at Graceland the same night!

Part Two:
The Music

The recordings

The Music

This section covers all of Nirvana's officially released music, beginning with studio, live and compilation albums, followed by their singles and EPs, and guest appearances on compilations.

Studio albums

BLEACH

US Sub Pop June 1989; UK Tupelo August 1989.

BLEW / FLOYD THE BARBER / ABOUT A GIRL / SCHOOL / PAPER CUTS / NEGATIVE CREEP / SCOFF / SWAP MEET / MR. MOUSTACHE / SIFTING / LOVE BUZZ / BIG CHEESE / DOWNER

Recorded 23 January, 11 & 30 June, 16 July, 24 & 29–31 December 1988 and 14 & 24 January 1989. The last three tracks all appear on the CD; the original US vinyl version included "Love Buzz", while the UK vinyl included "Big Cheese", and "Downer" only appeared on the CD. In the US, the first 1000 copies were on white vinyl, and some of the first 3000 copies had a limited edition poster. In the UK, the first 300 copies were on white vinyl, and the next 2000 on green; in Australia, the album was released on Waterfront, on different colours of vinyl.

Featuring a reverse-negative image of Cobain mid-headbang along with what would become the band logo, the *Bleach* cover was striking if somewhat one-dimensional (see p.35).

Bleach begins with the passive request "If you wouldn't mind…", while musically hitting the same hypnotic drone of "Love Buzz". But the band's aggressiveness comes bounding in by the time they reach the first chorus, and, by and large, doesn't let up throughout the rest of the album. Cobain himself later called *Bleach* "one-dimensional", and certainly the album does have its share – some would say more than its share – of dirgy sludge. But it's a far more complex and revealing album than you might realize on first listen.

Thematically, the album is laced with claustrophobia and a lacerating misanthropy and self-hatred, leavened by a welcome sarcasm (which always helped keep the band's music from lapsing into despair). The opening track, "Blew", sets the mood, with the singer trapped in a stifling relationship (an overriding theme of the album), alternately moaning and whining about his predicament. The dark mood continues on "Floyd The Barber", which casts the characters of the anodyne American sitcom *The Andy Griffith Show* as merry murderers.

Lyrically "About A Girl" is as acerbic as the other songs on the album, though belied by the sweet, tuneful melody critics invariably described as "Beatlesque". Sandwiched in between "Floyd" and "School", the song stood as a testament to the band's diversity, not to mention the underlying pop sensibility that would eventually help them cross over into the mainstream. "School", though inspired by the frustration of being an outsider, is a wonderfully engaging rant that quickly became a live favourite. "Paper Cuts" is as thuddingly oppressive as "School" is buoyant, said to have been based on the real-life story of a local family who kept their children locked in a room. Its slow grind is enhanced by the fact that it's the Melvins' Dale Crover on drums: along with "Floyd" and "Downer", the track was taken from the band's demo recorded with Crover on 23 January 1988 (the so-called "Dale Demo"). The song also has Cobain singing the group's name as "Nir-van-uh" instead of "Nir-vah-nuh".

Cobain takes shots at himself in both "Negative Creep" and "Scoff", though while he rails at how others perceive his inadequacies in the latter, he gleefully embraces them in the former, ably supported by a bed of crunchy riffage. "Negative Creep" also has a fadeout ending, a rarity in a Nirvana song. Cobain's gaze then turns outward again for two more small-town portraits in "Swap Meet" and "Mr. Moustache". "Swap Meet" depicts an unhappy couple who hawk their arts and crafts at the weekly sales events Cobain describes as a "battleground", stymied by both their impoverished surroundings and their inability to emotionally connect with each other (which some have read as a description of Cobain's own feelings about his relationship with his then girlfriend). "Mr. Moustache" takes a swipe at macho he-men, but in his (albeit sarcastic) request to gain insight from a "new vision" and "mighty wisdom", there are hints that Mr. Moustache may not be as closed-minded as he seems. It's possible that Mr. Moustache may

reflect Cobain himself to a degree; at the time he wrote the song he was living in Olympia, home to the progressive Evergreen State College, where more than a few students knew how to, as Mr. Moustache puts it, "question question". If "Mr. Moustache" represented a culture Cobain wanted to get away from, he recognized it had nonetheless left its mark on him, and in later interviews he'd express a defiant sense of pride in his working-class roots. The song's musical arrangement was a bit more complicated than other tracks on the album, with its pile-driving rhythm gradually slowing down after the last chorus (and another raging scream from Cobain) before finally coming to a halt.

"Sifting" is the album's longest track, running almost five and a half minutes. If nothing else, it showed that Nirvana could churn out a thick slab of hard rock as well as any band in Seattle – when Cobain later told MTV the *Bleach* songs were "slow and grungy and they are tuned down to really low notes and I screamed a lot", this is the kind of song he was referring to. The original US vinyl album also included the A-side of the band's first single, "Love Buzz". The song builds into its pop groove nicely, starting off with a bass line, followed in short order by the drums and finally guitar, another indication of Nirvana's love of a strong hook. On the UK album, the heavier "Big Cheese" was substituted for "Love Buzz", striking a more menacing note, and more of a vocal workout for Cobain as well. On the CD, *Bleach* ends with the furious blast of "Downer", a song first performed on Cobain's Fecal Matter tape. The Fecal Matter version is noticeably slower, but the song's arrangement is largely the same, as are the stream-of-consciousness lyrics. Cobain later dismissed the song as an attempt at being "Mr. Political Punk Rock Black Flag Guy... I was just throwing together words." He said the same of many of *Bleach*'s lyrics as well, although he was also writing more concisely by then: there are more words in one verse of "Downer" than in all of "School".

Overall, *Bleach* shows a band in the first stages of finding their own voice, revealing their influences while staking out their own turf. There are hints of the band's future direction, but at the time of its release no one could have guessed that Nirvana would produce something as commercially palatable as *Nevermind*. Still, it's worth noting that "Blew", "About A Girl" and "School" were deemed strong enough by the band that they remained in their live set right up to the very last show, long after the likes of "Mr. Moustache", "Sifting" and "Paper Cuts" had fallen by the wayside.

NEVERMIND

UK Geffen 23 September 1991; US DGC 24 September 1991.

SMELLS LIKE TEEN SPIRIT / IN BLOOM / COME AS YOU ARE / BREED / LITHIUM / POLLY / TERRITORIAL PISSINGS / DRAIN YOU / LOUNGE ACT / STAY AWAY / ON A PLAIN / SOMETHING IN THE WAY / ENDLESS, NAMELESS

Recorded May–June 1991. Due to a production error, "Endless, Nameless" is missing from initial copies of the CD. The album was also released on green vinyl in the Czech Republic.

There are few records that can rightly be hailed as landmark albums; *Nevermind* is one of them.

Cobain might have jokingly described the band's music as "the Bay City Rollers being molested by Black Flag and Black Sabbath", but it was a more concise description of Nirvana's sound, and the underlying reason for their broad appeal, than any critic ever

Nevermind has one of the twentieth century's most recognizable album covers (see p.65).

came up with. At last Cobain had hit upon the magic formula that mixed pop, punk and metal in just the right amounts to attract fans of all those genres – and more. And for all the perceptions of Nirvana's music being sad and depressing, on *Nevermind* the anger and energy are directed outwards, in contrast to the suffocating, implosive self-loathing of *In Utero* (and, to a lesser degree, *Bleach*).

Nirvana set the bar high by opening with what would quickly become the album's most noteworthy track, "Smells Like Teen Spirit". The main riff, played six times during the song's intro, is so catchy that by the time the verse begins, it's firmly lodged in your head, which makes its reappearance in the chorus that much more of a delight. And for all the ennui expressed in the lyrics, the music is irresistibly invigorating; one can see why, when Cobain brought the song's riff to rehearsal, the band readily jammed on it for over half an hour.

One of *Nevermind*'s greatest strengths is its running order. It took some nerve to kick off the album with one of its strongest tracks; most albums wait a bit to spring something so powerful on the listener. But Nirvana felt no such qualms, confident that each track could hold its own. After "Teen Spirit", the album launches into the appealing strut of "In Bloom", a song that cleverly both lampoons and embraces the band's audience at the same time. Its energy is tempered by the cool wash of "Come As You Are", with Cobain poetically expressing his vulnerability by noting he doesn't have a gun. An opening guitar hum then ushers in the hammering rhythms of "Breed". Lyrically, the song harks back to the minimalism of *Bleach*, with its sole verse repeated twice and the chorus three times. Nor would its musical frenzy have been out of place on *Bleach*, though it's also clear why Nirvana's music was best served by a hard-hitting drummer like Grohl. Butch Vig added some fun during the instrumental break by panning the guitar solo from the right to left channels.

Ever mindful of their pacing, the band then scales back to the loping beat of "Lithium", a song whose sing-along melody typically masks the disturbing quality of the lyric, which touches on the solace one can find in religion or madness. The final guitar note fades into the beginning of "Polly", a harrowing look into the mind of a rapist, made all the more disturbing by Cobain's detached singing, as if he's merely an observer at the horrific scene.

As the last song on the first side of the vinyl album, "Polly" provides a disquieting conclusion. But on the CD, the listener is thrust right back into the thrashing of "Territorial

Pissings", which opens with Novoselic's strangled delivery of the chorus of the Youngbloods' "Get Together", before giving way to Cobain's furious guitar riffing and Grohl's propulsive drums. It's an all-out, no-holds-barred punk attack, its raw sound achieved by plugging Cobain's distortion pedal directly into the mixing board (a cleaner-sounding version was also recorded, but isn't nearly as effective). Cobain strives to match the music vocally, with the result that his voice sounds like it's literally tearing itself to shreds. The song's abrupt ending leads into the bright pop of "Drain You", which draws on a similar chord structure to "Teen Spirit". Like the other songs on *Nevermind* that deal with relationships (barring "Come As You Are"), there's a veiled threat in its offer of intimacy, made explicit by the song's title. Cobain's mighty scream at the end of the song's instrumental break could be seen either as a welcome release or a cry of frustration.

Some critics have cited *Nevermind*'s second half as being weaker than its stunning beginning. But all the songs interlock together so well, changing even one would alter the character of the album. "Lounge Act" has been nominated as one of the lesser songs, and indeed the band played it live infrequently. But on *Nevermind*, it serves as a kind of flip side to "Drain You", about escaping a relationship that's become too stifling. Cobain heightens the sense of anxiety by going up an octave after the instrumental break, screaming out the rest of the song with increasing desperation. Instead of letting the final note fade away, an unusual ending was devised during the mixing process: gradually slowing the tape down so it sounds like the note is being stretched.

"Stay Away" had evolved from the song "Pay To Play", originally recorded with Vig in April 1990. But both the musical performance and the lyrics are harder and sharper in this version, due to the power of Grohl's drumming and Cobain's vastly improved singing. Although Cobain's lyrics often lend themselves to varying interpretations, the essence of a song is frequently summed up in its title – as it is here. The other lyrics may rail against conformity, but it's Cobain's burning desire to be left alone that takes precedence, with "Stay away!" being hurled out repeatedly through the song. Cobain further tweaks mainstream sensibilities during the fadeout by howling "God is gay!" before the song sputters to a stop.

The shimmering power pop of "On A Plain" lightens the mood again, with its instantly hummable melody. Lyrically, the song is an intriguing mix of throwaway lines and the occasional scrap of insight, due in part to the fact that Cobain was writing lyrics practically up to the moment of recording his vocal. Along with hints of discord at home, and frequent references to the difficulties of writing a song, the most revealing couplet is Cobain's frank admission of self-centredness. For all that, the song ends on a surprisingly optimistic note – which couldn't stand in greater contrast to the final song, the sombre and disconsolate "Something In The Way". This song underscores the fact that Nirvana not only realized that emotions didn't always have to be expressed at the highest volume, they were also capable of

pulling it off, with Cobain turning in one of his most expressive vocal performances.

The album had one further surprise to spring on the listener – at least those who didn't immediately take the CD out of the player. For after ten minutes of silence comes a six-and-a-half-minute noise fest, uncredited on the album sleeve, called "Endless, Nameless". It was a final piece of catharsis, culminating with Cobain smashing his guitar – as their stage shows often ended. The number not only helped lighten the mood after the downbeat "Something In The Way", it was a further demonstration of the band's versatility. From acoustic ballads to power pop, raw punk, speed metal and pure unadulterated noise, *Nevermind* encompasses a breadth of styles that made the "alternative rock" label far too limiting. Those limitations would soon come to chafe at Cobain. But the passage of time hasn't diminished *Nevermind*'s status as a rock classic, a rich, multifaceted work that's just as compelling and engaging as the day it was released.

IN UTERO

UK Geffen 13 September 1993; US DGC 21 September, 1993.

SERVE THE SERVANTS / SCENTLESS APPRENTICE / HEART-SHAPED BOX / RAPE ME / FRANCES FARMER WILL HAVE HER REVENGE ON SEATTLE / DUMB / VERY APE / MILK IT / PENNYROYAL TEA / RADIO FRIENDLY UNIT SHIFTER / TOURETTE'S / ALL APOLOGIES

Recorded 13–26 February 1993. CDs sold in Wal-Mart and Kmart stores had altered artwork on the back cover, and the title of "Rape Me" was changed to "Waif Me". The album was also issued on clear vinyl in the US.

Nirvana's third studio album is typically described as a combination of *Bleach* and

Frances Farmer

Farmer was born in Seattle in 1913 and attracted controversy even as a teenager, when her essay, "God Dies", won a writing contest in *Scholastic Magazine* in 1931, and then when she won a trip to the Soviet Union in 1935 through a Communist newspaper, *The Voice of Action*. Farmer studied drama at the University of Washington, and, following the Russian trip, secured a contract with Paramount Studios. She was soon receiving good notices for her work in such films as *Rhythm On The Range* (co-starring fellow Washington native Bing Crosby) and *Come And Get It*.

But Farmer's independent nature frequently put her at odds with the studio system, as they wanted to maintain control over every aspect of their stars' lives, and in 1942, Paramount dropped her. On 19 October 1942 she was arrested in Los Angeles for a traffic violation, resulting in a chain of events that led to her being hospitalized and diagnosed as a paranoid schizophrenic. By the end of 1943 she was back in Seattle under her mother's care, but was later committed twice to Western State Hospital.

Farmer's treatment at Western is the subject of much dispute. In *Shadowland*, a 1978 biography of Farmer, author William Arnold (a film critic at the *Seattle Post-Intelligencer*) speculates that she was given a lobotomy during her second stay; other sources contest this. In any case, after her release in 1950, her acting career never regained its previous heights. Farmer made only one further film appearance, in the 1958 B-movie *The Party Crashers*. She also appeared in television dramas, summer stock and college productions, then took a job offer in Indianapolis, Indiana, to host an afternoon TV movie showcase, *Frances Farmer Presents*. She died in Indianapolis in 1970 of cancer of the oesophagus.

Cobain was moved by Farmer's story, and even wrote to Arnold after reading his book while still in Aberdeen. "There was something about that book that made however many people who read it want to get a hold of me and talk to me," Arnold recalls. "And people came by the hundreds. I had people come from out of town and just appear at my doorstep, wanting to talk." Because he was inundated with so many requests, Arnold didn't answer Cobain's letter.

The *In Utero* cover is based on a postcard of a transparent woman owned by Cobain (see p.111).

Nevermind, which, while not an inaccurate assessment, is something of an oversimplification. For while it does draw on the rawness of *Bleach*, the songs are clearly those of a far more sophisticated songwriter. And though it contains the kind of pop-friendly melodies that would have fit nicely on *Nevermind*, it's a more complex work musically, utilizing dissonance and atonality as much as catchy hooks.

It's also been said that the band deliberately set out to record a more abrasive album in order to drive away the mainstream audience they'd acquired with *Nevermind*. In fact, *In Utero* is a more accurate representation of what the band sounded like in performance, as opposed to the pop sheen of *Nevermind*.

Cobain remained intrigued by Farmer's life, drawing parallels between her experiences and the persecution to which he felt that he, and later his wife, had been subjected once fame had arrived for Nirvana. "The story of Frances Farmer is so sad and it can happen to anybody," he told Michael Azerrad. "And it almost felt at a time that it was happening to us." In "Frances Farmer Will Have Her Revenge On Seattle", Cobain turns the victim into victor, envisioning the actress finally vanquishing her foes.

Cobain tried to contact Arnold again, leaving messages on his voice mail at work. Arnold, who hadn't been following the local music scene, had no idea who the persistent caller was, until the *Post-Intelligencer*'s Arts & Entertainment editor told him, explaining that Cobain had also contacted her, asking Arnold to call him. Arnold then received further voice mail messages from Cobain, which he recalls as "rambling", describing the impact Arnold's book had on him, and his speculation that he might be related to Judge John Frater, who had signed the first order to commit Frances. After returning from a trip, Arnold

had plans to contact Cobain; on the top of his to-do list for 8 April 1994 was the notation "Return the call of K.C. – the Nirvana guy!"

Instead, Arnold wound up writing an article entitled "Cobain Found a Kindred Spirit in Frances Farmer's Tragic Life" for the 14 April edition of the paper, saying of Cobain, "From his punkish-honesty-meant-to-shock to his outbursts of violence, Cobain's behaviour might be interpreted as the actions of a man determined to embody the spirit of Frances Farmer." Cobain's identification with Farmer also made Arnold think hard about how a writer's work can influence people in ways the writer can't foresee but that shouldn't be dismissed. "I felt like when you write something and it influences people, that gives you a certain kind of moral responsibility; you can't just ignore that," he says. He ended his article on a cautionary note for Cobain's fans: "It is a big mistake to judge your own life by the life of someone else, particularly a celebrity. Even the most appealing, soothing and seemingly positive of myths can be, if embraced too fervently, enormously destructive."

Cobain may have been trying to distance himself from *Nevermind*'s success by insisting that *In Utero* had the sound he'd been trying to capture on record all his life, but it was equally true that his music had a hard edge to it from the very beginning.

He likewise insisted that the songs on the album did not reflect his personal life, something belied by the very first song, "Serve The Servants", in which he deconstructs his own myth over a sturdy rock backing. After

shrugging off his newfound success, he refers to media harassment, his troubled relationship with his estranged father, and actually goes so far as to dismiss his parents' divorce – the key event of his childhood – as "such a bore". Many of these themes (childhood trauma and media harassment, particularly of his wife) would resurface throughout the album, as would disquieting references to Cobain's depressed mental state (as in this song's stark admission that he's "bored and old").

The first of *In Utero*'s songs to go to musical extremes was "Scentless Apprentice", an incendiary track that's startling in its vehemence; Cobain never sounded more frightening than he did in his frenzied screams of "Go away!" in this song. Its brutal assault is followed by the album's standout track, "Heart-Shaped Box", a wonderfully evocative example of Cobain's development as a songwriter. The song was a perfect fit for the soft/loud Nirvana formula, the striking imagery of the verses giving way to the sarcastic roar of the chorus.

"Rape Me" was originally going to be the album's lead-off track, but its opening was deemed to be too close to that of "Teen Spirit", so it was pushed back in the line-up. Lyrically, it fit in well with the album's pervasive sense of persecution, as did the following track, "Frances Farmer Will Have Her Revenge On Seattle". Cobain identified with the unconventional actress's struggles against the mainstream entertainment industry and the media, two of his own pet peeves, and accordingly the track seethes with a lurching anger that bursts to the surface and then subsides. But while Cobain paints Farmer as an avenging angel who rains down fire on those who have wronged her, he himself can only work up the energy to muse on the "comfort of being sad". Again, there's a thematic link to the next track, the otherwise tranquil "Dumb", which explores the same idea of sinking into passivity.

And there's yet another link to the next track, as if the songs are stepping stones leading the listener through the album, from being dumb to being "Very Ape". The high, wailing note that runs throughout the song like a siren gives it a new wave feel (hence its working title, "Perky New Wave"), while the swaggering lyrics recall the protagonist of "Mr. Moustache", who takes pride in his ignorance.

"Milk It" is another harsh, uncompromising number, with its mumbled verses and shrieking choruses pushing Cobain to his vocal limits. After Cobain's death, journalists were quick to point to the song's refrain that refers to suicide as the "bright side", though the song seems to focus more on the confining nature of dependency, devolving into a litany of medical terminology. The scent of illness permeates the subsequent track, "Pennyroyal Tea", further embodied by Cobain's listless vocal, the sound of someone who's beyond making any kind of effort.

Rousing itself out of its stupor, the album's next two tracks come charging in as if making one last attempt at escape. "Radio Friendly Unit Shifter" is built around a main riff that plays through the whole song. But instead of making it one-dimensional, it's almost exuberantly buoyant, and Nirvana would regularly use the song as the opening number on their final two tours. Such is the musical power of the song, most listeners probably overlooked (at least initially) the discontent that's lurking in the lyrics. "tourette's", the album's shortest song, is a more structured version of the jams the band played in rehearsal, with lyrics made all the more indecipherable by Cobain's screaming them out at the top of his lungs.

"All Apologies" provides a grand conclusion for the album, the lush haze of its music (particularly during the extended outro) typically at odds with the despondent lyric. Once again, the band added a track after a long gap: 24 minutes of silence before the stream-of-consciousness jam called "Gallons Of Rubbing Alcohol Flow Through The Strip" – though it wasn't much of a surprise, as the song's title is on the album cover. The track only appeared on overseas versions of the album, hence the accompanying sticker on the CD case, "Exclusive International Bonus Track".

There's an air of self-consciousness about *In Utero*, given that Cobain was fully aware the album would be scrutinized for any clues as to his mental state. But while some songs did indeed comment on his reactions to fame, family and fatherhood, Nirvana's music had constantly progressed and developed over the years, and it shouldn't have been any more of a surprise that *In Utero* was different to *Nevermind* than that *Nevermind* was different to *Bleach*. Opting to use Steve Albini as producer also gave the album a more visceral sound, and showed anyone who doubted it that Nirvana were far from a one-hit wonder. Instead, they remained eager to push themselves, striking out in a new, more challenging direction, instead of ploughing the same commercially successful field *Nevermind* had turned out to be. For all its personal turmoil, *In Utero* is also a complicated and complex piece of work. Which is why it remains Nirvana's most intriguing album, one that rewards repeated listenings.

Live albums

MTV UNPLUGGED IN NEW YORK

UK Geffen 31 October 1994; US DGC 1 November 1994.

ABOUT A GIRL / COME AS YOU ARE / JESUS DOESN'T WANT ME FOR A SUNBEAM / THE MAN WHO SOLD THE WORLD / PENNYROYAL TEA / DUMB / POLLY / ON A PLAIN / SOMETHING IN THE WAY / PLATEAU / OH ME / LAKE OF FIRE / ALL APOLOGIES / WHERE DID YOU SLEEP LAST NIGHT

Recorded 18 November 1993. In the US, the album was also issued on white vinyl.

Nirvana initially seemed an unlikely choice for the MTV series, given that much of the band's appeal was due to their glorious celebration of noise. Sceptics also wondered whether their music could adapt to a quieter setting. Not all the band's songs were abrasive rockers, though. The opening track, "About A Girl", was nearly "unplugged" in its original performance anyway, and was a good choice to start the set, a reminder that Nirvana didn't always feel the need to turn their amps up to 11. Stripped of their volume, it became more apparent just how melodic the songs actually were; Cobain proved to be just as evocative a singer, having little difficulty in connecting emotionally with the audience despite the uniqueness of the performance setting.

The cover of *MTV Unplugged in New York* reveals the intimacy of this astonishing live concert.

Leadbelly

It's hard to imagine what Leadbelly would have thought of Nirvana's performing style. But he would have been pleased that the band's performance of "Where Did You Sleep Last Night" helped introduce his music to another generation.

Leadbelly was born Huddie William Ledbetter in 1888 in Mooringsport, Louisiana. His parents worked as sharecroppers, but encouraged their son's budding musical talent. The first instrument he took up was the accordion, but he soon moved on to guitar, and in his teens began to perform at parties, juke joints and clubs, while continuing to work as a labourer.

As a young man, Leadbelly had frequent scrapes with the law. He escaped from his first stint in prison (for assault), but by 1918 was back inside, convicted of killing a man in a fight (which he always maintained was an accident). He was said to have received his nickname while in prison, in reference to his toughness. He secured an early release in 1925, in part by writing a song of appeal to Governor Pat Morris Neff. But his third stretch in prison, in Angola, Louisiana, in 1930, for attempted homicide, had unexpected consequences. For it was here in 1933 that he encountered John Lomax and his son Alan, musicologists on an expedition through the South, making recordings of traditional songs for the Library of Congress. The Lomaxes were impressed by Leadbelly, who by now had a wide range of folk and blues numbers in his repertoire, along with many original songs.

The following year, Leadbelly was released early from prison for good behaviour, and he quickly tracked down John Lomax, announcing his intention to work for him. Lomax hired him as his driver and assistant, while seeking to boost Leadbelly's performing career. Leadbelly was eventually able to tour and record for the rest of his life (apart from a brief interruption due to yet another prison sentence). He died in 1949 of amyotrophic lateral sclerosis, commonly known as Lou Gehrig's disease, a degenerative illness of the nervous system in which sufferers eventually lose control of their body movements (and for which there is still no cure). On the day Leadbelly could no longer hold his guitar, he cried.

Wisely, though to MTV's consternation, the band didn't perform any of their big hits. "Come As You Are" was as close as they came, another song well suited to the format, especially as it lacked the trademark soft/loud dynamic of "Teen Spirit" or "In Bloom" (though it's still intriguing to contemplate how those songs might have turned out had they been performed acoustically). The set included a high proportion of covers, six in total (out of fourteen songs), three of them Meat Puppets songs. It was later pointed out that a number of the songs mention death – a connection that was hard to miss during the repeated plays of *Unplugged* that ran on MTV after 8 April 1994, an experience

Unfortunately, Leadbelly never achieved much commercial success during his life. The year after his death, the folk group the Weavers took a song he had popularized, "Goodnight Irene", to number one in the charts, and the subsequent folk revival saw a number of his songs become standards. But many of the songs most associated with Leadbelly were those he didn't write. This was true of "Where Did You Sleep Last Night", variously known as "In the Pines" and "Black Girl". The song is believed to date back to the 1870s, originating in the Southern Appalachians, where it was passed down via oral tradition. The first printed version, credited to Cecil Sharp, was published in 1917, and consisted of just four lines. It was first recorded in 1925 by a private collector on a cylinder; the following year, the first commercial versions were released. There are well over 200 recorded versions of the song, with many lyrical variations, though the "in the pines" refrain is common to all, as is the song's accusatory theme. Leadbelly recorded at least six versions himself, the first released in February 1944.

Cobain first heard of Leadbelly through an article written by William Burroughs. His neighbour Slim Moon then lent him a copy of Leadbelly's *Last Sessions*, and he quickly became a fan; his early handwritten bios for Nirvana cited Leadbelly as an influence, and he frequently listed him as one of his favourite artists. In 1992 Cobain explained to journalist Everett True that he found Leadbelly's music "so raw and sincere. It's something I hold sacred. The songs are amazingly heartfelt... I'd hope that my songs approximate that honesty. That's what I strive for." Despite his praise for Leadbelly's work, Cobain didn't mention that he played the same guitar as Leadbelly's trademark instrument, a twelve-string Stella acoustic.

"Where Did You Sleep Last Night" was the only Leadbelly song Nirvana performed; they first played it in concert on 29 November 1989 in Geneva, Switzerland, and it remained in their set until 14 February 1994, when they performed it for the last time, at Le Zénith in Paris. But their most celebrated performance of the song undoubtedly the one that closed their *Unplugged* appearance. Cobain introduced the song by saying it was by "my favourite performer... our favourite performer, isn't it?", going on to relate an anecdote of how he'd been offered the chance to buy one of Leadbelly's guitars for $500,000 (a few months before, he'd told another interviewer the price was $55,000). The band's performance, highlighted by Cobain's keening vocal, brought the show to an electrifying close.

akin to watching Cobain perform at his own funeral.

There's a plaintiveness to Cobain's raw vocal delivery, especially on "Pennyroyal Tea", where he very nearly comes in on the wrong note after the second chorus (afterwards, he deflects Grohl's "That sounded good" with a playful "Shut up!"). In "Dumb", the line about being "just happy" had never sounded so despairing; "On A Plain" went from being an upbeat stream-of-consciousness bit of wordplay to a song steeped in regret and resignation; "Something In The Way" sounds as if Cobain can barely summon up the energy to get through the song. Only "Polly" makes less of an impression, as it sounds essentially the same as on *Nevermind*.

Nirvana were in their element performing live.

Most striking were the covers. The group had been performing "Jesus Doesn't Want Me For A Sunbeam" for years by this point, but this is undoubtedly the definitive version, with Novoselic's accordion adding a poignant touch. Equally resonant was the cover of David Bowie's "The Man Who Sold The World", performed here for the first time but added to the set list of subsequent shows. The Meat Puppets' covers aren't as stark as the originals, but on both "Plateau" and "Lake Of Fire" Cobain's at times fractured vocal sounds just as crazed as

Curt Kirkwood's did, while his version of "Oh Me" has an unexpected warmth.

Nirvana could easily have closed their set with "All Apologies", with its sense of finality in summing up Cobain's personal world view. But instead they went for broke, turning in an absolutely searing version of Leadbelly's "Where Did You Sleep Last Night". This was another song they'd been performing for a few years that still occasionally made their set lists. But Cobain never sounded as desperate as he did in this performance.

FROM THE MUDDY BANKS OF THE WISHKAH

UK Geffen 30 September 1996; US DGC 1 October 1996.

INTRO / SCHOOL / DRAIN YOU / ANEURYSM / SMELLS LIKE TEEN SPIRIT / BEEN A SON / LITHIUM / SLIVER / SPANK THRU / SCENTLESS APPRENTICE / HEART-SHAPED BOX / MILK IT / NEGATIVE CREEP / POLLY / BREED / TOURETTE'S / BLEW

Recorded various dates 1989–1994. There are a few errors in the track listing: the Astoria show is incorrectly listed as 5 December 1991, instead of 3 December, while the Seattle Center Arena show is incorrectly dated 5 January 1994, instead of 7 January.

If *Unplugged* showcased a more thoughtful, introspective side to the band, *Wishkah* endeavoured to capture the spirit of a typical Nirvana performance, drawing on shows that spanned the majority of the group's career.

The disc begins with Cobain's impassioned shrieks that kicked off the band's 3 December 1989 performance at London's Astoria, before segueing neatly into a bracing rendition of "School" from the Amsterdam Paradiso in 1991. Nine of the album's sixteen songs are from 1991 shows, mostly the Paradiso show, and a December performance at the Del Mar Fairgrounds in California that was also broadcast on radio, capturing the group in their first flush of fame. The songs from the Del Mar date ("Drain You", "Aneurysm" and a brisk "Teen

The cover design reflects the patchwork nature of the live album, taken from dates ranging from 1989 to 1994.

Spirit") are especially energetic, as Novoselic points out himself in the album's liner notes. The Paradiso songs ("School", "Been A Son", "Lithium" and "Blew") have a pleasing rawness, while "Negative Creep" is a fine performance from the Seattle Halloween 1991 show.

The band sound somewhat tired on the two songs from the Astoria show, "Polly" and "Breed", understandable given that the show was the last date of their first, gruelling European tour. "Breed", which was called "Immodium" at the time, also features different lyrics than would appear in the final version. The two tracks also feature Chad Channing on drums.

The performance of "Sliver", from a November 1993 date, is not one of the band's strongest. Nor is "Spank Thru", an unusual choice to begin with; taken from a November 1991 performance in Rome, it features a slurry, half-mumbled vocal from Cobain. And the only song taken from the band's landmark appearance at the Reading Festival in 1992 is "tourette's". But the *In Utero* songs – "Scentless Apprentice" and "Heart-Shaped Box" from 1993 shows, "Milk It" from a 1994 date – are uniformly strong, even more powerful live than they are on record.

Some fans were disappointed that the album didn't feature more rarities, as the shows the songs were drawn from had all been bootlegged. At less than an hour long, there certainly would have been room to include some more obvious contenders such as "In Bloom", "Rape Me" or "Radio Friendly Unit Shifter". But overall, the album is a good representation of Nirvana's live performance; indeed, they were still playing most of these songs in their final shows. The sound quality is also excellent throughout. And the band included a extra treat for those who bought the album on vinyl. Because the music itself only filled three sides of the double album set, the fourth side was made up entirely of stage chat.

Nirvana compilations

INCESTICIDE

UK Geffen 14 December 1992; US DGC 15 December 1992.

DIVE / SLIVER / STAIN / BEEN A SON / TURNAROUND / MOLLY'S LIPS / SON OF A GUN / (NEW WAVE) POLLY / BEESWAX / DOWNER / MEXICAN SEAFOOD / HAIRSPRAY QUEEN / AERO ZEPPELIN / BIG LONG NOW / ANEURYSM

Recorded various dates 1988–1991. Early copies of the CD featured Cobain's liner notes, credited to "Kurdt (the blond one)". In Europe, 15,000 copies were released on blue swirled vinyl.

A hardcore Nirvana fan would have had most – but not all – of the tracks on this album when it was released: "Downer" on the CD version of *Bleach*, "Mexican Seafood" on the *Teriyaki Asthma* compilation, "Beeswax" on the *Kill Rock Stars* compilation, "Stain" on the *Blew* EP, "Sliver" and "Dive" on the "Sliver" single, and "Turnaround", "Molly's Lips" and "Son of a Gun" on the *Hormoaning* EP.

But there were six tracks that were previously unreleased. "Hairspray Queen" and "Aero Zeppelin" were both from the Dale Demo. The new wave influence

of "Hairspray Queen" is evident in the looping bass and scratchy guitar work of the intro, while vocally Cobain is all over the map. During the verses, he's at his caterwauling best, adopting a more conventional rock delivery in the chorus, throwing in a mumbled spoken word passage, grunting and groaning his way to the song's conclusion; all in all, not too dissimilar to the material on his Fecal Matter tape.

"Aero Zeppelin" was an homage to/parody of the metal acts that ranked among the band members' earliest influences; even Cobain's guitar solo eschews squalling feedback for a more traditional approach. Lyrically, the song is a rather caustic attack on the mainstream music industry and its audience, who will consume anything if it's "packaged properly", illuminating the very contradiction that would eat away at Cobain as his music became increasingly popular.

"Big Long Now" is an out-take from the *Bleach* sessions. It was excluded because Cobain felt there were too many slow and heavy songs on the album, though it's perhaps stronger than other slow and heavy songs that did make the cut, such as "Sifting". The song's opening is an ominous guitar refrain followed by a haunting Cobain vocal that could almost be described as dreamy if it didn't sound so menacing. The chorus has him going up an octave as the band pounds out a four-note riff for added emphasis, an early sign of the anthemic qualities of Nirvana's best material. The song's ending is also atypical: the opening refrain is again repeated, gradually slowing to a halt.

The remaining unreleased songs are from a 1991 BBC radio session. "Aneurysm" isn't quite as powerful as the version on the "Teen Spirit" single, largely because it's taken at a faster pace (though the final scream is still impressive). "(New Wave) Polly" is given what Cobain called a "power pop" treatment (listen to Grohl's tight drum fills), presumably for fun, as the group had already recorded the song in a slower, more effective fashion on *Nevermind*. But the boost in tempo benefits "Been A Son", which had dragged slightly in its earlier released version recorded with Steve Fisk; the band also goes full throttle during the instrumental break.

NIRVANA

UK Geffen 28 October 2002; US DGC 29 October 2002.

YOU KNOW YOU'RE RIGHT / ABOUT A GIRL / BEEN A SON / SLIVER / SMELLS LIKE TEEN SPIRIT / COME AS YOU ARE / LITHIUM / IN BLOOM / HEART-SHAPED BOX / PENNYROYAL TEA / RAPE ME / DUMB / ALL APOLOGIES / THE MAN WHO SOLD THE WORLD

Recorded various dates 1988–1994. Also released as a double album vinyl set, including "Something In The Way". European CDs include the track "Where Did You Sleep Last Night". The Japanese CD includes both "Something In The Way" and "Where Did You Sleep Last Night".

Once the lawsuit between Love and Novoselic and Grohl had been settled, the path was cleared for release of "You Know You're Right", the last song Nirvana recorded. It was chosen as the leading track for what's essentially a "best of" release. Offering a hint of how Nirvana's next record might have sounded, with its brooding verses and expansive chorus, it stands alongside such classics as "Teen Spirit" and "Heart-Shaped Box" with ease, though its darkness is closer in mood to the latter song. The ending mirrors that of "Teen Spirit", which had Cobain screaming "a

A simply designed black and silver cover graced the first post-Nirvana best-of album (see p.145).

denial" nine times; here, he repeats the song's title like a mantra a total of seventeen times. Yet while the ending of "Teen Spirit" suggests a fight, "You Know You're Right" is an admission of defeat, and considering the events of the next few months, it's tempting to speculate how much it reflected Cobain's own state of mind.

The rest of the album features a fairly standard selection of songs. All the singles from *Nevermind* and *In Utero* are included, along with what would have been the latter album's third single ("Pennyroyal Tea"), as well as two of the more acclaimed *In Utero* tracks ("Rape Me" and "Dumb"). *Bleach* is short-changed, with only "About A Girl" present. "Sliver" is an obvious inclusion, "The Man Who Sold The World" less so.

"Been A Son" is a more offbeat choice and, happily for collectors, the compilers chose the rarer version that originally appeared on the now out of print *Blew* EP (they also used the rarer Scott Litt mix of "Pennyroyal Tea", which previously only appeared on the edition of *In Utero* released to Wal-Mart and Kmart stores).

The Recordings

The songs were also newly mastered for this release, giving them a clearer, crisper sound.

WITH THE LIGHTS OUT

UK Geffen 22 November 2004; US DGC 23 November 2004.

CD1: *HEARTBREAKER (live) / ANOREXORCIST (radio perform-ance) / WHITE LACE AND STRANGE (radio performance) / HELP ME I'M HUNGRY (radio performance) / MRS. BUTTERWORTH (band rehearsal) / IF YOU MUST (band demo) / PEN CAP CHEW (band demo) / DOWNER (live) / FLOYD THE BARBER (live) / RAUNCHOLA-MOBY DICK (live) / BEANS (home demo) / DON'T WANT IT ALL (home demo) / CLEAN UP BEFORE SHE COMES (home demo) / POLLY (home demo) / ABOUT A GIRL (home demo) / BLANDEST (studio out-take) / DIVE (band demo) / THEY HUNG*

HIM ON A CROSS (The Jury Session) / GREY GOOSE (The Jury Session) / AIN'T IT A SHAME (The Jury session) / TOKEN EASTERN SONG (band demo) / EVEN IN HIS YOUTH (band demo) / POLLY (band demo)

CD2: *OPINION (radio performance) / LITHIUM (radio performance) / BEEN A SON (radio performance) / SLIVER (home demo) / WHERE DID YOU SLEEP LAST NIGHT (home demo) / PAY TO PLAY (compilation track) / HERE SHE COMES NOW (compilation track) / DRAIN YOU (band demo) / ANEURYSM (B-side) / SMELLS LIKE TEEN SPIRIT (band rehearsal) / BREED (Butch Vig mix) / VERSE CHORUS VERSE (band rehearsal) / OLD AGE (band rehearsal) / ENDLESS, NAMELESS (radio performance) / DUMB (radio perform-ance) / D-7 (compilation track) / OH, THE GUILT (split single track) / CURMUDGEON (B-side) / RETURN OF THE RAT (compilation track) / SMELLS LIKE TEEN SPIRIT (Butch Vig mix)*

Nirvana and KAOS Radio

Nirvana had only played a handful of shows when they were offered their first opportunity to appear on radio. It was early 1987, and the band was then called Skid Row. Their first non-party gig, a few weeks after their first show at a party in Raymond in March, was at the closing night of the GESCCO (Greater Evergreen Student Community Cooperative Organization) Hall in Olympia, where they shared the bill with Danger Mouse and Nisqually Delta Podunk Nightmare. John Goodmanson and Donna Dresch of Danger Mouse were impressed with the Aberdeen crew. "I was super into them," Goodmanson recalls. "I remember after they played Donna getting mad at me that I liked their band better than I liked our band."

Goodmanson and Dresch happened to host back-to-back radio shows Monday nights on KAOS, the radio station at Evergreen State College (his was called "The Toy Train Crash Backside Bone Beefcake Show", hers "Out Of Order"). They invited Skid Row to appear on both shows one night in April (the exact date's unknown).

The group began with a new cover they'd added to their set, "Love Buzz", which at this stage featured a more experimental guitar solo, perhaps to make up for Cobain's less confident vocals. On "Floyd The Barber" he even sounds somewhat strangled, not quite letting go into the full-throated screams he'd develop later. The tempo on this and most of the other songs is also noticeably slower than when the group later recorded them: "Downer" is almost meandering compared with the breakneck pace it would later be performed at.

"Mexican Seafood" is suitably raw, and then comes one of the set's highlights, the raucous "White Lace And Strange", a song recorded in 1969 by an obscure garage rock band called Thunder & Roses; the band sounds more energized on this song than they do on their own material. The loping beat of "Spank Thru" made it the poppiest song in the set, nicely juxtaposed with the most aggressive song played that night, "Anorexorcist". "Hairspray Queen" reflected Cobain's new wave/post-punk leanings, and while "Pen Cap

CD3: *RAPE ME (home demo) / RAPE ME (band demo) / SCENT-LESS APPRENTICE (band rehearsal) / HEART-SHAPED BOX (band demo) / I HATE MYSELF AND I WANT TO DIE (band demo) / MILK IT (band demo) / MOIST VAGINA (band demo) / GALLONS OF RUBBING ALCOHOL FLOW THROUGH THE STRIP (album bonus track) / THE OTHER IMPROV (band demo) / SERVE THE SERVANTS (home demo) / VERY APE (home demo) / PENNYROYAL TEA (home demo) / MARIGOLD (B-side) / SAPPY (compilation track) / JESUS DOESN'T WANT ME FOR A SUNBEAM (band rehearsal) / DO RE MI (home demo) / YOU KNOW YOU'RE RIGHT (home demo) / ALL APOLOGIES (home demo)*

DVD: *LOVE BUZZ / SCOFF / ABOUT A GIRL / BIG LONG NOW / IMMIGRANT SONG / SPANK THRU / HAIRSPRAY QUEEN / SCHOOL / MR. MOUSTACHE (tracks 1–9 band, rehearsal) / BIG CHEESE (live) / IN BLOOM (Sub Pop version) / SAPPY / SCHOOL / LOVE BUZZ / PENNYROYAL TEA / SMELLS LIKE TEEN SPIRIT / TERRITORIAL PISSINGS / JESUS DOESN'T WANT ME FOR A SUNBEAM / TALK TO ME (tracks 12–19, live) / SEASONS IN THE SUN (band demo)*

Recorded various dates 1987–1994.

Around two-thirds of the material on this set was already available – legally or otherwise – but to fans who weren't obsessively scouring the Internet, *With The Lights Out* is a veritable treasure trove.

The opening track, "Heartbreaker", comes from the band's very first show in Raymond in 1987, and though not the most exciting

Chew" was a song soon dropped from the group's repertoire, this version features a wildly off-kilter vocal from Cobain who clearly hasn't worked out the song's lyrics yet but isn't about to let that get in the way of giving a good performance. The final song, credited as "Help Me I'm Hungry" on *With The Lights Out*, is now believed to be titled "Vendetagainst", and here comes off as an afterthought to the set, with Cobain delivering a rambling stream-of-consciousness monologue against a backing of bass and drums.

Though admittedly on the ragged side, it was nonetheless an impressive performance from a group that had been performing for little more than a month. The set was, however, plagued by numerous pauses between songs, when band members can be heard asking "Are we still on?" "You can hear they seem a little confused about whether they're still on the air or not," Goodmanson explains. "We didn't have very good communication between the performance room and the control room; it was all hand gestures."

Some of the songs were slated to appear on a local cassette label, but the plans for its release fell through. Instead, the session became Nirvana's first demo, and helped secure them their first date at Tacoma's Community World Theater on 18 April.

The band never did another session for KAOS, but Cobain performed solo on 25 September 1990, when he was an apparently spontaneous guest on Calvin Johnson's *Boy Meets Girl* show, having called Johnson up and suggested he come in and "share some new tunes with you". Johnson later recalled that eight songs were performed, though only three have been released to date: "Opinion", which was never performed again, "Lithium", which Cobain introduced by saying "that's gonna be on our new album", and "Been A Son". Johnson also recalled Cobain performing "Dumb" (essentially complete but not recorded until *In Utero*), "Polly", and the two singing the Wipers' "D-7" together. Cobain accompanied himself on acoustic guitar, and, stripped of high volume, revealed for the first time just how expressive a singer he could be.

The Music

The Jury sessions

In August 1989, Cobain and Novoselic joined Mark Lanegan and Mark Pickerel, the lead singer and drummer of Screaming Trees, to collaborate on a blues band. Lanegan and Pickerel had been steadily developing an interest in the genre over the years. Pickerel's job at a record store in the Trees' home town of Ellensburg, Washington, had given him the opportunity to explore the owner's extensive collection of obscure blues tracks on his stash of cassettes. The two were also interested in modern interpretations of the genre, Pickerel citing the early Gun Club records and Nick Cave's *Kicking Against the Pricks* as examples, as well as Americana of the 1950s and 60s – what came to be called "alt-country", a decade before the term became widely used.

It wasn't a genre many musicians in the Northwest were interested in at the time. "At the beginning of the 'grunge' explosion out of the Seattle it seemed like most bands, the first genre of music that they tried to play was punk rock and it seemed like after they conquered punk rock they went on to try and reinvent heavy metal," Pickerel says. "But no one in the Northwest had really done anything to reinvent early Delta blues, early rockabilly, early country western or anything like that."

Before long, the two came up with the idea of approaching Novoselic and Cobain (whose interest in Leadbelly was known to Lanegan) with a view to reinventing the genre themselves. "What we were trying to do was a modern-day version of Cream or Led Zeppelin. It was going to include everyone from Lightning Hopkins to Leadbelly to Robert Johnson, whoever. But we certainly wouldn't have shied away from doing something like a Johnny Cash song or a Ray Price song if the right song was out there. Mark and I were both already big admirers of Kurt and Nirvana, so Mark knew that I would jump at

the chance to start, for lack of a better term, a blues supergroup in Seattle."

Cobain and Novoselic were receptive to the idea, and everyone spent time combing their record collections for likely candidates, which they brought to the band's rehearsals, with the idea of doing a session devoted to Leadbelly, then covering other blues artists. But Pickerel was surprised to see a strange dynamic developing between Lanegan and Cobain during rehearsals. "Mark is normally a very aggressive, dominant personality when it comes to rehearsing and recording, and just being a musical visionary," he explains. "And I'm assuming that Kurt was the same way in his working environment. But when you put the two of them in the same room together, I felt like there was so much mutual admiration and respect for each other that neither one of them really wanted to be the instigator. I remember Kurt and Lanegan standing around staring at their feet the whole time, while Krist and I waited for direction from people who we were used to taking directions from. It seemed like neither one of them were willing to be the aggressive bandleader that they normally had been in the past. It was sort of strange to see Mark all of a sudden become sort of shy and unwilling to do anything to offend Kurt."

After two rehearsals, the musicians went into Reciprocal Recording on 20 August with Jack Endino producing. They started out with "Where Did You Sleep Last Night", with Lanegan on vocals, which Endino considered the strongest song of the session. He also noted the hesitancy between Lanegan and Cobain that kept the session from really catching fire. This was perhaps most evident on "Grey Goose", which remained an instrumental, neither Lanegan nor Cobain suggesting they record a lead vocal for it. "It was really unusual to watch those two," Pickerel notes. "They looked like junior high kids at a dance, a couple of wallflowers, and neither one of them would dance with each other. You could tell that they wanted there to be some productivity. I think everybody had high expectations for it. But it just didn't seem like either one of those guys would take the initiative to make statements like 'I want to sing this song', or, 'I think you'd be great for the first verse, and why don't I come in for the chorus and I'll take the second verse'. I'd never seen either one of those guys behave that way, before or since! But it was kind of cute."

A welcome dose of energy arrived with the next song to be cut, "Ain't It A Shame", a rollicking number that featured one of the best Cobain vocals ever captured at a recording session. Cobain then cut "They Hung Him On A Cross" as a solo perform-ance, accompanying himself on guitar. As a result, "Where Did You Sleep Last Night" became the only song at the session with a Lanegan vocal. "He was basically looking on," says Endino. "Probably in the control room with me while we were recording them, thinking, 'Hmm, should I sing on these?'"

The group spent six hours in the studio on the first day, with a one-hour session held 21 August. Both "Where Did You Sleep Last Night" and "Ain't It A Shame" were mixed on 28 August, with the assump-tion they'd be released on a single. Asked what he should put down as a name, Endino recalls someone calling out "The Jury!", which was duly written down. Pickerel thinks he may have made the suggestion, since he had first mentioned the name at rehearsals, to little enthusiasm; Cobain preferred the name Lithium.

But the purported "Where Did You Sleep Last Night"/"Ain't It A Shame" single never happened. "There was a great Singles of the Month club single, but at the time Kurt didn't feel comfortable with his vocals on it for some reason," Pickerel recalls. "And Jonathan Poneman always said it was one of Kurt's great vocal performances. What it was about that song that Kurt shied away from, I really don't have any idea. But I always thought it was amazing." Instead, "Where Did You Sleep Last Night" was remixed and used on Lanegan's first solo album, *The Winding Sheet*, released on Sub Pop in 1990 (Cobain also contributed backing vocals to "Down In The Dark").

Nor did The Jury ever reconvene. Both bands soon signed to major labels (Nirvana to DGC, Screaming Trees to Epic), "and it just seemed like we didn't cross paths as much as we did earlier on," Pickerel says. "I really had high hopes for it. I wished that we had already rehearsed more tracks, I wish that we'd recorded sixteen songs and put out a full-length record or something like that. I really wanted it to be a working band that rehearsed every few months, recorded once a year, and maybe went out and did a tour and went to Europe. But it just wasn't meant to be, I guess."

Fortunately, the nascent band's offerings didn't go unheard: "Ain't It A Shame", "They Hung Him On A Cross" and "Grey Goose" were all exhumed for *With The Lights Out*. "Ain't It A Shame" had become legendary in Nirvana circles since it was first revealed in *Come As You Are*, not least because it had never been bootlegged, and it easily lived up to its pre-release hype on the box set. "They Hung Him On A Cross", which all the session's participants had forgotten about until the tapes were retrieved from Sub Pop's vaults, was another compelling perform-ance. You can't help but wonder whether a Kurt Cobain solo album might have given him a welcome respite from Nirvana, allowing him to explore other musical directions. The same could of course be said of The Jury; who knows what could have developed had the group decided to spend another evening sitting around listening to cassettes in the hopes of discovering further inspiration.

The Recordings

A collection of CDs and a DVD providing an overview of Nirvana's entire career, the box set that sports a cover of the band in their "Knack" outfits was six years in the making (see pp.145–148).

choice from that particular show, it serves to illustrate the band's earliest musical influences. Compare the track with three from a 1988 show ten months later in Tacoma ("Downer", "Floyd The Barber", "Raunchola/Moby Dick") and the extent of the band's development is obvious: musically, they're far more skilled, Cobain's delivery is increasingly confident, and it also helps that Dale Crover is on drums.

The tracks that had been previously released officially ("Pay To Play", "Here She Comes Now", "Aneurysm", "D-7", "Oh, The Guilt", "Curmudgeon", "Return of the Rat", "Marigold", "Sappy" and "Gallons of Rubbing Alcohol...") appeared on B-sides or compilations (some now out of print), or as bonus tracks. Of the previously unreleased radio tracks, two are from a 1991 BBC appearance ("Dumb", "Endless, Nameless"), while the more interesting ones come from Cobain's September 1990 solo appearance on Calvin Johnson's KAOS radio show. Though he'd described them as "new tunes", only "Opinion" was actually new; Nirvana were already performing "Lithium" and "Been A Son". But these are wonderfully intimate performances.

Early versions of songs provide a fascinating insight into how they developed. Songs like "Dive", "Even In His Youth", "Heart-Shaped Box", "Drain You", "I Hate Myself And I Want To Die" (slightly retitled from the Beavis & Butthead compilation, which had only the first "I"), "Milk It" and "Moist Vagina" are not too dissimilar to the final versions. But when first recording "Polly", at a 1989 session, the band opted for a harder and faster performance, instead of the stripped-down arrangement they later used. And the first version of "Rape Me" is given a disturbing touch by Cobain's daughter heard crying throughout. In a rehearsal of "Scentless Apprentice" you can actually hear the song in the process of being written. There's also the first known recording of "Smells Like Teen Spirit", captured at a band rehearsal on a boombox; the sound quality's understandably raw, but there's still a visceral thrill at hearing the song in its earliest stages.

Butch Vig's rougher mixes of "Teen Spirit" and "Breed" are also included. Then there are the songs that got away. "Token Eastern Song" was recorded twice by the band, once with Steve Fisk (the version on *WTLO*) and once with Craig Montgomery, and was a regular feature in their shows in 1989, but they never released it in any form. The droning main riff inspired the song's title; perhaps, coming too late for *Bleach* and too early for *Nevermind*, it simply fell through the cracks. "Verse Chorus Verse" and "Old Age" were both recorded during the *Nevermind* session, but were later dropped. The versions here are unfinished, but it's interesting to speculate how they might have changed *Nevermind*'s character if they'd been fully developed. "Blandest" was initially considered for the B-side of "Love Buzz" but was dropped in favour of the much stronger "Big Cheese".

Also included are three songs from The Jury sessions ("Ain't It A Shame", "Grey Goose", "They Hung Him On A Cross"), a February 1994 rehearsal version of "Jesus Doesn't Want Me For A Sunbeam" with a lovely cello line from Melora Creager, and a jam from the Brazil 1993 sessions belatedly titled "The Other Improv".

The most intimate tracks are Cobain's own home demos, where he recorded himself singing to his own guitar accompaniment. Some are similar to their later recorded versions ("Polly", "Pennyroyal Tea" and "Where Did You Sleep Last Night", though the last is less fraught than the *Unplugged* performance); some show the songs in the stages of being worked out ("About A Girl", "Sliver", "Rape Me", "Very Ape", "You Know You're Right" and "All Apologies", all with different lyrics). And there are a handful of tracks that only exist as demos: the jokey "Beans" with Cobain distorting his voice, and the acoustic "Don't Want It All" and "Clean Up Before She Comes" (the latter, recorded when Cobain lived in Olympia, undoubtedly refers to his girlfriend's pleas he do his share of the housework). And then there's the haunting "Do Re Mi" (with Pat Smear on guitar), which begins with words from a child's prayer and ends up being a cry from the heart of almost unbearable poignancy.

In contrast to *Live! Tonight! Sold Out!!*, most of the DVD focuses on Nirvana's pre-fame years. The highlight is undoubtedly a rehearsal session at Novoselic's mother's home

in December 1988, as the band prepared to record *Bleach*. Friends and family members sit around the rehearsal room drinking beer, as the band plays and mugs for the camera; the fun they're having as they burn through Led Zeppelin's "Immigrant Song" is unmistakably evident. Other notable footage includes "Love Buzz" from Grohl's live debut with the band, the first public performance of "Teen Spirit" and non-bootlegged footage from the 1990 Motor Sports and 1992 Crocodile Café shows. Studio and candid footage is edited together for the bitter-sweet "Seasons In The Sun". Tour footage and home movies appear as linking sequences on each of the DVD's menus.

SLIVER: THE BEST OF THE BOX

UK Geffen 31 October 2005; US DGC 1 November 2005.

SPANK THRU *(Fecal Matter tape)* / HEARTBREAKER *(live)* / MRS. BUTTERWORTH *(band rehearsal)* / CLEAN UP BEFORE SHE COMES *(home demo)* / ABOUT A GIRL *(home demo)* / BLANDEST *(out-take)* / AIN'T IT A SHAME *(The Jury Session)* / SAPPY *(band demo)* / OPINION *(solo radio performance)* / LITHIUM *(solo radio performance)* / SLIVER *(home demo)* / SMELLS LIKE TEEN SPIRIT *(rehearsal)* / COME AS YOU ARE *(rehearsal)* / OLD AGE *(band demo)* / OH, THE GUILT *(split-single track)* / RAPE ME *(home demo)* / RAPE ME *(band demo)* / HEART-SHAPED BOX *(band demo)* / DO RE MI *(home demo)* / YOU KNOW YOU'RE RIGHT *(home demo)* / ALL APOLOGIES *(home demo)*

The Fecal Matter tape (see p.13) rests on top of the pile of Nirvana cassettes on *Sliver*'s cover, its title revealed for the first time.

The Music

Recorded various dates 1985–1994.

Those who didn't wish to spring for *With The Lights Out* could pick up this single CD of highlights. And to entice those who'd already purchased the box set, three previously unreleased tracks were included. "Come As You Are" was taken from the same cassette that provided the first known recorded version of "Smells Like Teen Spirit"; longer than the final version, its lyrics also haven't been fully worked out yet, Cobain repeating the first verse three times. Also included is the first studio version of "Sappy" (which would later be titled "Verse Chorus Verse"), recorded with Jack Endino. It's the version with the most "rock" feel out of the five known versions and, like the one released (on the *No Alternative* compilation), it begins without an instrumental intro. But of greatest interest to fans was the first official release of material from the Fecal Matter tape, an early version of "Spank Thru". It's remarkably similar to the version that would be professionally recorded in 1988 – the arrangement and even the lyrics are the same, though Cobain's vocal and instrumental prowess are much improved.

Singles and EPs

Love Buzz / Big Cheese

US Sub Pop. Recorded 11 & 30 June, 16 July & 27 September 1988. Released November 1988 in a limited edition vinyl run of 1000 individually hand-numbered 7-inch singles.

The first single's back cover image, shot on infra-red film, illustrates Cobain's prominence in the band.

The decision to release a cover song as Nirvana's first single wasn't quite as unusual as it seemed. First, it was felt by all to be the best song then in Nirvana's repertoire. And if it was a cover, then at least it was an obscure one; while rock fans might be acquainted with Shocking Blue's "Venus" (a number-one US hit in 1970), "Love Buzz" was a track on the Dutch band's second album, *At Home* (released in 1969).

That the band approached their recording debut with tongue in cheek is evident from the ten-second sound collage that preceded the song proper (at least on the single version), ending with an exhortation from the *Rocky & Bullwinkle* cartoon character, Natasha Fatale, for the listener "to do a Twist, the Surf, a wild Watusi, a Frug, or a swinging Hully Gully!". Nirvana's version retains the psychedelic feel of the original but is unmistakably modern as well, the band locking into a trancey groove from which Cobain could shoot off into improvisational hijinks during the instrumental break – especially in live performance.

The flipside, said to refer to Sub Pop co-founder Jonathan Poneman, is more trademark grunge, with an eerie opening two-note guitar wail that explodes into righteous heaviness. It's more of a vocal workout for Cobain as well, though both sides of the single hint at the ferocious rock growl that lurks within him.

The single was the first released in the subscription "Sub Pop Singles Club", though it was also briefly available through mail order on its own for a mere $3.50. "Why don't you trade those guitars for shovels?" (a phrase Krist Novoselic's father was fond of saying to the band) was etched in the run-out groove on the "Love Buzz" side. The opening sound collage, and another sound collage that played during the song's instrumental break, are missing from the remixed version of the song that appears on the *Bleach* album.

Blew

BLEW / LOVE BUZZ / BEEN A SON / STAIN

UK Tupelo. "Blew" recorded 24 & 29–31 December 1988, 14 & 24 January 1989; "Love Buzz" recorded 11 & 30 June, 16 July & 27 September 1988; "Been A Son" and "Stain" recorded September 1989. Released December 1989 on both 12-inch vinyl and CD.

This four-track EP was ostensibly issued to tie in with Nirvana's first European tour. As it wasn't actually released until after the tour concluded on 3 December 1989, it didn't serve as much of a promotional tool – but it did give fans some new music, which showed the band already moving away from the grungy sounds of *Bleach*.

"Been A Son" and "Stain" were recorded right before the tour in September 1989 at a new studio for the

A UK-only EP, *Blew*'s back cover image was even less animated than the front, featuring a photo of an empty gynecologist's office.

band, the Music Source in Seattle, and with a new producer, Steve Fisk. Both songs address the nature of inadequacy. "Been A Son" laments the fate of those born female, not male, over another melody described as "Beatlesque", especially in its use of harmonies. "Stain" has one verse, repeated three times over the course of the song, but what's interesting here is Cobain's use of perspective: he sings the verse in the third person, then makes it clear who he thinks the "stain" is by singing the chorus in the first person. Fisk was especially pleased with the duelling guitar solos during the instrumental break, which he describes as being like "squabbling hens".

Sliver / Dive

UK Tupelo, US Sub Pop. "Sliver" recorded 11 & 24 July 1990; "Dive" recorded 2–6 April 1990. Released UK January 1991, US September 1990.

In the US this single was only available as a 7-inch, the first 3000 copies in black, blue or pink vinyl. The first 2000 copies of the UK 7-inch were on green vinyl. The UK 12-inch features a live version of "About A Girl" from the 9 February 1990 show at Portland's Pine Street Theatre; the UK CD adds "Spank Thru" from the same performance.

This single represented a huge musical leap forward for Nirvana. "Sliver", written from a child's perspective, addresses the childhood trauma of being abandoned by one's parents. "Mom and dad go off somewhere and leave the kid with his grandparents and he gets frightened," Cobain told *Melody Maker* at the time. "But, hey, you mustn't get too worried about him – grandpa doesn't abuse him or anything like that." Nonetheless, after a restrained start, the music, and Cobain's vocals, become increasingly energetic throughout the song, culminating in an agonized cry of relief when the boy and his parents are reunited. "Now we specialize in happy endings," Novoselic said in the same *Melody Maker* article. The original single featured a conversation between a hungover Novoselic and Jonathan Poneman,

accidentally recorded on Novoselic's answering machine, tacked on at the end of the song. "Sliver" also marks the only recorded studio appearance of Dan Peters on drums.

"Dive", culled from the April 1990 sessions with Butch Vig, was harder rock in comparison, the pop/hard rock split mirroring that on

Top ten Nirvana rarities

Despite innumerable stories proclaiming "the death of vinyl", it remains a hot commodity in the collector's circuit. This listing of the top ten most wanted Nirvana releases was compiled by Enrico Vincenzi of sliver.it/nirvana, the most highly detailed Nirvana discography currently available online. Values were calculated by averaging recent sale prices of items in mint or near mint condition; naturally, auctions can result in a lower or higher figure.

1. "Love Buzz" single, Sub Pop SP23, 1988, US

Nirvana's first single is highly desirable simply for being the band's first release, though it's heightened by the fact that only 1000 hand-numbered copies were offered to the public (an additional 200 were in sleeves with a red slash in place of a number). The single can command between $2000 and $2500, with higher prices for low-numbered copies.

2. *Bleach* album, Sub Pop SP34, 1989, US, first pressing

In order to enhance the collectability of their releases, Sub Pop frequently issued their records on coloured vinyl. Not that simply being on coloured vinyl makes

a record collectable; as in other cases, it helps if it's a limited run. When Sub Pop originally issued *Bleach* in 1989, the first 1000 copies were on white vinyl, which range in value from $400 to $600.

3. *Bleach* album, Sub Pop SP34, 1992, US, third pressing

Nirvana's success spurred sales of *Bleach*, leading Sub Pop to re-press it in a variety of colours on vinyl. A white/green "iceberg" vinyl is especially prized as there are comparatively few in existence, since it was thought to be too close in colour to the first white vinyl pressing. As such, it was only given out to Sub Pop's employees and friends, and ranges in value from $800 to $1000.

4. *Bleach* album, Sub Pop SP34, 1992, US, re-pressing

This unique re-pressing is on red and white vinyl, and was shrink-wrapped with a copy of the "Sliver" single (on blue vinyl). There were 500 individually numbered copies with a sticker on the shrink-wrap, and an unknown quantity of copies that weren't numbered. The set ranges in value from $500 to $700, with lower numbers commanding a higher price.

their first single. It's another song propelled by Novoselic's bass line, and with its thick guitars and scraped vocal from Cobain, it could easily have fit on *Nevermind* (indeed, five of the eight songs recorded with Vig would appear on that album, though four of them would be re-recorded).

Molly's Lips

US Sub Pop. Recorded 9 February 1990. Released January 1991. The single's run was limited to 7500 copies, 4000 on green vinyl. In the run-off groove on the Nirvana side was the word "Later".

Nirvana ended their career on Sub Pop as they began it, releasing a 7-inch as part of the

5. *Bleach* album, Sub Pop/Waterfront DAMP 114, 1992, Australia

A special edition of *Bleach* was prepared for Nirvana's 1992 tour of the country. The album is on green vinyl, packaged in a silver and green sleeve, which is itself packaged in a white cloth outer sleeve, with the album name, song titles and tour dates silk-screened on it. The set also includes a poster, and is valued at $800–1200.

6. "Sliver" single, Sub Pop SP73, 1990, US, re-pressing

Of all the coloured pressings of "Sliver", the rarest is on white vinyl. As with the "iceberg" vinyl *Bleach*, it was largely made available to Sub Pop employees and associates. It ranges in value from $500 to $700.

7. "Here She Comes Now" single, Communion COMM23, 1991, US

This song was originally released in 1990 on the compilation *Heaven And Hell*. The following year, Nirvana's song was paired with the Melvins' "Venus In Furs" as a single, and released in a run believed to be 1000 copies. The single was pressed in a variety of colours, and ranges in value from $100 to $300, with the rarer colours (white-green, orange, mustard) more valuable.

8. *Hormoaning* EP, Geffen GEF21711, 1992, Australia

This EP was released as a tie-in with Nirvana's February 1992 Pacific Rim tour. In Australia, the vinyl record was pressed on red and blue swirled vinyl, in a run of 4000 copies, and ranges in value from $200 to $300.

9. "Pennyroyal Tea" CD single, Geffen GED21907, 1994, Germany

"Pennyroyal Tea" was set to be the third single from *In Utero*, planned to coincide with Nirvana's spring 1994 tour of Europe and the UK. But the single was hastily pulled in the wake of Cobain's suicide. Most copies were recalled and destroyed; only a few hundred copies of this German edition, with a picture sleeve, are known to exist. It ranges in value from $300 to $400.

10. "Pennyroyal Tea" CD promo single, Geffen NIRPRO, 1994, UK

This UK promo misspelled the song title as "Penny Royal Tea", and it's only available in a plain slim CD case. It's believed that fewer than 100 copies exist; it ranges in value from $600 to $800.

This split single with labelmates the Fluid was the last Nirvana 7-inch to bear the Sub Pop logo.

Sub Pop Singles Club (#27). The release was also a split single, with The Fluid's "Candy" on the flipside.

The track was drawn from the recording of the same show that provided live cuts for the UK "Sliver" single. Cobain wasn't happy with the band's workmanlike performance (and, typically, he'd only learned one verse of the song), but as Sub Pop had been granted the right to release a final Nirvana single, he couldn't do much about it. Indeed, the version the band recorded for a John Peel radio session nine months later, with Dave Grohl on drums, is superior, perhaps one reason why the song has never been officially released in any other format.

Smells Like Teen Spirit / Even In His Youth / Aneurysm

UK Geffen, US DGC. "Smells Like Teen Spirit" recorded May–June 1991; "Even In His Youth" and "Aneurysm" recorded 1 January 1991. Released UK 9 September 1991, US 10 September 1991. Also released as a picture disc in Germany and the UK.

Cobain's stated intention with "Teen Spirit" was to write "the ultimate pop song", but no one had expected the song to break the album as massively as it did. It was felt that college radio would be the most receptive to the track – not an unreasonable assumption in a year in which Bryan Adams and Mariah Carey were the biggest acts on mainstream radio – which would lay the groundwork for the future crossover single, "Lithium". But "Teen Spirit" struck an immediate chord with its audience, becoming the spark that lit the fuse for the resulting Nirvana explosion. But it also sowed the seeds for Nirvana's eventual demise; ironically, "Teen Spirit" turned out not to be the beginning, but the beginning of the end for the band.

The single version is about thirty seconds shorter than the album version, with a shorter intro and instrumental break; the edits don't detract too much from the song, though the album version is the more effective.

Both the bonus tracks, "Even In His Youth" and "Aneurysm", were drawn from the January 1991 session in Seattle and feature rather tortured vocals from Cobain, who remains in his upper register throughout both songs. They also share a lyrical brevity, consisting of a sole verse and chorus. It was drummer Dave Grohl's first studio session with the group, and for the first time, you hear the essence of the Nirvana machine that would produce *Nevermind* on display, guitar, bass and drums in lurching synchronization.

In an ironic touch given the harsh nature of the music, the single's cover has the

The European cover lacked the teenage girl-style handwriting of the US version, sticking instead with Nirvana's traditional Onyx font.

title in cursive writing, with hearts dotting the "i"s and an exclamation point at the end, emulating the handwriting of a teenage girl. The rear cover has one of Charles Peterson's best known photos of Cobain, playing guitar while seemingly standing on his head, shot at a 3 March 1991 show in Vancouver, BC.

Hormoaning

TURNAROUND / ANEURYSM / D-7 / SON OF A GUN / EVEN IN HIS YOUTH / MOLLY'S LIPS

Note Grohl's T-shirt; Cobain would subsequently provide cover art for Sonic Youth's own Australian tour EP, "Whores Moaning" (see p.53).

Australia Geffen, Japan DGC. "Turnaround", "Son Of A Gun", "Molly's Lips", "D-7" recorded 21 October 1990; "Aneurysm", "Even In His Youth" recorded 1 January 1991. Released Australia December 1991 in a limited run of 15,000: 10,000 on CD, 4000 as a 12-inch on red and blue swirled vinyl, and 1000 on cassette. Released in Japan January 1992 on CD only.

This EP was released in advance of Nirvana's Pacific Rim tour in February 1992. "Aneurysm" and "Even In His Youth" had previously appeared on the "Smells Like Teen Spirit" single, and the rest came from their 1990 appearance on John Peel's radio show. It was their first radio session with Dave Grohl on drums, and the only session to feature all covers. Both "Son Of A Gun" and "Molly's Lips" were originally recorded by Scottish duo the Vaselines, and Nirvana's versions are a good deal more raucous. The band also rocks

up Devo's "Turnaround", though Cobain does a good job of conveying the band's robotic feel in his vocal delivery. And after a slow intro, Nirvana's version of the Wipers' "D-7" blasts off with fury and becomes positively scorching.

Come As You Are / School / Drain You

UK Geffen, US DGC. "Come As You Are" recorded May–June 1991; "School" and "Drain You" recorded 31 October 1991. Released UK 2 March 1992, US 3 March 1992. Also released as a 12-inch picture disc in the UK and Germany.

With its cover depicting microscopic life forms, there's a perceptible link to later *Nevermind* singles artwork.

The CD version of the "Come As You Are" single featured two previously unreleased live tracks from Nirvana's 31 October 1991 show in Seattle, great versions of "School" and "Drain You". In the UK, the CD single also included *Nevermind*'s "hidden" track, "Endless, Nameless".

Nevermind: It's An Interview

DGC. Recorded May–June 1991, 31 October 1991 & 10–12 January 1992. Released 31 March 1992.

This promo-only release combined band interviews (conducted separately by Kurt St. Thomas, then Music Director at Boston radio station WFNX) with studio and live tracks, taken from the band's Halloween 1991 show in Seattle, including complete versions of "About A Girl", "Aneurysm", "Drain You", "On A Plain" and "School". "Drain You" and "School" also appeared as bonus tracks on the "Come As You Are" single, and footage of the "About A Girl" performance was later released on *Live! Tonight! Sold Out!!*. But the live versions of "Aneurysm" and "On A Plain" are only available on this release.

Lithium / Been A Son / Curmudgeon

The disturbing cover was designed, front and back, by Cobain (see p.86).

UK Geffen, US DGC. "Lithium" recorded May–June 1991; "Been A Son" recorded 31 October 1991; "Curmudgeon" recorded 7 April 1992. Released UK 20 July 1992, US 21 July 1992. The UK CD added "D-7".

Two more previously unreleased tracks appeared on the "Lithium" single. The performance of "Been A Son" was a fairly straightforward run-through of the song from what was one of the band's best shows on their fall 1991 tour. "Curmudgeon" begins with a wonderful droning guitar line that continues throughout the song, which features a particularly bawling vocal from Cobain. The squalling guitar work during the instrumental break was a clue to the direction Nirvana would pursue on *In Utero*. Another element that captured attention was that the inner sleeve printed all the

lyrics to *Nevermind* (something that should have been considered for "Curmudgeon" as well). "Curmudgeon" is also available, remixed, on *With The Lights Out*, but "Been A Son" is only available on this single.

In Bloom / Sliver / Polly

UK Geffen. "In Bloom" recorded May–June 1991; "Sliver" and "Polly" recorded 28 December 1991. Released 30 November 1992. Also released as a 12-inch picture disc.

The fourth single from *Nevermind*, with its strikingly symbolic cover, was only released outside the US.

The US elected not to release a fourth single from *Nevermind*, but overseas markets did, adding two previously unreleased live tracks from a performance at the Del Mar Fairgrounds, California. The songs, from what's generally acknowledged as one of the band's best performances, are only available on this single.

Oh, The Guilt

US, UK Touch and Go. Recorded 7 April 1992. Released 22 February 1993. Released in a "limited edition" of 100,000 on 7-inch vinyl, cassette and CD. In France it was released on blue vinyl; in Australia as a picture disc.

Perhaps mindful of the fact they'd be sharing the single with the abrasive Jesus Lizard (whose song "Puss" is on the flip side), Nirvana didn't hold back on their contribution. The song is reminiscent of *Bleach* in

A dual image for a split single with The Jesus Lizard; the back has Polaroid-style portraits of both bands.

its musical heaviness and lyrical repetition, as well as playing on words that sound the same but have different meanings. But where the band were still finding their voice on *Bleach*, they're now fully in command of their talents, and thus the song exudes a magnificent sense of strength. As it happens, "Puss" was produced by the man who would also produce *In Utero* – Steve Albini. The original version featured the sound of a cigarette lighter being flicked, which was mixed out of the version on *With The Lights Out*.

Heart-Shaped Box / Milk It / Marigold

UK Geffen. Recorded 13–26 February 1993. Released 23 August 1993.

The first single from *In Utero*, another non-US release, featured Cobain's photography on the front cover.

"Heart-Shaped Box" was unsurprisingly chosen as *In Utero*'s first single, but what did come as a surprise to many was that the previously unreleased track on the record, "Marigold", was written and performed by Dave Grohl and not Kurt Cobain. Thus far, the only

releases featuring any sign of Grohl's singing talents had been the *King Buzzo* album and his own *Pocketwatch* tape – and both of those had been recorded under pseudonyms. "Marigold" in fact was first released on the *Pocketwatch* tape, with Grohl accompanying himself on acoustic guitar. The arrangement of this version is similar, though there's more instrumentation (electric guitar, bass and drums) and the harmonies are more prominent. Still, the additional instruments don't intrude on the song's delicate, haunting beauty. It also clearly shows that however much he might like rocking out, Grohl has little difficulty revealing his softer side. The single's cover art featured a photograph by Cobain of a heart-shaped box resting in a bed of flowers.

All Apologies / Rape Me / MV

UK Geffen. Recorded 13–26 February 1993. Released December 1993.

Cobain's request to Robert Fisher for the "All Apologies" single was for "something with seahorses".

This is the last Nirvana single released while the band was together. It has one previously unreleased track, "Moist Vagina", which was discreetly retitled "MV" on most versions. Starting out as a slow, almost plodding number, the music soon rises to match Cobain's screaming out the word "Marijuana!", concluding with what sounds like an extended dry gargle. The song was never performed live, and is only available on this single.

Unreleased tracks

Over the course of Nirvana's career, there were a number of songs that fell by the wayside. Some were recorded but never released; some were only performed live and never recorded; some never made it past the home demo stage. Over the years, some of these tracks have appeared on B-sides and compilations, as well as *Incesticide*, *With The Lights Out*, and S*liver: The Best Of The Box*. Others have made it into the collector's circuit. But a number of officially unreleased studio tracks still remain in the vaults, starting with "Spank Thru", recorded at the Dale Demo session. From the "Love Buzz" single session, there are alternate takes of "Big Cheese" and "Love Buzz" and early takes of "Mr. Moustache", "Blew" and "Sifting". During the *Bleach* sessions the band recorded new versions of "Hairspray Queen" and "Floyd The Barber", neither of which have been bootlegged. "Breed", "Lithium" and "Sappy" from the April 1990 sessions at Smart Studios remain officially unreleased (though "Breed" did appear on a promo CD issued to promote *With The Lights Out*), and there are alternate mixes of other songs from the session.

Most of the tracks recorded with Craig Montgomery in January 1991 remain officially unreleased: early versions of "All Apologies", "On A Plain", "Radio Friendly Unit Shifter", "Token Eastern Song" and "Oh, The Guilt". The only unreleased song from the *Nevermind* sessions is "Sappy", which also remains unbootlegged. There are also alternate mixes of other songs recorded during the sessions.

None of the unreleased material from the 1992 sessions has made its way to the collector's circuit: instrumental versions of "Return Of The Rat", "Frances Farmer Will Have Her Revenge On Seattle", "Dumb", "Pennyroyal Tea", "Rape Me", "Radio Friendly Unit Shifter" and "tourette's". From the January 1993 session in Brazil, "Scentless Apprentice", "Very Ape" and "Onward Into Countless Battles" (aka "Meat") are unreleased, though widely bootlegged, but the initial version of "Heart-Shaped Box", with Cobain complaining throughout about the sound coming through his headphones, has yet to surface. Most of the unreleased material from the *In Utero* sessions hasn't reached the collector's circuit either: there are alternative versions of about half of the album's songs, as well as a brief jam by Grohl called "Dave Solo", and a band jam called "Lullaby".

Only two tracks have been released from the band's last session in January 1994: "You Know You're Right" and an excerpt of a jam that appeared on the *With The Lights Out* DVD. Most of the songs were by Grohl and Novoselic, but there are a few with contributions by Cobain: the earlier takes of "You Know You're Right", the full jam (which ran over twenty minutes) and a shorter instrumental called "Jam After Dinner".

Many songs from the band's radio sessions remain unreleased, including the following.

KAOS, April 1987: "Love Buzz", "Floyd The Barber", "Downer", "Mexican Seafood", "Spank Thru", "Hairspray Queen", "Pen Cap Chew".

BBC Radio 1, 26 October 1989: "Love Buzz", "About A Girl", "Polly", "Spank Thru".

VPRO Radio, 1 November 1989: "Love Buzz", "Dive", "About A Girl".

BBC Radio 1, 3 September 1991: "Drain You".

BBC Radio 1, 9 November 1991: "Something In The Way".

VPRO Radio/VARA Radio, 25 November 1991: "Where Did You Sleep Last Night", "Here She Comes Now" and various jams.

Cobain during a radio recording at studios in Hilversum, the Netherlands, November 1991; at least two tracks from the session remain unreleased (see opposite).

Contributions to compilations

Spank Thru

US Sub Pop. Recorded 11 & 30 June, 16 July & 27 September 1988. Originally released on the limited edition EP box set *Sub Pop 200*, December 1988.

For all their purported heaviness, the first tracks Nirvana released all evinced clear pop leanings. "Spank Thru" dates back to Cobain's 1985 Fecal Matter tape, and while the performance is stronger on the *Sub Pop 200* release, the arrangement is essentially the same. The song's opening jangly guitar stands in stark contrast to something like "Paper Cuts", while lyrically it seems to send up all the clichés of a classic rock love song. This is especially apparent on the Fecal Matter version, but you can still hear sarcasm in the Sub Pop version, especially on the lovelorn chorus about broken hearts; Cobain's scream on the word "heart", which he drags out with relish, makes his lack of emotional devastation clear, especially as he then goes on to brag about the delights of self-gratification.

The song's appearance on *Sub Pop 200* put Nirvana in good and diverse company;

The *Sub Pop 200* compilation album features the unmistakeable artwork of Seattle comics artist Charles Burns.

the box set also featured contributions from fellow Sub Poppers Soundgarden, Tad and Mudhoney, the power-pop Fastbacks, spoken-word artist Steven Jesse Bernstein and alt-rocker Terry Lee Hale.

Mexican Seafood

US C/Z. Recorded 23 January 1988. Originally released on the limited edition EP *Teriyaki Asthma Vol. 1* in November 1989. The first five *Teriyaki Asthma* EPs were later compiled as *Teriyaki Asthma Vol. 1–5*, released in a limited edition vinyl run of 2000 in November 1991, and subsequently on cassette and CD.

All but one of the tracks from the January 1988 Dale Demo eventually ended up being officially released, and "Mexican Seafood" made its first appearance on the initial release in C/Z Records' *Teriyaki Asthma* series, a 7-inch EP that also featured contributions from Helios Creed, Coffin Break and Yeast. The song addresses a favourite Cobain topic – illness (in this case, possibly sexually transmitted) and bodily functions. It's a scenario that allows him to make the appropriate grunts and groans (indeed, the song ends with a series of moans), and the jagged musical accompaniment also suits the mood. But, with a hint of embarrassment, Cobain himself later said of the track, "God – I used to be, like, so-boy."

Nirvana featuring on the first EP in C/Z Records' *Teriyaki Asthma* series.

Do You Love Me?

US C/Z, UK Southern. Recorded spring 1989. Originally released on *Hard To Believe: A Kiss Covers Album*, August 1990.

This shambolic cover of a Kiss song was not only Nirvana's sole recording session with second guitarist Jason Everman, it also marked the group's first time in a 24-track studio, at Evergreen State College in Olympia, Washington. Not that the group took advantage of them; Cobain and Novoselic were more concerned with having separate channels for their improv commentary, which by the song's end has replaced both verse and chorus (in one in-joke, they appear to pronounce the word "money" as "Mu-uh-ud-honey"). As the musical side breaks down completely, Cobain finally bellows "Fuckin' turn it off!" and the proceedings thankfully come to an end. The song was only known to have been performed live once.

Here She Comes Now

Nirvana's Velvet Underground cover, released as a single on the Communion label, was one of their longest songs.

UK Imaginary, US Communion. Recorded 2–6 April 1990. Originally released on *Heaven And Hell: A Tribute To The Velvet Underground*, UK 1990, US 1991, and as a single in the US with the Melvins' "Venus In Furs".

Nirvana's cover of the Velvet Underground song stretched on for five minutes, making it one of the longer numbers in the band's catalogue. Again, Cobain only learned the first verse and chorus; more interesting is the song's arrangement, which starts out with Cobain singing quietly to an equally subdued accompaniment, then jumping an octave the final time he sings the verse. The music becomes increasingly louder as well, a rising tension building throughout the song. But there's no culminating moment of release, and the song never gets as frenzied on record as it became in its occasional live performances.

Beeswax

US Kill Rock Stars. Recorded 23 January 1988. Originally released on *Kill Rock Stars*, 21 August 1991, in a vinyl limited edition run of 1000 copies, and later on CD with additional tracks.

Yet another song from the Dale Demo was offered to the Kill Rock Stars label for their very first release, issued at the time of the International Pop Underground Festival held 20–25 August 1991. Musically, the most interesting thing about the song is the grinding, descending riff that runs through the verses. Lyrically, the song does seem to be a case of Cobain throwing together words simply to give himself something to sing, with references to cartoon character Pepé Le Pew, Toni Tennille, Sonny Bono and having his "titillate spayed".

Return Of The Rat

US Tim/Kerr Records. Recorded 7 April 1992. Originally released on *Eight Songs For Greg Sage And The Wipers*,

20 June 1992, in a limited edition run of 10,000 of a box set of four singles, 4000 of which were on coloured vinyl. In 1993 the album was released on CD with six additional tracks and thus retitled *Fourteen Songs*.

Nirvana originally intended to give their cover of the Wipers' "D-7", previously recorded for a 1990 John Peel session, to this tribute record. But resistance from their label in licensing the track made them decide to simply record a different song. This energetic, propulsive version basically follows the original arrangement, though there are some differences: it's in a different key, Cobain doesn't copy the song's guitar solo, but rather uses it as a starting point for his own and, being thirty seconds longer, it's not quite as fast-paced. The band captured the song in two takes, and the casualness of the session was evident by Cobain's sudden cough after the first chorus, at least on the Tim/Kerr releases (when remixed for *With The Lights Out*, the cough was removed). The song is one of the few numbers Nirvana recorded that they never played live.

Verse Chorus Verse

US Arista. Recorded 13–26 February 1993. Originally released on *No Alternative*, 9 November 1993.

Three and a half years since it had first been recorded in a studio, a version of "Sappy" was finally released, though it was now retitled "Verse Chorus Verse". It's certainly the best of the four versions the group recorded, with a decidedly more energetic feel, thanks to Grohl's drumming. The musical arrangement also gives the song a lift, alternating between moments when Cobain's backed solely by guitar, then the blast of the full band – the typical Nirvana soft/loud formula, in fact. The lyrics, seemingly about the illusion of attaining happiness, represent another typical Cobain theme, though how being stuck in a laundry room figures into the equation is anyone's guess.

The song was originally released on *No Alternative*, a compilation album benefiting different AIDS organizations. But it appeared as a "hidden" track, and thus was not featured in the track listing. Nirvana's participation, and the song's title, were revealed in the album's promotional material.

I Hate Myself And Want To Die

UK, US Geffen. Recorded 13–26 February 1993. Originally released on *The Beavis and Butt-head Experience*, UK 22 November 1993, US 23 November 1993.

Nirvana's contribution was the lead-off track on this compilation "hosted" by the MTV cartoon characters (who themselves cover "I Got You Babe" in a duet with Cher). The song's title had at one point been considered for the title of *In Utero* – as a joke, Cobain always insisted. Instead, it wound up as the title for this number, which had no title when it was originally recorded (on tape boxes from the session, it was identified by the drawing of a fish). Certainly that explains the lack of any real tie between the title and the actual song. The music is an upbeat, friendly thrash-along, while the nonsense lyrics touch on some favourite Cobain subjects, including illness; during the instrumental break, he also mumbles his way through one of National Lampoon humorist Jack Handey's satiric "Deep Thoughts". In keeping with most tracks post-*Nevermind* that were solely B-sides or given to compilations, "I Hate Myself..." was never performed live.

Pay To Play

US DGC. Recorded 2–6 April 1990. Originally released on *DGC Rarities Vol. 1*, 5 July 1994.

Anxious to not be seen as cashing in on a tragedy, DGC took pains to point out that this release was on the label's schedule well before Cobain's death. "Pay To Play" was the fifth song to be released from the April 1990 Smart Studios sessions (when it was re-recorded for *Nevermind*, it became "Stay Away"). The arrangement of the two songs is the same, though the lyrics are different; and the drumming isn't as powerful on this version. The original title, referring to the practice of clubs making bands buy tickets for their own shows, which they were then responsible for selling, comes across as a more generalized gripe, as opposed to "Stay Away", which, coupled with Cobain's more frenzied screaming, is a more personal cry of anguish. But until the release of *With The Lights Out*, "Pay To Play" offered a rare chance to listen to a Nirvana song in different stages of development. The track listing for the album incorrectly lists the recording date of the song as being August 1990.

Radio Friendly Unit Shifter

US Epic. Recorded 18 February 1994. Released on *Home Alive: The Art Of Self Defense*, 20 February 1996.

Nirvana contributed a live recording of "Radio Friendly Unit Shifter" from a show in Grenoble, France, on their final European tour. It's a solid performance of the song used to open all of their shows that year. Proceeds from this release benefited the Seattle organization Home Alive, a group formed in the wake of the murder of Gits lead singer Mia Zapata.

Rape Me

US Dreamworks. Recorded 25 September 1993. Released on *SNL 25: Saturday Night Live: The Musical Performances, Volume 2*, 21 September 1999.

One year after being denied permission to perform the song on MTV, Nirvana found another more receptive media outlet on NBC's long-running comedy programme. It was the band's second (and final) appearance on *SNL*, and marked the debut of Pat Smear on guitar. It's a strong performance that finds Cobain in good voice; just listen to him hold that final note.

25 Essential Nirvana songs

This section looks at the songs we consider to be the "core catalogue" of Nirvana's releases. Covering all the band's singles and key album tracks, songs are listed in the order they were released.

1. Love Buzz

Robby Van Leeuwen; recorded 11 & 30 June, 16 July 1988; original mix available on a single, remix on *Bleach*.

Though the very first Nirvana song released to the public was a cover, it nonetheless anticipated the band's future style in many ways. For despite their punk/metal influences, the key to their ultimate success was the appreciation for a solid pop hook, something intrinsic to all of Nirvana's best material.

Novoselic's insinuating, Eastern-flavoured bass line kicks off the song and provides a sturdy framework for Cobain's antics, both vocally and on guitar. And it's Cobain's performance that sells the song. It was Novoselic who'd brought the track to his attention, but Cobain never bothered learning more than the first verse and chorus (indeed, in early performances, he didn't make it beyond the first line of the first verse). Nor did he need to: his slurring vocal commands attention, in part because you can sense the underlying power, which he finally unleashes on the last word of the chorus, screaming out "Buzz!" with

a vengeance. Cobain's drony guitar regularly spirals off into cascading riffs, and he used the song's instrumental break for more guitar tomfoolery. Nothing along the lines of the pompous solos you might hear in heavy metal, though; Cobain's tendency was to coax as much squalling feedback as he could out of his instrument – and in a live setting during the early years, this often meant playing his guitar on his back or while crowd surfing. On the single version, another sound collage Cobain created can just about be heard during the instrumental break.

The payoff comes at the song's conclusion, when guitar, bass and drums all hammer away in unison, creating a rising tension that bursts into sudden release on the final note. It's rare for a band to exude such confidence on a first single and Nirvana were just getting started.

2. Floyd The Barber

Kurt Cobain; recorded 23 January 1988; available on *Bleach*.

Rather than over-analyse his lyrics, Cobain was prone to dismiss them as meaningless, something his impenetrable vocal delivery seemed to emphasize. Yet even his early songs often had clear narratives, and "Floyd" was particularly straightforward, displaying a decided – if dark – sense of humour toward its subject matter.

The "Floyd" of the title refers to the character Floyd Lawson, from *The Andy Griffith Show*, a 1960s American sitcom set in the fictional town of Mayberry, North Carolina. Cobain reworks the idyllic setting into something far more sinister, and an innocent trip to Floyd's barber shop becomes a nightmare straight out of Sweeney Todd, with the song's narrator lashed to the chair, blindfolded with a hot towel, "shaved" and "shamed" by the town's residents.

After a brief wail of guitar, the opening thudding beats set an ominous tone, which becomes increasingly fraught. Cobain's agonized vocal is too energized to fall into despair, adding a masochistic touch to the proceedings. The song's ending sounds a despondent note: the guitar and bass drop out in turn, leaving the drums to pound out the final beats. Yet there's also something mischievous about the idea of turning the mom-and-apple-pie loving residents of Mayberry into a gang of murderous souls.

3. About A Girl

Kurt Cobain; recorded 24 & 29–31 December 1988, 14 & 24 January 1989; available on *Bleach*.

"About A Girl" struck a mellower note in contrast to the more aggressive material on *Bleach*, though the band's pop leanings were already clearly in evidence on tracks like "Love Buzz" and "Spank Thru". The song's inspiration was two-fold, drawing on a comment by Cobain's girlfriend that he hadn't written a song about her, and the occasional arguments the two had about his reluctance to get a job. Not surprisingly, the resulting song was tinged with animosity. Nothing in the Nirvana catalogue could be considered a straightforward love song by any stretch of the imagination; instead, relationships are depicted as a manipulative battle of wills, with a dependency on the loved one something both desired and feared. "About A Girl", with its caustic chorus that has Cobain blithely singing about taking advantage while being hung out to dry, is the first such example.

But these spiteful sentiments weren't immediately apparent, given that Cobain created an appealingly tuneful musical setting for the lyrics, replacing the bludgeoning force of *Bleach*'s other tracks with a quietly strummed guitar and an equally restrained backing from Novoselic and Channing. Cobain later claimed to have listened to *Meet The Beatles!* for hours before composing the song, though its melancholy feel is more reminiscent of the *Rubber Soul/Revolver* period, blending Paul McCartney's melodicism with John Lennon's verbal bite. The instrumental break bumps up the energy a notch, a tambourine adds a playful touch, and, in the best pop song tradition, the track clocks in at under three minutes. But it's the haunting, wistful quality that dominates, something that was even more apparent in Nirvana's *Unplugged* performance.

4. School

Kurt Cobain; recorded 24 & 29–31 December 1988, 14 & 24 January 1989; available on *Bleach*.

The heart of "School" is a guitar line that Novoselic joked was such a trademark "Seattle Sound" riff it verged on cliché. Undeterred, the band used the riff as a starting point, crafting an energetic thrasher whose underlying playfulness is irresistible. For lyrical inspiration, Cobain turned to the insularity of Seattle's music scene, and his disillusionment at finding that the cliquish environment he'd faced in high school was replicated in adult life. Even more impressively, he summed up the situation in a mere fifteen words.

The track opens with a rising guitar whine that finally explodes into the main riff, with some exceptionally propulsive pounding by Channing leading into the chorus, as Cobain shrieks "No recess!" as if his life depended on it. In a neat trick, his voice drops to a lower register during the bridge, before vaulting back into the stratosphere, a technique that would be put to good use in future Nirvana songs. And like "In Bloom", the song's in-joke was even more apparent in live performance; though ostensibly a put-down of Seattle scenesters – and by extension anyone who likes to categorize and pigeonhole people – those very same folks would mosh with abandon when the song was played, blissfully unaware that the joke was on them.

5. Blew

Kurt Cobain; recorded 24 & 29–31 December 1988, 14 & 24 January 1989; available on *Bleach*.

The first known performance of "Blew" was on 19 March 1988 – and six years later it was still in the band's set list, the penultimate track at their very last show on 1 March 1994, an indication of just how attached they were to the song. Ironically, while it most frequently closed the band's sets, it's the opening track on *Bleach*, setting the stage for much of what follows.

After four opening bars of bass playing the main riff, the full band kicks in, followed by Cobain's surprisingly tentative beginning, "If you wouldn't mind...", a request that could be read as shy, sarcastic or both. The minimalist lyrics (one verse repeated twice, the chorus repeated three times, a closing line repeated four times) don't reveal much beyond a sense of claustrophobia. It's also the first Nirvana song to use the word "shame", which would crop up in later songs, as would the themes of insecurity, inadequacy and defeat.

But if the song conveys the feeling of being trapped, it also hints at escape. After drawling his way through the first verse, Cobain's voice leaps an octave when he gets to the chorus (dragging out "sha-a-a-me") and maintains the intensity by keeping his voice in the upper register for the rest of the song. The final line, telling the listener they "could" do anything, is another tentative suggestion to match the song's first line, an expression of desire from someone lacking the confidence to make a decisive move – though it can also be seen as a call to consider the wide range of one's own potential.

6. Been A Son

Kurt Cobain; recorded September 1989, available on *Blew*; radio version recorded 9 November 1991, available on *Incesticide*.

The jump between the heaviness of *Bleach* and the hard-rock/pop sheen of *Nevermind* isn't as surprising if you look at the songs Nirvana released between those two albums. And if Cobain submerged his pop tendencies on *Bleach*, they burst into full flower on this song. The lyric addresses the societal preference for boys over girls (said to be a reflection of Don Cobain's own feelings). But given the pressure Cobain himself felt from his father and step-father to engage in manly pursuits like sports and hunting, coupled with his disdain for stereotypical macho behaviour, it's possible he saw a reflection of himself in the lyric – from "be a man" to "been a son".

Musically, there's a buoyancy to the track surpassing everything the band had done previously (and, in typical Nirvana fashion, at odds with the more cynical lyric). The pop quotient is further pushed by Cobain's harmonies, which producer Steve Fisk proudly noted were "*Rubber Soul*, John Lennon kind of harmonies". The version the band recorded at a BBC radio session just over two years later is even poppier: taken at a faster clip, with a smoother instrumental break in contrast to the somewhat gnarly bass solo in the studio

version (which Novoselic had never liked), and with a more abrupt ending as opposed to the studio version's slow fade, it's a much tighter, and better performance.

7. Sliver

Kurt Cobain; recorded 11 & 24 July 1990; available on *Incesticide*.

"Sliver" was one of Cobain's most transparently autobiographical songs and proved to be one of the easiest to record; the basic track was laid down in an hour on the first day, with Cobain recording his vocals during the second session.

The song begins in a deceptively low-key fashion, with a simple bass line. Then Cobain's drawling vocal comes in, recounting an evening when he was left at his grandparents while his parents went out. But the child in the song doesn't want to be left behind, and the whine of the guitar going into the first chorus echoes his constant lament of wanting to go home. Musically, the song stays on the bright side, so the boy's feelings of abandonment aren't particularly angst-ridden. But in spite of the brisk pace (aided by the fact that the song has no bridge), the song is also streaked with sadness, elements that work to create an underlying tension. The sense of urgency is further heightened when Cobain's voice goes up an octave on the third verse, and is thrown into greater relief on the final verse, when the instrumentation is kept at a subdued level, making his vocal sound even louder. Cobain tops it off by going into the final chorus with a rising scream.

In contrast to other Nirvana songs that provoked debate about what they "really" meant, "Sliver" had an appealing simplicity and boosted the band's profile by being so accessible.

8. Dive

Kurt Cobain; recorded 2–6 April 1990; available on *Incesticide*.

If this version of "Dive" hadn't appeared as the B-side of the "Sliver" single, it might well have been re-recorded for *Nevermind*, as half of the songs recorded with Butch Vig in April 1990 were. It clearly points the way to *Nevermind*, with its fusion of punk, metal and pop, and was one of the harder tracks recorded during the Vig sessions.

Had the band played up the heavier side of the song, it also wouldn't have been out of place on *Bleach*. But the underlying pop melodicism gave the song a lightness that helped make it a crowd favourite. Lyrically, too, the song has a braggadocio missing from most other Nirvana songs, though the tongue-in-cheek sarcasm harkens back to earlier numbers like "Spank Thru". An ostensible plea to a would-be lover, the force of the chorus, with its demand for total immersion, exudes the kind of attitude that says "if I'm not picked, it's your loss", with Cobain singing more to please himself than any partner by that point. The song also varies from Nirvana's trademark soft verse/loud chorus pattern: after a typically brooding bass intro, it kicks into high gear and stays there throughout.

9. Aneurysm

Kurt Cobain; recorded 1 January 1991; available on *With The Lights Out*.

Cobain's fascination with bodily functions and medical conditions frequently expressed itself in both his songwriting and his visual art. Here, the title refers to a swelling in a blood vessel, usually the arteries around the heart or brain, which, if it bursts, can result in death. But Cobain's song is more of an invitation to come over and party, though ultimately with a darker subtext.

Unusually for Nirvana, the song begins with a lengthy guitar intro that lasts nearly a minute and a half, with a rising guitar line building to a descending riff repeated eight times, creating a whiplash effect. It was Dave Grohl's first studio session with the group and his powerful drumming takes on a life of its own. The lyrics are nearly superfluous, especially as they consist of a single verse and chorus.

On the surface, the song's lyrical twists are humorous, an encouragement to dance until you "have a fit". But Cobain had just started using heroin, and the lyrics seem to hint at this, particularly in the final line about "pumping straight to my heart". That it's a woman who's delivering "it" to the singer's heart speaks to a romance, but the fact that Cobain frequently called the drug "heroine" in his diaries suggests another reading, too.

The studio version of the track, which first appeared on the B-side of the "Smells Like Teen Spirit" single, features a spectacularly bloodcurdling scream from Cobain. The band recorded a less powerful version for BBC radio that ended up on *Incesticide*.

10. Even In His Youth

Kurt Cobain; recorded 1 January 1991; available on "Smells Like Teen Spirit" single, *Hormoaning* EP.

The autobiographical elements of this song are starkly apparent: a taut depiction of an inadequate son who's a disappointment to his father, his family and, ultimately, himself. And as if to emphasize the despair of the situation, the first line in each stanza of the verse is repeated three times.

Nirvana first demoed the song in September 1989 with Steve Fisk. At that time it had a frantic, caterwauling intro, which was cut and later appeared in "Endless, Nameless", and the chorus and instrumental break had yet to be fully worked out. When the band recorded it again with Craig Montgomery, they tightened up the arrangement, giving the song more of an emotional punch. Grohl's drumming is also more imaginative than in the original demo. The instrumental break echoes the repetition in the verses, with Cobain simply playing a variation on the same riff eight times. Nor does the lyric offer any hope of redemption. After quoting from a child's prayer ("If I die before I wake"), the wish to not come back "a slave" has become a wish to not come back at all the last time the chorus is sung. And the "yeah, yeah"s of the song's final section are heavy with resignation. Not untypically for Nirvana, though, the energetic musical backing belies the lyrics' mood of despair.

Perhaps the song hit too close to the emotional bone even for Cobain, for it was performed live only in 1989 – which makes it all the more interesting that the song was revived during the January 1991 session.

11. Smells Like Teen Spirit

Kurt Cobain, Dave Grohl, Krist Novoselic; recorded May–June 1991; available on *Nevermind*.

"Smells Like Teen Spirit" is, of course, the definitive Nirvana song, a song so linked with their legend that it figures in even the briefest reference to the group. It's now possible to hear this landmark song in the process of evolution.

The demo of the first known performance of the song appears on *With The Lights Out* and shows the musical arrangement to be fairly well worked out, even at that stage of recording, the chief difference being the length of the chorus (and with the exception of three lines, the lyrics had yet to be finalized). The final version of the song epitomized the Nirvana formula, with the soft/loud, push/pull dynamic evident from the very beginning: four bars of a single guitar strumming the main riff, eight bars of the whole band crashing in, then right back to four bars of more restrained playing as the intro leads into the verse. Cobain used the same effect with his vocal, sounding jaded, almost disinterested, in the verse, in sharp contrast to the chorus, when his voice rises to a roaring scream. It's a dichotomy evident in the lyrics as well, which convey a weary sense of defeat in the verses, the song's second line even noting "It's fun to lose". Conversely, the chorus is almost playful in its demand "Entertain us!", followed by lines juxtaposing various nonsense words. And linking the verse and chorus is another instance of word play, with Cobain alternating between the words "hello" and "how low".

Cobain was always reluctant to ascribe any meanings to his songs ("It's your crossword puzzle," he told one interviewer), but he did concede "Teen Spirit" in part reflected his feelings about his generation's apathy. Yet the defeatist lyrics imply that it's not worth making the effort anyway. Cobain even critiques his own inability to cope in the second verse, when he notes that he's worst at what he does best, a line that could serve as his epitaph (the rest of the verse neatly encapsulating the band's own story). The exploration of contradictions and conflicts are root themes of much of Cobain's songwriting, and in "Teen Spirit" they're left unresolved, shrugged off with a resigned "whatever, never mind". But the force with which Cobain screams "a denial" nine times at the song's conclusion – alternately a cry of frustration and a victorious shout of release – makes the case that ultimately it's important to rage about *something*.

The song's lyrical ambiguity was another factor in its wide appeal: with no clear message, it was possible for listeners to read anything into it they wanted. Musically, the song is incredibly potent, even seductive, in the way it draws the listener in. Though the intro suggests a much louder song is going to follow, the musical backing immediately drops

to a minimal level during the verse, the guitar playing a two-note refrain, the bass playing four notes, and the drums a simple beat. The intensity rises during the "hello/how low" section, the guitar playing with more urgency, then the drums paving the way for the sudden eruption into the chorus. Then it's right back to the minimal instrumentation of the verse again. The building of tension throughout the song makes the final chorus especially cathartic, wringing out every last drop of emotion in a thoroughly satisfying manner.

12. In Bloom

Kurt Cobain; recorded May–June 1991; available on *Nevermind*.

If "Teen Spirit" had been a broad swipe at generational indifference, "In Bloom" had a more direct target – the band's own audience.

As in "Teen Spirit", the crunching intro gives way to a minimalist instrumental backing in the verse, with only the bass and drums playing at first, the guitar coming in toward the end, followed by a series of rapid-fire drumbeats and Cobain's "He-e-e-e-y!" leading into the chorus. On introducing the song at one show in 1990, Cobain explained, "It's about reproduction", and the verses do touch on the fecundity of nature. But the chorus is a none too subtle taunt aimed at the masses who will follow anything with a good beat; the person who sings along to the pretty songs, but "knows not what it means", a phrasing Cobain used in early drafts of the song before opting for a less formal tone. He also gives his pen portrait an extra sting by making the ignorant fan a gun-totin' redneck. Most subversive of all, the jab is paired to the kind of instantly catchy melody that you can't help singing along with, rather proving Cobain's point. The song's inspiration has long been said to be Cobain's friend Dylan Carlson, but Carlson hasn't commented on the matter.

Nirvana first recorded the song in 1990, and it was chosen for their first video, done for Sub Pop. That recording is very close to the *Nevermind* version, the biggest difference being Grohl's contribution; in his hands, the drums become as melodic as any sound instrument, and his harmonies on the chorus add further colour to the song. Ironically, though written well before the release of *Nevermind*, "In Bloom" foreshadowed the type of arena rock audience Nirvana would ultimately attract.

13. Come As You Are

Kurt Cobain; recorded May–June 1991; available on *Nevermind*.

"Come As You Are" is one of the more laid-back Nirvana songs, subdued to the point of being languid. The mood is immediately set by the watery sound of Cobain's guitar (achieved through the use of an Electro-Harmonix Small Clone), giving the song a dreamy feel throughout.

The song also has an unusual structure, as it doesn't really have a chorus, unless you count the last word of the two verses, "memory", which Cobain stretches out to "memor-i-a".

It also catches Cobain in a remarkably non-judgemental frame of mind, welcoming all-comers no matter their affiliation. Not that this is expressed directly aside from the title; rather, the idea is conveyed through a clever pairing of opposites ("mud"/"bleach") and transitions ("come as you are/were"). The first known demo (available on the compilation *Sliver*) has only one verse, which largely matches the first verse in the final version of the song; it's the final version that lyrically expands the all-inclusive aspect of the song. Cobain also wears his vulnerability on his sleeve, as revealed by his repeated insistence that he's unarmed.

There's still a touch of sharpness; Cobain never wrote a song without some sort of edge. Though you can ostensibly come as you are (or were), he adds a qualifying note by suggesting you can also come as "I want you to be"; his acceptance has its limitations after all. Like all of Nirvana's best work, a song's sentiments are never entirely what they seem on the surface.

14. Lithium

Kurt Cobain; recorded May–June 1991; available on *Nevermind*.

"Lithium" combines a playful attitude with a twisted – some might say sinister – sensibility, matched with one of the most pop-friendly melodies Nirvana ever produced. The title refers to the drug used to treat bipolar disorder and, indeed, the opening lines of the song allude to schizophrenia. "People who are secluded for so long go insane," Cobain said in the press release for *Nevermind*, "and as a last resort they often use religion to keep alive." To *Musician*, Cobain also said the song drew in part on his memories of break-ups and bad relationships, "feeling that death void that the person in the song is feeling – very lonely, sick".

You might expect a song depicting someone on the verge of a breakdown to be laced with despair. But Cobain makes the thought of straddling the thin line between sanity and insanity sound almost joyous, especially when the lazy, carefree quality of the verses surges into the celebratory roar of the chorus, itself nothing more than a sustained series of "Yeah!"s. It's the kind of chorus that inspires fist pumping and jumping up and down in unison, though it also leads to a disturbing litany the second and third time the chorus is sung, Cobain alternately affirming "I like it/miss you/love you/kill you", perhaps a suggestion that insanity ultimately wins this balancing act.

The song was another *Nevermind* track first recorded with Butch Vig in April 1990, a version that mirrors the final one in most respects. The chorus has a decidedly rawer feel in the earlier version, while Novoselic recalls he changed his bass part for the later version. It also has a fade-out ending, unusual in a Nirvana song. But the final track is in a lower key, which gives the verses a more wistful feel, features a more powerful drum performance by Grohl, and instead of a fade-out, comes to a crashing halt that hangs suspended in the air, the fate of the song's protagonist left unresolved.

15. Polly

Kurt Cobain; recorded 2–6 April, 1990; available on *Nevermind*.

Nirvana first recorded "Polly" in September 1989 with producer Steve Fisk. At that point, they took the song at an upbeat tempo, similar to the way they'd record it for the BBC the following month (though the Fisk version featured heavier drums). In November 1991, at another BBC session, they'd record an even faster version they jokingly called "(New Wave) Polly".

But the definitive version of the song was recorded in April 1990 during the band's first session with Butch Vig, a version deemed so effective it was later used on *Nevermind* without being re-recorded. This version was the one most like Cobain's original home demo of the song, which had him singing to his own acoustic guitar accompaniment, a restrained treatment that stood in stark relief to the dramatic qualities of the narrative. Cobain based his song on a real-life incident, the abduction and rape of a fourteen-year-old girl on her way home from a concert in Tacoma. Interestingly, for a writer who generally lampooned macho men and their redneck attitudes in his songs, Cobain wrote from the perspective of the attacker, creating a devastating portrait of a soul devoid of empathy. Instead of an obvious caricature, Cobain's character study benefits from subtlety, with the dispassionate narration of the rapist casting his crime as something committed out of mere boredom, making the scenario even more horrifying. And contrary to Vig's belief that Cobain's singing of the line "Polly said" before the final verse was an error, live recordings of shows before the session reveal that he had got into the habit of adding this line to the song already.

Cobain's cool portrayal was too unnerving for some, and he found himself having to explain to more than one interviewer that just because a song was written in the first person, it didn't necessarily mean he was referring to himself. It was ironic that one of Nirvana's most powerful songs would be one of their quietest.

16. Drain You

Kurt Cobain; recorded May–June 1991; available on Nevermind.

Cobain cited this as one of his favourite songs, better than "Teen Spirit", and it was one he never got tired of playing live (indeed, on their final tours, Nirvana ended up playing it more frequently than "Teen Spirit").

"Drain You" is one of two songs on *Nevermind* with a "cold" opening, where the vocals begin at the start of the song ("On A Plain" is the other) and it's the most invigorating slice of power pop on the album. It's also a love song, but as usual the focus is less on the bliss of being in love and more on how dependency and submission are intrinsic to relationships. This is frighteningly apparent in the first verse, with the baby/lover who not only demands to be the centre of their partner's universe, but also plans to exercise their "duty"

in draining them fully. Yet in comparison to the bitterness expressed in "About A Girl" and "Heart-Shaped Box", "Drain You" is decidedly more light-hearted, largely due to the upbeat nature of the music.

This was even truer of the demo, recorded with Grohl and Dale Crover in San Francisco in April 1991, when Cobain and Grohl were on the way to LA to record *Nevermind*. At that stage, Cobain wasn't even sure he wanted Nirvana to record the song, but Crover's drum part (Grohl played bass) gave the song a new direction. The song's most glorious moment comes at the end of the extended instrumental break. Instead of playing a guitar solo, Cobain lets Grohl's drumming hold sway, occasionally breaking in with short guitar riffs, while making odd vocal squeaks that Vig drops in variously in the right or left channels. Then Cobain's guitar comes in again, followed by a titanic scream, Grohl pounding the drums to breaking point, driving the energy upwards, until with a last gasp of relief the band charges back into the song. You won't find such free-spirited exaltation anywhere else on the album.

17. Something In The Way

Kurt Cobain; recorded May–June 1991; available on Nevermind.

Even for Nirvana, "Something In The Way" is an exceptionally bleak song, distilling a lifetime's worth of alienation into nine lines. Though the first line refers to the occasional night Cobain spent sleeping under bridges, the broader theme is one of complete and utter abandonment.

Cobain told Michael Azerrad he built up the drama of the scenario into a "fantasy". But for someone who'd spent most of his teen years being shuttled between relatives, crashing with friends, and at times having no proper home at all, Cobain's personal experience of loss and desolation was all too real.

Successfully capturing the feel of the song in the studio proved to be tricky. A band arrangement didn't work, so Cobain came into the control room, sat on the couch, and sang the song to Vig, while playing the same guitar he'd used to record "Polly". Vig immediately realized the intimate sound was just what the song required, and recorded Cobain on the spot, turning off the phones, air conditioner, and anything else that might make any noise. Cobain's final vocal is so exposed, it sounds as if he's sitting right next to you, and Novoselic and Grohl had to work hard to keep from eroding the song's delicacy when they recorded their parts. A cello line during the chorus adds to the haunting mood. But it's Cobain's vocal that's most impressive here, a heart-rending performance that's bereft of hope, the concluding "yeah, yeah"s delivered with a weary sigh.

18. Scentless Apprentice

Kurt Cobain, Dave Grohl, Krist Novoselic; recorded 13–26 February 1993; available on *In Utero*.

This song is one of the few credited to all three members of the band, and also one of the most punishing. Grohl came up with the song's main riff, which the band jammed on for a while,

Cobain eventually coming up with an ascending riff to match it (the first rehearsal of the song can be found on *With The Lights Out*).

In interviews, Cobain spoke enthusiastically about the song being written in a collaborative fashion. But though he acknowledged its lyrical inspiration, he never made clear whether he'd had the idea already in mind, or if it arrived after the music had been conceived. He drew on the storyline of Patrick Süskind's best-selling novel *Perfume: The Story of a Murderer*, the tale of a perfumer's apprentice in eighteenth-century France, whose acute sense of smell leads him to commit murder in an attempt to capture the scent of virgin women.

While the verses reference the book's plot, the emotional heart of the song lies in its chorus. The rage of the song burns at a high level of intensity throughout, but Cobain manages to push himself to the limit as the verses rise to the chorus and his bloodcurdling screams come out on top in a blast of pure, unmitigated fury. Unlike the angry cry that ends "Teen Spirit", though, the "Go away" of "Scentless Apprentice" is more of a plea, tinged with fear and desperation. The band's playing is also exceptionally brutal, helping to make this one of Nirvana's most compelling songs.

19. Heart-Shaped Box

Kurt Cobain; recorded 13–26 February 1993; available on *In Utero*.

"Heart-Shaped Box" is one of Nirvana's most beautifully crafted songs, and certainly the most evocative. A slow, descending guitar line introduces the song and repeats itself throughout the verses, rising to meet the passion of the chorus – the Nirvana formula, in fact, but with a noticeable poignancy that's missing from other examples like "Teen Spirit" or "Lithium". This is primarily due to the strength of the song's lyrics. Cobain claimed his initial inspiration was "little kids with cancer", but the lyrics instead examine a relationship with an unsettling mix of devotion and sarcasm. Typically, the strong desire for intimacy (a wish to "eat your cancer") is matched by the dread of what commitment might bring – in this instance being ensnared by such symbols of female entrapment as "meat-eating orchids" and "umbilical noose". In the song's original title, the "box" was a coffin, suggesting an even greater degree of suffocation.

Yet far from bemoaning his enslavement, Cobain ridicules his submissiveness in the chorus, dismissing the proffered "priceless advice" with a withering snarl, then ramming the point home by repeating the phrase four times at the song's conclusion, as Grohl's drums create a driving thunderstorm underneath. As a result, the song is constantly turning back in on itself, creating an inner tension that never attains full release, ending abruptly with a squall of feedback.

20. Rape Me

Kurt Cobain; recorded 13–26 February 1993; available on *In Utero*.

The intro of "Rape Me" mirrors that of "Teen Spirit", which was written around the same time. It stands as one of Nirvana's most disquieting songs, seeming to invite abuse. Yet the force of Cobain's vocals makes the song stand as a defiant indictment of such an assault.

Cobain was one of the few major rock stars to speak openly about the atrocity of rape, an attitude that stood out within a culture many see as celebrating the objectification, if not outright abuse, of women. He not only denounced the act itself (calling it "one of the most terrible crimes on earth"), he also felt that one of the most effective ways of combating it was to change men's attitudes, as he told *NME* in 1991: "What really needs to be done is teaching men not to rape. Go to the source and start there." As such he understood how powerful it would be to hear a man singing a song entitled "Rape Me".

When Nirvana first began performing the song in June 1991, the bridge had no lyrics. By the time the band recorded the song, Cobain had added four lines that attacked the media harassment he felt he'd suffered, giving the song a metaphorical as well as literal meaning. As he'd had to explain that despite the first-person perspective of "Polly" he hadn't been referring to himself, so he had to explain that "Rape Me" was not meant to advocate assault, insisting to *Rolling Stone* "I was trying to write a song that supported women". One would think that the fury of Cobain's performance, particularly his anguished cries at the song's end, when he screams "Rape me!" nine times, might have been sufficient to make that point.

21. Dumb

Kurt Cobain; recorded 13–26 February 1993; available on *In Utero*.

Much as he claimed to be an outsider, there was a part of Cobain that wished to fit in – or was at least a bit envious of those who could do so. "Dumb" has one of the most beguiling melodies in Nirvana's catalogue, but the song's underlying theme – ignorance is bliss – gives it a dark shading.

Though the instrumentation isn't as minimal as on "Polly" or "Something In The Way", it does remain discreetly in the background, the better to highlight Cobain's world-weary vocal. As he sings of his ability to pretend to be like everyone else, or to lose himself in a druggy haze (in one of the few Nirvana songs to have an explicit drug reference), Cobain sinks ever deeper into apathy; it's the sound of someone who's given up, but is past caring about it. Yet the song never spirals down into abject gloom. Cobain's skill as a songwriter is such that what could have become a morose rumination on the meaninglessness of existence instead has something of a light feel due to both the heart-tugging pull of the melody, and lyrics that simply shrug off disappointment instead of wallowing in it.

22. Pennyroyal Tea

Kurt Cobain; recorded 13–26 February 1993; available on *In Utero*.

The herb pennyroyal is said to induce abortion; among its more benign uses, as a tea it can calm an upset stomach. Cobain may have disputed pennyroyal's abortifacient qualities in his journal, but as a metaphor it works nicely in the song, suggesting desire for a spiritual, as much as a physical, cleansing, a plea to wash away one's inner demons.

The song is replete with references to all manner of ailments, effectively weighing the singer down with the heavy burden of illness. And unlike other songs that utilize the Nirvana quiet verse/loud chorus formula, Cobain sounds just as tired during the choruses as he does in the verses. Instead of the explosiveness of the chorus bringing its usual sense of release and relief, the singer remains mired in disaffection, as the ensuing rush of the music threatens to bury him beneath a wall of sound. It's a state of mind perfectly captured in the phrase "anaemic royalty" – feeling weak in spite of being seen as powerful. The sense of defeat also comes through strongly in the song's lumbering conclusion, the band playing more and more slowly, Cobain moaning half-heartedly, until everything comes to a halt, as if collapsing with exhaustion.

Cobain wasn't happy with how the song came out, telling *Rolling Stone* he wanted to re-record or remix it, as "that's a strong song, a hit single". Scott Litt did remix the song, a version that's available on the *Nirvana* compilation. It does have a cleaner sound, with Cobain's harmonies brought out more in the chorus, though his final groans are more buried in the mix.

23. All Apologies

Kurt Cobain; recorded 13–26 February 1993; available on *In Utero*.

Cobain recognized the universal pull of this song, dubbing it an "alternateen anthem" in his journal, and its melodic quality was evidenced in its early title, "La La La". The song is deceptively simple, beginning with a single melodic line that's played throughout most of the song, creating a hypnotic effect; it's the kind of strong hook that lodges in your head on first hearing it. A demo of the song, recorded in January 1991, has an even lighter, jaunty pop quality.

But the song's inherent tunefulness couldn't mask the mournful tone of the lyric. Despite Cobain's insistence that the song was meant to be sarcastic, his lyrics are wracked with guilt. Accompanying the declarations that it's all his fault and he'll rightfully assume the blame is a nod to the outsider-looking-in theme of "Dumb", in his admiration of those who can be "easily amused", as well as a final sense of giving up in his admission that he has nothing left to say and nothing more to write. So pervasive is the sense of futility that some critics later saw the song as being akin to a suicide note. That he chose to rhyme "married" with "buried" also raised eyebrows, though Cobain would insist he'd written the lines before he was married.

"All Apologies" has an undeniably elegiac quality, leading to its grand closing, a line that alternately ends "all we are" and "all we all are", a mantra-like phrase that constantly cycles back in on itself. As if not wanting to let the moment go, the song's outro is unusually long for a Nirvana song, running for over a minute and a half, initially as a fuzzy wash of sound, the instrumental backing gradually becoming less intense, until the final, predominant sound is that of Cobain's plaintive vocals.

24. Where Did You Sleep Last Night

Traditional, arranged by]; recorded 18 November 1993; available on *MTV Unplugged In New York*

Nirvana's performance of this nineteenth-century folk song on *MTV Unplugged* was one of the most extraordinary moments in the band's career. Cobain and Novoselic had previously played on Mark Lanegan's version, but with this performance the band made the song their own.

Though the song's origins date back to the 1870s, it was popularized by blues musician Huddie "Leadbelly" Ledbetter, who first recorded the song in 1944 (and would go on to re-record it numerous times). It's also been recorded by hundreds of artists as varied as the Grateful Dead, Marianne Faithfull, Link Wray and Dolly Parton, and is variously known as "Black Girl" and "In The Pines".

In Nirvana's hands, this lament about a man's unfaithful partner starts out slow, then steadily rises in power until it's burning with a white-hot intensity. The number opens with Cobain's forceful guitar playing, the other instruments (including cello) gradually joining in, creating

The Music

a swirling maelstrom of sound by the time it reaches the instrumental break. Then, heightening the tension, the instruments drop out again, save for Cobain's guitar, played so quietly it's as if he's singing a capella. Just as suddenly, the instruments come back in full force, and Cobain's voice jumps an octave for the rest of the song, delivering an absolutely scalding vocal, as if the song's being drawn out from the very depths of his soul. By the time he reaches the last line, he's not even singing complete sentences any more, merely hitting on key words – "the pines... sun... shine..." – until he gets to "shiver", dragging the word out and leaving it hanging suspended in mid-air as he pauses, takes a breath, and pushes out the last four words of the song in a tortured gasp. It's a masterful performance, whether you're watching the show or listening to the recording.

25. You Know You're Right

Kurt Cobain; recorded 30 January 1994; available on *Nirvana*.

"You Know You're Right" was not only the last Nirvana song ever recorded, it was also one of the last songs Cobain wrote. At the beginning of his career, Cobain had regularly made demos, but after the completion of *In Utero*, he appears to have only made a few. A demo for this song was included on *With The Lights Out*, with the notation that it was recorded in 1994; it would be interesting to know if it was done before or after the January recording session, as it has completely different lyrics to the final version.

In its final recording it has the softest beginning of any Nirvana song, with Cobain lightly plucking his guitar strings so they sound like chimes. For all his talk during the fall of 1993 of taking Nirvana in another direction musically, "You Know You're Right" adheres to the band's usual quiet/loud dynamic. After the opening "chimes", the verse comes in at a low boil, gradually building into a mighty chorus.

Lyrically, the song conveys a strong sense of loss, of giving up on any hope of reconciliation, and a need to leave behind all the turmoil and conflict of the past. Precisely what that turmoil and conflict is, isn't specified, beyond a two-line mention of a distant, self-centred woman in the second verse. Certainly one can read signs of foreboding in the lyric, but the overwhelmingly sad and downbeat mood is hardly unusual in a Nirvana song.

As in "Heart-Shaped Box", there's a heavy dose of sarcasm, as Cobain sardonically notes things are "so swell" before the chorus, a long, drawn-out cry of "hey" that leads to an equally mocking repetition of the song's title. There's no bridge or instrumental break; after the second chorus, Cobain simply repeats the song's title above the crash of the music (which here has the same touch of Eastern flavour found in "Love Buzz" and "Token Eastern Song"), and in a typical piece of word play alternates between singing "you're right" and "your rights". As the song ends, the band is playing as quietly as they were at the beginning, coming to a stop with a final, understated drumbeat – and bringing Nirvana's recording career to a close not with a bang but with a whisper.

Solo music

Of the three main members of Nirvana, Dave Grohl has had the most active recording career; since 1987, he's appeared on at least one record a year, both his own releases and as a guest artist. His post-Nirvana band, Foo Fighters, has also enjoyed great commercial success. In comparison, Krist Novoselic has released few records, in part because of his increasing involvement in politics. And for all his comments about how much he wanted to pursue different musical directions, Kurt Cobain didn't often collaborate with anyone outside of Nirvana.

Kurt Cobain

Kurt Cobain released no solo albums and made only made a handful of guest appearances on other records. In his first guest spot he played guitar on a single by Olympia band The Go Team, "Scratch It Out"/"Bikini Twilight", released in July 1989 on K Records. It's as lo-fi as you'd expect for a project recorded in a garage.

His next appearance was playing guitar on a cover of "Where Did You Sleep Last Night" for Mark Lanegan's solo album *The Winding Sheet*, released in May 1990 on Sub Pop. Cobain also contributed backing vocals to "Down In The Dark".

Cobain also contributed to some tracks for his friend Dylan Carlson's drone metal band Earth in October 1990, in a session at Smegma Studios in Portland, Oregon. He played guitar and contributed vocals on "A Bureaucratic Desire For Revenge, Parts 1 & 2", a heavy, hypnotic number which was first released on the Sub Pop EP *Extra-Capsular Extraction*,

with Cobain credited as "Kurt Kobain". The track subsequently appeared on another EP called *A Bureaucratic Desire For Revenge*, as well as the Sub Pop compilation albums *10.1990* and *Revolution Come & Gone*; a limited edition promo video for *Extra-Capsular Extraction* was also produced, assembled from found footage of aircraft carriers and mid-twentieth-century softcore porn (chiefly couples spanking each other).

Earth's *Sunn Amps and Smashed Guitars Live*, released in 2001 on No Quarter, features another track recorded at the same session, "Divine and Bright", with Cobain's vocals consisting entirely of him reciting the song's title. The track also appeared on a US single.

Nirvana's promotion of the Melvins in the media led to their being signed by a major label. Cobain lent a hand on their debut album for Atlantic, *Houdini*, released in 1993, producing six tracks, and playing guitar on "Sky Pup" and percussion on "Spread Eagle Beagle".

In November 1992, Cobain was given the chance to work on a record with one of his idols, beat writer William Burroughs, in a project set up by Cobain's friend, Thor Lindsay of Portland's Tim/Kerr. Each recorded his part separately, Burroughs reading a short story, "The 'Priest' They Called Him", and Cobain recording a backing track at the Laundry Room. Through Cobain's squalling guitar, you can pick out the melody of the carol "Silent Night", in keeping with the story's holiday setting. The one-sided single was released on Tim/Kerr in July 1993 as a 10-inch single (also available as a picture disc and on yellow vinyl) and CD. The cover art had Krist Novoselic dressed as a priest and in the credits Cobain's name was spelled "Kurtis Cohbaine".

In October 1993, Cobain visited the recording sessions for Hole's *Live Through This* in Atlanta, Georgia, and recorded backing and harmony vocals for a number of tracks. The only one to surface to date is a version of "Asking For It"; though the song was not officially released, a copy was provided to Seattle radio station KNDD and subsequently bootlegged.

Dave Grohl

This section looks at Grohl's albums with Foo Fighters, followed by an overview of his pre-Nirvana work, side projects and guest appearances.

FOO FIGHTERS

UK, US Roswell/Capitol, 4 July 1995.

THIS IS A CALL / I'LL STICK AROUND / BIG ME / ALONE + EASY TARGET / GOOD GRIEF / FLOATY / WEENIE BEENIE / OH, GEORGE / FOR ALL THE COWS / X-STATIC / WATTERSHED / EXHAUSTED

Recorded 17–24 October 1994. The Japanese edition had bonus tracks "Winnebago" and "Podunk"; an "Australian Tour Pack" edition featured both those tracks plus "How I Miss You", "Ozone" and live versions of "For All The Cows" and "Wattershed".

The cover of Foos' first album continued the sci-fi theme with a Buck Rogers-style pistol.

Foo Fighters came as a revelation to those who weren't aware of Grohl's musical pedigree – a drummer who could also write songs, play guitar and sing more than adequately? Comparisons to Nirvana were inevitable, but Grohl managed to firmly establish himself as a performer in his own right. This album is the most pop-friendly release in the Foos' catalogue, though with enough hard edges to keep the energy up – as seen in the album's opening track (and first single), which begins with harmonies backed by the clear strum of a guitar, only for the full band to kick in at the twenty-second mark (a similar effect is used in the opening of "Floaty"). Grohl also exposed his softer side, as in the light ballad "Big Me" (the album's biggest single in the US), while "For All The Cows" took Nirvana's soft verse/loud chorus formula to a sharp extreme. And the closing track, "Exhausted", managed the neat trick of juxtaposing a soft vocal against harsh musical backing that grinds away with the intensity of a slow burn. But most of the album thrashes along happily, while never getting too carried away (though the frenzy of "Weenie Beenie" comes close). For all its moments of heaviness, Foo Fighters never sounded this poppy again; the passion with which Grohl howls out the title of "I'll Stick Around" is a sign of where the band's sound was headed.

THE COLOUR AND THE SHAPE

UK, US Roswell/Capitol, 20 May 1997.

DOLL / MONKEY WRENCH / HEY, JOHNNY PARK! / MY POOR BRAIN / WIND UP / UP IN ARMS / MY HERO / SEE YOU / ENOUGH SPACE / FEBRUARY STARS / EVERLONG / WALKING AFTER YOU / NEW WAY HOME

Recorded October 1996–February 1997. The Japanese edition included bonus track "Dear Lover"; an Australian "Tour Pack" edition included "Down In The Park", "Drive Me Wild", "Baker Street" and "Requiem". In 2007, a ten-year anniversary edition was issued (on the band's new label, RCA), with all these bonus tracks, plus a previously unreleased track, "The Colour And The Shape". An acoustic version of "See You" was offered through iTunes.

This has been called Grohl's "divorce album", because it came together following the break-up with his wife; but it became something of a divorce album for the first line-up of Foo Fighters as well, as original drummer William Goldsmith left before the album's completion. Certainly the album begins in a chastened mood, with Grohl sounding suitably broken on "Doll". After a minute and a half, the album explodes in "Monkey Wrench", but despite the roar of the music, a careful listen to the lyrics reveals that it's a song of almost desperate vulnerability; though he screams with defiance about being "Free!" at the end of the song's spoken-word middle eight section, he still sounds like a man dangerously close to the end of his tether. In fact, Grohl's punishing vocals are the bedrock of much of the album, as you can hear on tracks like "My Poor Brain", "Wind Up" and "My Hero". A barrage of power chords, however majestic, doesn't necessarily provide

The UK spelling in the title, which doesn't appear on the front cover, was said to be a reference to British producer Gil Norton.

substance, but as if unable to resist playing a song without slamming in a loud chorus, tracks like "Up In Arms", "Enough Space" and "February Stars" pull a similar "Doll"/"Monkey Wrench" trick in having their quiet beginnings smothered by a loud second half. Conversely, quieter songs like the old-time swing of "See You" and the haunting "Walking After You" provide a fine showcase for Grohl's expressive vocals, which prove to be far more evocative than his go-for-the-jugular rock screaming.

Playing with the dynamics also makes a song more interesting. "Everlong" begins rather like "Exhausted" (intense backing, quieter vocal), but once you feel the song's locked into its runaway groove, you're thrown off balance by a sudden drop into near silence. The album's closing song and longest track, "New Way Home", has similar ebbs and flows, plus a great conclusion, as the tempo scales back then gradually surges forward to a breakneck pace. Overall, *Colour* is an album whose music shows the band's confidence growing by leaps and bounds.

The Music

THERE IS NOTHING LEFT TO LOSE

UK, US Roswell/RCA. UK 1 November 1999, US 2 November 1999.

STACKED ACTORS / BREAKOUT / LEARN TO FLY / GIMME STITCHES / GENERATOR / AURORA / LIVE-IN SKIN / HEADWIRES / AIN'T IT THE LIFE / M.I.A.

Recorded March–June 1999. Early pressings came with a Foo Fighters temporary tattoo, like the one on Grohl's neck on the cover. An "enhanced CD" edition featured the "Learn to Fly" video and other extras, while Japanese and Australian CDs had the bonus track "Fraternity". In 2001, the album was reissued in Europe with a second disc featuring the videos of "Learn to Fly", "Generator", "Breakout" and "Next Year".

There had been three line-up changes in the band since the recording of *Colour*, and when sessions for their third album began they were also between labels. Undeterred, Foos didn't bother finding a second guitarist; Grohl, bassist Nate Mendel and drummer Taylor Hawkins simply decamped to Grohl's new home studio in Virginia and recorded the album as a trio. Armed with a strong set of songs, *There Is Nothing Left To Lose* is one of the band's most satisfying albums.

Grohl had returned to Virginia as he was fed up with the superficiality of the LA scene, a rage that's fully on display in the album's opening track, the scathing "Stacked Actors". But despite the occasional turns of

Some early pressings came with a temporary tattoo like Grohl's on the cover.

abrasiveness, *There Is Nothing...* focuses more on melody, as in the blissfully tuneful "Learn To Fly", a hook-laden pop treat that soared to the top of *Billboard*'s Modern Rock chart. The singles "Breakout" and "Generator" were just as catchy (Grohl used a "talk box", a device popularized by Peter Frampton, on the latter song), while tracks like "Next Year" and "Ain't It The Life" neatly walk the mainstream rock line without veering over into the realm of the power ballad.

But what really makes the record work is that all the tracks fit well together: it feels like a complete album, as opposed to a collection of a few good tracks surrounded by filler. There's also an understated poignancy in many of Grohl's vocals that gives less prominent tracks like "Headwires" and "Live-In Skin" an extra emotional pull. "M.I.A." brings the album to an abrupt end, the drums cutting off in mid-stroke.

ONE BY ONE

UK, US RCA. UK 21 October 2002, US 22 October 2002.

ALL MY LIFE / LOW / HAVE IT ALL / TIMES LIKE THESE / DISENCHANTED LULLABY / TIRED OF YOU / HALO / LONELY AS YOU / OVERDRIVE / BURN AWAY / COME BACK

Recorded 6–18 May 2002. A Special Edition came with a bonus DVD featuring videos of "All My Life", "Walking A Line" and "The One". The Japanese edition featured bonus track "Danny Says"; a Norwegian edition featured four songs from a 4 December 2002 performance in Oslo ("Times Like These", "Low", "Aurora", "Monkey Wrench"). A second edition of the album released in Europe featured "Walking A Line", "Sister Europe", "Danny Says", "Life Of Illusion" and live versions of "For All The Cows", "Monkey Wrench" and "Next Year".

As well as the regular white cover pictured here, the album came in a limited-edition black version.

One By One is the result of Grohl's perception that the last album had been too "mellow". The album comes charging out of the starting gate with its opening track, and barely looks back in its determination to leave anything soft in the dust. And that first track is also the album's best. Beginning with a nervy guitar line, followed by an equally tense vocal by Grohl, the song then whipsaws back and forth between all-out throttling and restraint, with a lyric that continually circles around the nature of frustration (Grohl admitted that the chorus was "a little dirty"). The closing song, "Come Back", has one of the most interesting arrangements to come from the band. Halfway through the nearly eight-minute track, the crush of noise neatly scales back to the sound of quietly strummed acoustic guitars, the band gradually coming back in over the next two minutes, topped by Grohl's triumphant proclamation "I will come back!"

Between those two songs, it's more of a mixed bag. There's other strong material, like "Times Like These", which skilfully combines heartfelt lyrics, plaintive, even wistful, vocals and a solid power pop backing, and the catchy if pummelling "Low", both pulled out as singles (along with "All My Life" and "Have It All"). "Tired Of You" also benefits from the distinctive sound of Brian May's guitar. But the album's clean, well-produced sound comes at the expense of the band's personality. The songs have been polished until they shine – but they've also had the rough edges rubbed away, leaving you with music that's just a tad too slick. There isn't even as much sense of pleasure: both "Disenchanted Lullaby" and "Halo" have a tendency to drag, "Overdrive" is all revved up but ultimately goes nowhere, and "Lonely As You" has more of Grohl's throat-shredding screams, but little else. Grohl himself has acknowledged the album's shortcomings: for all its acclaim (it was another Grammy winner and the first Foos album to top the UK charts), he's always cited *One By One* as his least favourite album.

IN YOUR HONOR

UK, US RCA. UK 13 June 2005, US 14 June 2005.

IN YOUR HONOR / NO WAY BACK / BEST OF YOU / DOA / HELL / THE LAST SONG / FREE ME / RESOLVE / THE DEEPEST BLUES ARE BLACK / END OVER END / STILL / WHAT IF I DO? / MIRACLE / ANOTHER ROUND / FRIEND OF A FRIEND / OVER AND OUT / ON THE MEND / VIRGINIA MOON / COLD DAY IN THE SUN / RAZOR

Recorded January–March 2005. The album was also released in the DualDisc format, with a CD on one side, and a DVD on the other, with a 5.1 mix of the album and a "making of" documentary. The UK vinyl edition had the bonus track "The Sign".

In Your Honor marked the first time the same Foo Fighters line-up had recorded two albums in a row. Grohl had originally thought of releasing a single acoustic album, but unable to completely eschew his love of volume, expanded the album to a two-disc set, the first typical Foos hard rock, the second acoustic.

The hard rock disc takes the sound of the hardest material of *One By One* and throws it into overdrive, with Grohl screaming his way throughout, sounding rather like Cheap Trick's Robin Zander (in fact the entire band sounds like a heavier version of Cheap Trick). As usual, the performances are tight, the sound clean, but with nary a change in stylistic mood it's also somewhat one-dimensional; when a record's one powerhouse anthem after another, it becomes a bit numbing by the third song. Of course, the band was going all out because their softer side would be more than adequately displayed on the second disc. There was a political subtext to songs like "Best Of You" and "No Way Back", Grohl explaining the former was about breaking out of confinement and the latter about "feeling controlled by a government that you didn't elect". But instead of being too explicit, the lyrics lent themselves to different interpretations, giving them a broader appeal.

The acoustic disc's most noted track was "Friend Of A Friend", which, Grohl revealed, not only dated from his 1992 solo cassette *Pocketwatch*, but was also specifically written about Cobain and Krist Novoselic during Grohl's first few weeks in Nirvana. It's a pen portrait made all the

Foos' first double album's split identity is signalled by its hard/soft cover image.

more astonishing for its prescience, a delicate sketch of Cobain, even then wanting to lock himself away from the world.

The rest of the acoustic disc provides a new, refreshing take on Grohl's singing and songwriting skills. Unable to utilize rock screaming to vault himself back into a song's chorus, his emotions and vulnerability are on full display, with consistently winning results. Judicious use is made of assorted guest stars: John Paul Jones plays piano on "Miracle" and mandolin on "Another Round", Josh Homme plays guitar on the brooding, vaguely unsettling "Razor", and, most unexpectedly, Norah Jones duets with Grohl on the lovely "Virginia Moon", a song lightly tinged with an old-time swing. Taylor Hawkins also made his lead vocal debut on a Foos record, with "Cold Day In The Sun", a bright poppy track in contrast with the rest of the album's folkish feel.

SKIN AND BONES

UK, US Roswell/RCA. UK 20 November 2006, US 7 November 2006.

RAZOR / OVER AND OUT / WALKING AFTER YOU / MARIGOLD / MY HERO / NEXT YEAR / ANOTHER ROUND / BIG ME / COLD DAY IN THE SUN / SKIN AND BONES / FEBRUARY STARS / TIMES LIKE THESE / FRIEND OF A FRIEND / BEST OF YOU / EVERLONG

Recorded 29–31 August 1996. The iTunes bonus track "Ain't It The Life" can also be found on the DVD.

Recorded during the Foos' acoustic tour in the fall of 2006, the CD presents an edited version of the concert (the DVD of the same title has the complete show). On the CD version, a mere five songs are from *In Your Honor*, skewing the set in

The circle of Foo Fighters' live acoustic album cover is faintly reminiscent of the *Unplugged* album design.

favour of well-known tracks like "Everlong", "Times Like These" and "Next Year". The mood isn't quite as scaled back as on *In Your Honor* either, with the live histrionics nearly overwhelming some songs, like "My Hero". That said, the band (which also includes former Foo Pat Smear, and guests like Petra Haden and Rami Jaffee, who also appeared on *In Your Honor*) are clearly relaxed and having fun, which adds to the enjoyment. It's nice to see Grohl revive the sole Nirvana track he did a vocal for, "Marigold". The haunting title track, the only new song performed during the tour, is another highlight.

ECHOES, SILENCE, PATIENCE & GRACE

UK, US Roswell/RCA. UK 24 September 2007, US 25 September 2007.

THE PRETENDER / LET IT DIE / ERASE/REPLACE / LONG ROAD TO RUIN / COME ALIVE / STRANGER THINGS HAVE HAPPENED / CHEER UP, BOYS (YOUR MAKE UP IS RUNNING) / SUMMER'S END / BALLAD OF THE BEACONSFIELD MINERS / STATUES / BUT, HONESTLY / HOME

Recorded March–June 2007. The UK edition featured the bonus track "Once And For All"; the Japanese edition featured the additional track "Seda" (both tracks were also available through iTunes). A Wal-Mart edition featured live versions of "The Pretender" and "My Hero" as part of their *Soundcheck* series.

Foos' sixth studio album strikes a good balance between out-and-out rockers and more contemplative material. As usual, the album begins with its strongest track (and first single), "The Pretender", which starts out with a quiet, almost sorrowful vocal from Grohl, before the full band kicks in with typical gusto. Yet Grohl's vocal is coloured with a melancholy yearning, as it is on much of the rest of the album – in contrast to the bright optimism of the band's earlier work.

The band also has more fun playing with the dynamics of a song, as on "Let It Die", most of which is in singer-songwriter vein, before exploding into screaming angst. "Erase/Replace" unexpectedly throws a middle eight of lush harmonizing into the midst of its hard rock setting, though it's an effect that feels overused after a while. "Come Alive" and "But, Honestly" are other songs that start out quietly before building to a roar, when they might have worked just as well had they remained low-key throughout.

Songs like "Statues" and the album's closing track, "Home", show the emotional depths the band can reach when operating with more restraint. "Statues" is a haunting reflection on mortality, while "Home" is even more heartfelt. The song's simple arrangement has Grohl accompanying himself on piano, with a string

Like most Foos' album covers, the sixth has a strikingly spare design.

quartet gradually coming in, making the song essentially a solo cut. It's when Grohl is at his most vulnerable that the music packs more of an emotional punch.

Pre-Nirvana bands

Grohl's first band, Mission Impossible, released a split single with Lünchmeat on Sammich Records in 1985, and appeared on the *Alive And Kicking* compilation released by WGNS/Metrozine in 1985. His second band, Dain Bramage, released the album *I Scream Not Coming Down* on Fartblossom in 1987. His albums with Scream are more readily available: *No More Censorship* (RAS, 1988), *Live At Van Hall In Amsterdam* (Konkurrel, 1989), *Your Choice Live Series 010* (Your Choice, 1990), *Fumble* (Dischord, 1993) and *Live At The Black Cat* (Torque, 1998).

Side projects

Throughout his time in Nirvana and Foo Fighters, Grohl has always found time to go off and record his own material, giving him the opportunity to explore different musical avenues.

Grohl's first solo album, *Pocketwatch*, was released under a pseudonym (Late!) on the now-defunct label Simple Machines in 1992. Grohl recorded a number of songs in Virginia in December 1990 and July 1991, and had given a cassette to Jenny Toomey, Simple Machines' co-founder. Toomey liked the songs and asked if the label could release it, dubbing copies from the cassette Grohl had given her.

Like the original Foo Fighters demo, Grohl plays all the instruments and does all the vocals, aside from a backing vocal by producer Barrett Jones on "Petrol CB". Three of the tracks were later re-

From recording in 1991, it was five years till the album with its organic-looking cover was released.

recorded: "Color Pictures Of A Marigold" (retitled simply "Marigold") with Nirvana, appearing as a B-side on "Heart-Shaped Box", "Winnebago", which appeared on *Foo Fighters*, and "Friend Of A Friend", which appears on *In Your Honor*, and as a live version on *Skin and Bones* (though it's the *Pocketwatch* version that's the most haunting). The ten-track cassette illustrates Grohl's versatility, not only on the various instruments, but in tackling different musical styles, and provides an excellent look at his budding songwriting skills.

Around the same time he was making *Pocketwatch*, Grohl formed a studio band in Virginia with his friends, which had Tos Nieuwenhuizen on guitar, Barrett Jones on drums, Bruce Merkle on vocals and Grohl on bass. But the songs stayed in the vault until released on Jones' Laundry Room Records label in 1996 as *Harlingtox A.D.*, with the band credited as Harlingtox Angel Divine.

In 1992, each member of the Melvins released a solo record, patterned after the solo albums the members of Kiss released in 1979. Grohl teamed up with Buzz Osborne on *King Buzzo*, released on Boner/Tupelo, playing drums and co-writing three of the EP's tracks; the fourth track, "Skeeter", is the same track that appeared on *Pocketwatch*, where it's titled "Just Another Story About Skeeter Thompson". Grohl is credited as "Dale Nixon", an alt-rock in-joke, as it's the pseudonym Greg Ginn used on Black Flag's *My War* album.

Music From The Motion Picture Touch (Roswell/Capitol, 1997) is effectively a Grohl solo album since he wrote and performs all the material. The film itself, an indie comedy about a modern day faith healer, attracted little interest, and the soundtrack is largely instrumental. Of the tracks with vocals, "How Do You Do" would have fit right in on *Foo Fighters*; "This Loving Thing (Lynn's Song)" has a plaintive vocal by X's John Doe; and "Touch" has Grohl singing with Veruca Salt's Louise Post (Doe and Post also co-wrote the tracks with Grohl, who used the pseudonym "Late" in the credits). Grohl first demoed the "Bill Hill Theme" and "Final Miracle" back in January 1994, at Nirvana's final recording session (when it had the self-explanatory title "New Wave Groove"); "Spinning Newspapers" is the kind of catchy instrumental Grohl can probably pop off in his sleep.

The cover is a big clue to the inspiration behind the Melvins' solo albums.

In 2003, Grohl's Probot project gave him the excuse to fully indulge, and pay homage to, his love of heavy metal. Grohl recorded the backing tracks for eleven songs, then approached a different singer to perform on each track, asking them to provide the lyrics as well. Among the participants were Lemmy (Motörhead), King Diamond, Cronos (Venom) and Snake (Voivod). Jack Black of Tenacious D also appears on the album's hidden track, "I Am The Warlock". The album was released in 2004 on Roswell/Southern Lord.

Guest appearances

Grohl has appeared on innumerable albums over the years, listed here in chronological order. *Backbeat: Music From The Motion Picture* (1994); Mike Watt's *Ball-Hog Or Tugboat?* (1995); The Stinky Puffs' *A Little Tiny Smelly Bit of...* (1995); Puff Daddy's *It's All About The Benjamins* (1997); The Earthlings' *Earthlings?* (1998); Verbena's *Into The Pink* (1999); Reeves Gabrels' *Ulysses (Della Notte)* (1999); Tony Iommi's *Iommi* (2000); Tenacious D's self-titled album (2001); Queens of the Stone Age's *Songs For The Deaf* (2002); Cat Power's *You Are Free* (2002); David Bowie's *Heathen* (2002); The Bangles' *Doll Revolution* (2003); Killing Joke's self-titled album (2003); Honky Mofo's self-titled album (2004); Queens of the Stone Age's *Over The Years And Through The Woods* (2005); Nine Inch Nails' *With Teeth* (2005); Garbage's *Bleed Like Me* (2005); the soundtrack *Tenacious D: The Pick Of Destiny* (2006); Rye Coalition's *Curses* (2006); Juliette

The Music

and the Licks' *Four On The Floor* (2006); Pete Yorn's *Nightcrawler* (2006); Jackson United's *Harmony And Dissidence* (2008).

Krist Novoselic

Krist Novoselic's post-Nirvana musical career has been less prolific than Dave Grohl's, but decidedly more eclectic. He played bass for a reformed Flipper from 2006 to 2008, recording album unreleased at the time of writing.

SWEET 75

UK Geffen, 18 August 1997; US DGC, 26 August 1997.

FETCH / LAY ME DOWN / BITE MY HAND / RED DRESS / LA VIDA / SIX YEARS / TAKE ANOTHER STAB / POOR KITTY / ODE TO DOLLY / DOGS / CANTOS DE PILON / NOTHING / JAPAN TREES / ORAL HEALTH

Recorded June–August 1996.

Novoselic referred to Sweet 75's music as "power lounge" in interviews at the time of the album's release, trying to convey that the sound wouldn't fit readily under the "alternative rock" banner. It was a fair assessment, given the band's diverse influences: the Latino rhythms underpinning tracks like "Cantos De Pilon" and "La Vida" (with Peter Buck contributing mandolin on the former, and Herb Alpert providing a trumpet solo on the latter), flourishes of slinky jazz, blues (most

The offbeat, non-alt rock nature of Sweet 75's album was signalled by the cover.

evident in singer Yva Las Vegas' raw vocals, as reflected by her nickname, "Brillo"), and, yes, even Country and Western on the rollicking "Ode to Dolly" (Parton, that is). Sometimes it feels as if too much is going on. "Take Another Stab" meanders along for over five minutes with no clear sense of direction, and the energy starts flagging around mid-album. But when all the elements come together, the band's offbeat musical approach has an intriguing pull, as on the menacing "Nothing", where Novoselic's guitar both digs in and breaks out into a spate of freeform noise. Other highlights include the jaunty swing of "Japan Trees", the melancholy kiss-off "Oral Health" (fittingly, the album's last track), which has the best melding of the Latin/alt-rock genres. Many of these songs wouldn't be out of place on an indie film soundtrack. A non-album track, "Soap Zone", was included on the single "Lay Me Down".

LIVE FROM THE BATTLE IN SEATTLE

US Alternative Tentacles, 8 May 2000.

BATTLE IN SEATTLE / LET'S LYNCH THE LANDLORD / NEW FEUDALISM / ELECTRONIC PLANTATION / FULL METAL JACKOFF

Recorded 1 December 1999.

"Well, what can we say about the past couple days besides 'The People Have Spoken?'" Jello Biafra crows at the beginning of this release, which documented the sole performance of "The No WTO Combo" that had formed in protest at the WTO Conference held in Seattle in late 1999. In addition to

The poster art for Alternative Tentacles' NO WTO live album: an expression of punk political fury.

Biafra, the group included Novoselic on bass, Soundgarden's Kim Thayil on guitar (in his first live performance since Soundgarden's split) and Sweet 75's last drummer, Gina Mainwal. The first track is a fifteen-minute talk by Biafra, with the musicians gradually coming in behind him. "Landlord" and "Jackoff" are Dead Kennedys songs; "New Feudalism" and "Electronic Plantation" are originals. All burn with suitably righteous

punk fury. Whatever your politics, the music is undeniably invigorating.

EYES ADRIFT

UK Cooking Vinyl, 27 January 2003; US spinART, 24 September 2002.

SLEIGHT OF HAND / ALASKA / INQUIRING MINDS / UNTRIED / BLIND ME / DOTTIE DAWN & JULIE JEWEL / SOLID / PYRAMIDS / TELESCOPE / SLOW RACE / WHAT I SAID / PASTED

Recorded March 2002.

The sole album by Novoselic's second post-Nirvana band is uneven, being a bit too laid-back at times, but elsewhere exhibiting a willingness to experiment that keeps you wondering where it's going next. The music is closer to the Meat Puppets' offbeat take on roots rock than Nirvana-esque grunge, beginning with the breezy "Sleight Of Hand", which sweeps you away with ease. "Alaska" bumps the pop quotient up a few notches, while "Telescope" crunches along with authority. Other tracks, like "Untried", "Blind Me" and "What I Said", are a tad lugubrious – or strangely mesmerizing, depending on your mood.

The album also features the first serious vocals by Novoselic, previously best known for bawling out a line from "Get Together" at the beginning of Nirvana's "Territorial Pissings" (Nirvana's early shows sometimes featured a cover of Cher's "Gypsies, Tramps And Thieves"

Eyes Adrift's album was more Meat Puppets than Nirvana.

with an equally caterwauling Novoselic vocal). He takes the lead vocal on "Inquiring Minds", a critique of tabloid journalism, and "Dottie Dawn and Julie Jewel", a rockabilly-infused ode to his dogs. Best of all is the closing track, "Pasted", which begins with an otherworldly wail of guitar, then has Novoselic ruminating on the nature of deity and celebrity over a folky background. But the song's just getting started: slowly, guitars and drums create a swirling mass of sound that spirals up and down over the course of fifteen minutes, before finally burning out, like a star gone supernova.

Guest appearances

Novoselic has made a few guest appearances on various albums, listed here in chronological order. Mike Watt's *Ball-Hog Or Tugboat?* (1995); The Stinky Puffs' *A Little Tiny Smelly Bit of…* (1995); the track "Time Of The Preacher" on the Willie Nelson tribute album *Twisted Willie* (1996), which also featured Johnny Cash, John Carter Cash, Kim Thayil and Sean Kinney from Alice In Chains; Sky Cries Mary's *Moonbathing On Sleeping Leaves* (1997); and as an engineer On Krishna Das' *Live On Earth… For A Limited Time Only* (1999).

Part Three:
Nirvanaology

Nirvana in print

Soon after *Nevermind* topped the charts, books about Nirvana began hitting the bookshelves. Initially, there was a rash of quickie knock-offs that devoted more pages to pictures than text (a rare exception was a 16-page pamphlet by Everett True that was included with copies of *Melody Maker*). There was another flurry in 1994, starting with Dave Thompson's *Never Fade Away: The Kurt Cobain Story*, which appeared within a month of Cobain's death. But there are a number of books that examine Nirvana more thoroughly, beginning with Michael Azerrad's *Come As You Are*, the only notable book about Nirvana published prior to Cobain's death. Most focus on Cobain, though there's an increasing number of Dave Grohl biographies, while Krist Novoselic has published his own book, and Courtney Love's journals are available alongside those of her late husband. And we can surely expect more books in the future, as Nirvana's music continues to be debated, and other participants decide to tell their version of the tale. Books are listed in order of first publication; some are out of print, but readily available to buy online.

Route 666: On the Road To Nirvana

Gina Arnold (US: St. Martin's Press, 1993)

Despite the Nirvana cover shot and subtitle, Arnold's book isn't a Nirvana bio but an overview of the American alternative music scene from whence they sprang. But Nirvana are at the heart of the story, with the opening and closing chapters focusing on them, along with an additional chapter on the band previously published in *Option*, and chapters on Sub Pop and Olympia's music scene.

Come As You Are: The Story Of Nirvana

Michael Azerrad (US: Main Street Books/Doubleday; UK: Virgin Books; 1993)

After writing *Rolling Stone*'s first cover story on the band in 1992, Michael Azerrad was asked by the band's management to write Nirvana's biography. Azerrad had access to the band members, their family, close friends and business associates, and turned out a remarkably detailed account given the short time frame he was given to work on it (the book was first published in October 1993).

Among this book's interesting images is the cover shot, taken from a Michael Lavine photo shoot in January 1992.

Some feel that being tapped by the band's management to tell the story compromises the book's integrity. Others have pointed out that Cobain gave his own spin on events, making the book inaccurate in places. In his defence, Azzerad later explained that Cobain's worst period of drug use occurred after he'd finished writing the book; nor was Cobain ever entirely honest about the drug use he did admit to. And if Cobain tells a few tall tales, it's also the only time he took an interviewer through his entire life story. For that reason alone *Come As You Are* remains essential reading. In addition to rare photos, the book also reproduces a selection of set lists, lyrics, posters and other ephemera. The book's second edition, published after Cobain's death, has an additional chapter.

Cobain

The Editors of *Rolling Stone* (US: Rolling Stone Press, 1994)

This lavishly illustrated book reproduces all of *Rolling Stone*'s original articles on the group (including those from its 2 June 1994 memorial issue), along with some new material – such as a new review of *Bleach*, which the magazine hadn't reviewed on its initial release. The authors were given the chance to write new introductions to their work. Ira Robbins notes the "concerted pitching" needed to get the magazine to agree to run a review of *Nevermind*, and it's interesting to compare his decidedly restrained review with the enthusiastic ones running in the UK press at the same time.

Screaming Life

Charles Peterson, Michael Azzerad (US: HarperCollinsWest, 1995)

Touch Me I'm Sick

Charles Peterson (US: powerHouse Books, 2003)

Charles Peterson made his name as the house photographer for Sub Pop Records, and his photos were intrinsic to the development of the Seattle scene, a visual counterpart to the raw urgency of the music, capturing the bands in all their grungy, sweaty glory. The best shots in both books are from the pre-grunge explosion era, when bands and audiences were packed into tiny clubs so tightly, they virtually merged; it's a wonder Peterson was able to emerge from so many moshpits with his camera intact. As the bands take off, a sense of isolation begins to creep in: instead of crowd-surfing, Kurt Cobain now stands on arena stages several feet above his audience. *Screaming Life* was Peterson's first book, and has more commentary on the photos (along with an essay by Michael Azzerad); *Touch Me*

I'm Sick has a superior presentation, but both provide an unmissable depiction of the grunge scene in its ascendancy.

The Nirvana Companion: Two Decades Of Commentary

John Rocco, ed. (US: Schirmer Books, 1998)

An invaluable collection of previously published Nirvana articles, drawn from a variety of sources, including the first ever article on the band, "It May Be The Devil, And It May Be The Lord… But It Sure As Hell Ain't Human", which appeared in August 1988 in the Seattle rock publication *Backlash*. The *Seattle Times*' Patrick McDonald contributes an interesting article about Aberdeen in early 1992, during Nirvana's first flush of fame, and there are other articles from *The Advocate*, *Billboard*, *The New York Times*, *Melody Maker*, *Spin* and *Goldmine*, among others. The editor also contributes an essay on William Burroughs, and shorter "notes" on other relevant topics (Sonic Youth, Leadbelly, Frances Farmer).

The Complete Guide To The Music Of Nirvana

James Hector (UK, US: Omnibus Press, 1998)

Hector's book provides a concise analysis of every officially released Nirvana song and record, the first two Foo Fighters records and a smattering of interview discs and video releases. It's better written and more comprehensive than the similarly styled *Teen Spirit: The Stories Behind Every Nirvana Song* by Chuck Crisafulli. The book was updated in 2004, though it misses out the release of *With The Lights Out*. Oddly, though the cover identifies Hector as "the pseudonym for a well-known rock writer and Nirvana expert", the book's title page gives the game away by crediting Mark Paytress as the author.

Guitar World Presents Nirvana And The Grunge Revolution

Jeff Kitts, Brad Tolinski and Harold Steinblatt, eds. (US: Hal Leonard Corp., 1998)

Drawn from the archives of *Guitar World* magazine, this book has six Nirvana-related articles, and one each on Foo Fighters and Sweet 75, along with articles on Pearl Jam, Soundgarden and Alice In Chains.

Nevermind: Nirvana

Jim Berkenstadt and Charles R. Cross (Schirmer Trade Books, 1998)

This in-depth look at the creation of Nirvana's landmark album was part of the now discontinued "Classic Rock Albums" series. There's a track-by-track analysis of the songs initially recorded with producer Butch Vig in 1990 and at the *Nevermind* sessions in 1991 (including unreleased tracks), then it's step-by-step through the process of mixing, mastering, choosing cover art, making the first video and promotion. The emphasis is on the "how" not the "why", making for a straightforward, fact-based account. There are also interviews with many of the key players, including Butch Vig.

Kurt Cobain: The Cobain Dossier

Martin Clarke and Paul Woods , eds. (UK: Plexus Publishing Ltd, 1999)

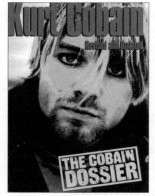

A classic shot of Kurt adorns the cover, originally from an *NME* shoot by Martyn Goodacre, see opposite.

Another collection of previously published articles (plus a few new ones), *The Cobain Dossier* is well worth picking up. Highlights include Keith Cameron's infamous "Love Will Tear Us Apart" article that brought to light the discord within the band; Robert Hilburn's "Cobain To Fans: Just Say No", one of the first in a series of interviews Cobain did to rehabilitate his image in late 1992; "Sounds Dirty: The Truth About Nirvana" by *England's Dreaming* author Jon Savage; "Kurt Cobain's Final Tour", Amy Dickinson's description of how some of Cobain's ashes ended up at a Buddhist monastery; and "8 Fragments For Kurt Cobain" by poet Jim Carroll (former husband of Rosemary Carroll, who served as Nirvana's attorney).

Nirvana: Winterlong

Martyn Goodacre, Steve Gullick and Stephen Sweet (UK: Vision On, 1999)

This photo book comprises the work of three British photographers who captured Nirvana at key points in their career, especially in the UK: their first UK tour in 1989, their first UK tour with Dave Grohl in 1990, and their first appearance at the Reading Festival in 1991. A number of the shots became notable in their own right, such as Sweet's December 1992 pictures of Cobain holding his daughter with "Diet Grrrl" written on her stomach, Gullick's November 1993 shot of Cobain stretched out on a couch backstage playing his guitar, and Goodacre's October 1999 haunting close-up of Cobain, eyes thick with mascara, that first appeared on the cover of *Select*'s July 1993 issue and became the cover shot of *NME*'s memorial issue. Gullick and Sweet's photos were repackaged in the book *Nirvana* (Vision On, 2001).

Loser: The Real Seattle Music Story

Clark Humphrey (US: MISCmedia, 1999)

Seattle-based Humphrey, a longtime chronicler of pop culture, produced the first comprehensive look at the area's music scene. Those who only became aware of Seattle via the early 1990s grunge explosion might be surprised to learn what a rich musical history the region has, from 1950s acts like The Fleetwoods, The Wailers and The Ventures, to Jimi Hendrix and cult favourites The Sonics in the 1960s, and Heart in the 1970s – not to mention the wealth of lesser-known acts. But the story really picks up during the punk era, and then it's another seventy pages until Nirvana enter the story. Humphrey doesn't just cover those who went on to great success, but seemingly everyone who ever released a record locally. Just as revealing is Art Chantry's design, which drew on hundreds of artefacts – photos, posters, record sleeves, bumper stickers, buttons, ticket stubs, band logos and newspaper headlines – to illustrate the book's pages, items which in themselves tell a pretty good story. Humphrey's fact-based style tends to be overly dry, but it's still a rewarding read for anyone interested in digging deeper into the intricacies of the Seattle music scene.

Nirvana: The Day By Day Eyewitness Chronicle

Carrie Borzillo (US: Thunder's Mouth, 2000; UK: Carlton Books, 2000, as *Eyewitness Nirvana: The Day By Day Story*)

Borzillo's book presented the first comprehensive listing of events in the Nirvana world from 16 May 1965 (Krist Novoselic's birth) to 30 April 1994 (when Hole's *Live Through This* debuted on the Billboard charts). Today, online sites may provide more accuracy as far as show dates are concerned (especially for the group's early years), but the veteran *Billboard* writer fleshes out her account with extensive interviews with friends, associates, co-workers and fellow musicians; interviews with those rarely spoken to before (such as Melora Creager,

cellist on Nirvana's final tour) add further insight. Borzillo also draws on accounts from contemporaneous articles and court documents, which helps to put events in context. The book was republished in 2003 as a heavily illustrated hardback coffee-table book, under the writer's married name, Carrie Borzillo-Vrenna; it's entitled *Nirvana: The Day By Day Illustrated Journals* in the US (Barnes & Noble), *Kurt Cobain: The Nirvana Years The Complete Chronicle* in the UK (Carlton Books).

Heavier Than Heaven: A Biography Of Kurt Cobain

Charles R. Cross (US: Hyperion; UK: Sceptre; 2001)

Cross, the former editor of *The Rocket* magazine, had previously written a book about the making of Nirvana's *Nevermind* (see p.227). For his Cobain biography, he scored a real coup in gaining Courtney Love's cooperation, for she granted him access to Cobain's extensive journals and other personal effects, which offered a greater insight into his state of mind throughout his life and career than had been captured in any interview. Some have said that Love's involvement led Cross to skew the story in her favour, but he has insisted that Love had no final say over what went in the book. Others feel

Cross over-dramatizes the account, as when he describes in detail the last minutes of Cobain's life. But there is much new information in the book, which draws on a wealth of interviews (over 400 by the author's count) and four years of research. Cross clarifies many of the details of Cobain's life that had been vague before, especially in his childhood years, and corrects previous accounts (for example, that Cobain never spray-painted any "Abort Christ" graffiti on walls in Aberdeen). The focus is on Kurt Cobain (in both the text and on the cover) though, not Nirvana, and it's the most thorough look at the man to date.

On The Harbor: From Black Friday To Nirvana

John C. Hughes and Ryan Teague Beckwith, eds. (US: *Daily World*, 2001)

Kurt Cobain spent three-quarters of his life in Aberdeen, Washington, but most people have little sense of what the town was like beyond the typical "backwoods redneck" stereotypes. *On The Harbor*, written by reporters from Aberdeen's *Daily World*, covers ninety years of the town's history, from a 16 October 1903 fire that destroyed the downtown area (the "Black Friday" of the title) to the later success of Nirvana. It's a history that encompasses labour strikes, unsolved murders, presidential visits, brothel raids and an abandoned nuclear plant, stories that give a fuller picture of the regional culture. The Nirvana chapter features some interesting pictures: of preppy, teenage Cobain; Krist's mother, Maria Novoselic,

proudly displaying one of her son's gold records in her beauty parlour; and Krist speaking at a city council meeting in neighbouring Hoquiam in July 1994, in an unsuccessful bid to have the Lollapalooza festival held in the town.

Our Band Could Be Your Life: Scenes From The Indie Underground 1981–1991

Michael Azerrad (UK, US: Little, Brown, 2001)

The *Come As You Are* author puts Nirvana's explosive success in context by profiling key bands of the pre-*Nevermind* era, many of whom Nirvana readily acknowledged as influences – Sonic Youth, Butthole Surfers, Hüsker Du, Dinosaur Jr. and Black Flag.

Journals

Kurt Cobain (US: Riverhead Books; UK: Penguin Books; 2002)

On the one hand, reading Cobain's *Journals* can be a frustrating experience. Only 272 pages are offered from an archive of 23 notebooks, little of the material is dated, and while a note says that some of the letters Kurt wrote were drafts and others were never sent, there's nothing to distinguish which is which in the main text. These aren't "journals" in the sense of recounting the events of each day, but pages of notebooks (like the scrawled-on example used reproduced for the book's cover) in which Cobain sketched out ideas for song lyrics, artwork and letters, in addition to ruminating on issues that

concerned him at the time. A fascinating peek inside Cobain's mind, especially if you're interested in seeing how his song lyrics evolved, or reading his own, often contradictory, views of his work. The 2003 paperback edition includes new pages not featured in the first edition. Courtney Love's *Dirty Blonde: The Diaries of Courtney Love* (Faber & Faber, 2006) also has some Cobain-related material and photographs, though the primary focus is naturally enough on Love's exploits.

GodSpeed: The Kurt Cobain Graphic

Barnaby Legg, Jim McCarthy, Flameboy (UK, US: Omnibus Press, 2003)

In mythologizing Cobain's story to such an extent, this graphic novel seems almost like a storyboard for the inevitable feature film. The text draws on other Nirvana bios (Azerrad's and Cross's books are obvious references), but it's also wildly inventive in places, as when *Nevermind*'s record release party is shown as being held in an impossibly ritzy setting; the result, as the book's cover copy explains, of choosing to tell the story in a manner which "fluctuates between subjective dream-state and objective reality". It's one of the more off-beat presentations of Cobain's life, but nonetheless moving on occasion.

Uncut Presents Nirvana

Steve Sutherland, ed. (UK: NME Originals, magazine, 2003)

If you can get hold of it, this magazine is an invaluable resource for any Nirvana fan interested in watching the story unfold as it happened, for the magazine reproduces original articles, interviews and reviews that ran in the UK weeklies *Melody Maker* and *New Musical Express* from 1989 (when Everett True wrote the introductory "Sub Pop Seattle: Rock City" for *Melody Maker*) to a 2002 *NME* review of Kurt Cobain's *Journals*. The UK music press regularly championed Nirvana years before their US counterparts, and the extensive interviews and critiques convey a real sense of the heady atmosphere as Nirvana rose from the underground to crash the mainstream.

Of Grunge And Government: Let's Fix This Broken Democracy!

Krist Novoselic (US: RDV Books/Akashic Books, 2004)

This short treatise focuses on one of Novoselic's passions – electoral reform – but also touches on his years in Nirvana. Nirvana were never considered an overtly political band, but this book provides a reminder that they often promoted progressive causes through their benefit shows and interviews. The book also shows how Nirvana's success led to Novoselic becoming increasingly involved in politics.

Kurt Cobain: Oh Well, Whatever, Nevermind

Jeff Burlingame (US: Enslow Publishers Inc., 2006)

Burlingame's book does a creditable job in boiling Cobain's story down to 134 pages and has an insider's touch, as Burlingame grew up in Aberdeen and was an acquaintance of Cobain's in his teens, before going on to write for Aberdeen's *Daily World*. As a result, his book has some fresh anecdotes from the locals and a smattering of rare photographs.

The Dave Grohl Story

Jeff Apter (Omnibus, 2006)

A comprehensive look at Grohl's life and career, pretty evenly divided into three sections. Though Grohl will now and forever be associated with Nirvana, Apter gives an excellent chronicle of Grohl's years as a budding musician (often overlooked in other accounts) and offers an in-depth look at Washington, DC's punk/hardcore scene where he built up his chops. Then, after the Nirvana years, Apter spends more time examining Grohl's post-Nirvana career in Foo Fighters and his numerous side projects. An updated paperback edition was published in 2008. As a better

written and more detailed book, Apter's bio is recommended over both *Dave Grohl: Foo Fighters, Nirvana and Other Misadventures* and *Dave Grohl: Nothing To Lose*.

In Utero

Gillian G. Gaar (US: Continuum, 2006)

A detailed account of the making of *In Utero*, by the author of this book, covering recording sessions, and the creation of the album's artwork and video. Has interviews with Krist Novoselic, producers Jack Endino, Craig Montgomery and Steve Albini, "Heart-Shaped Box" director Anton Corbijn, and art director Robert Fisher, among others.

Nirvana: The True Story

Everett True (UK: Omnibus, 2006; US: DaCapo, as *Nirvana: The Biography*, 2007)

True's unabashed egotism does put some people off and others have said his book is more an Everett True memoir in which Nirvana pops up as an occasional character. But there's no denying his depth of involvement with the band. True first met Nirvana in 1989 while covering Sub Pop acts for *Melody Maker*, and ended up becoming friends with the group: interviewing them through 1993, accompanying them on tour and performing with them on occasion, and even staying with Cobain and

Love (whom he dubbed "Kurtney") from time to time.

True's is the biggest Nirvana book to date, the main text running nearly 600 pages, and it makes no pretence at being an "objective" account (he freely takes shots at other Nirvana authors, especially Azerrad and Cross). But it's also a highly passionate retelling of the story, by someone who was as much a friend as a journalist; by the end he truly sounds like a man whose heart has been broken. And True opens up the story, putting Nirvana's career in a larger context by covering the growth of the Seattle and Olympia music scenes. Gossipy and cutting in turn, it's also highly entertaining.

True's earlier book, *Live Through This: American Rock Music in the Nineties* (Virgin Publishing, 2001) covers much of the same Nirvana turf, but also discusses other non-Pacific Northwest-based independent rock bands of the period.

Bumping Into Geniuses: My Life Inside The Rock And Roll Business

Danny Goldberg (UK, US: Gotham Books, 2008)

Goldberg's extensive resume includes writing for *Billboard*, working with artists like Led Zeppelin, Bonnie Raitt and Warren Zevon as publicist or manager, and executive positions at Atlantic Records, Mercury Records and Warner Bros. Records. It was while running the management company Gold Mountain Entertainment in the 1990s that he became one of Nirvana's managers, and he writes extensively of his time working with the band, giving the kind of account only an insider can; more than a decade after Cobain's death, the frustration Goldberg feels at not being able to help him is still palpable.

Cobain Unseen

Charles R. Cross (UK, US: Little, Brown, 2008)

A beautifully presented and designed collection of Cobain's personal memorabilia, from his childhood immunization records to the heart-shaped box he gave to his wife in 1994. Along with pictures of his guitars and rock T-shirts (Cheap Trick, Mudhoney, Frightwig), there are reproductions of his artwork and journal entries, and dozens of photos, most previously unseen.

The accompanying text by Cross is like a condensed version of *Heavier Than Heaven*, though it does feature some new material. The book also includes a CD with a brief spoken word piece from Cobain.

Nirvanaology

Nirvana on film

There are relatively few official Nirvana DVDs, some obvious holes being a collection of Nirvana's videos and a concert shown in its entirety, but the current releases do capture some of the band's best moments. A couple of feature films have been based on the Nirvana/Cobain story, and at the time of writing, a biopic based on Charles Cross's *Heavier Than Heaven* was reportedly in the works. As yet there's no in-depth documentary on the band, but there's a distressing number of unofficial documentaries, which cobble together interviews with folks who had a passing acquaintance with someone in the band, journalists providing filler, brief snippets of performance footage, and a soundtrack that for copyright reasons sounds almost-but-not-quite-like Nirvana. The following listings are in order of release date; unless indicated, all are available on DVD.

Sub Pop Video Network Program One

Released on VHS 1991, DVD 2003 (Sub Pop)

Until the release of the *With The Lights Out* box set, this was the only place to get the original version of Nirvana's "In Bloom" video (the soundtrack using the recording the band had done with Butch Vig in April 1990). Other artists featured include Mudhoney, Tad and Beat Happening.

1991: The Year Punk Broke

Released on VHS 1992 (Geffen Home Video)

Shot during the European summer festival season of 1991, this film is a good representation of the calm before the storm, though the backstage shenanigans seem more suited to a home movie. Along with five songs by Nirvana, there's also live footage of Sonic Youth (performing eight songs), Dinosaur Jr., Babes in Toyland, Gumball and the Ramones. Long rumoured to be imminently released on DVD.

Live! Tonight! Sold Out!!

Released on VHS 1994, DVD 2006 (DGC/UMe/Chronicles)

This release mostly covers Nirvana's breakthrough year of 1991, with live clips from eight different shows. These include some incendiary moments, such as the infamous fight that broke out at a Dallas show when a bouncer punched Cobain in the head; equally disturbing is when Cobain painfully rasps his way through "Come As You Are" in Amsterdam. But there are plenty of light-hearted moments as well, providing a welcome reminder that at their best Nirvana were hardly doom rockers: their main credo was to have as good a time as possible. Thus you see them cracking jokes in interviews, if they're not sending up the situation entirely. The highlight in this regard is the band's appearance on *Top Of The Pops* performing "Smells Like Teen Spirit", with Cobain singing in a bass voice.

The film is constructed to roughly approximate a live show, beginning with "Aneurysm", frequently among the first songs in the band's set, and ending with the "Endless, Nameless" destruction jam. The final shot, of Cobain dragging himself offstage at the end of the 23 January 1993 show in Brazil, is shattering. There's no voiceover narration, but the use of home movies, interview clips and news footage provides a narrative arc. The DVD adds five more songs from the band's Amsterdam show in 1991 (not 1992, as the liner notes state).

Hype!

Released on VHS 1997, DVD 2004 (Lions Gate Home Entertainment/Republic Pictures)

Doug Pray's documentary on the Seattle music scene only has brief footage of Nirvana. But it happens to be the most exciting in the film – the first ever public performance of "Teen Spirit" (the footage of the same song on the *With The Lights Out* DVD is shot from another angle). The rest of the film is highly entertaining too, with plenty of live footage and interviews showcasing one of the great unsung strengths of the Seattle scene, namely the ability to not

take oneself too seriously (that said, Jack Endino's thoughtful insights make him the film's star raconteur). DVD bonus features include the director's commentary, out-takes and additional live material.

Kurt & Courtney

Released on DVD 1998 (Fox Lorber)

British documentarian Nick Broomfield's film is arguably better known for the controversy it provoked than its actual content. The film explores some of the conspiracy theories surrounding Cobain's death, with Broomfield speaking to, amongst others, Love's estranged father Hank Harrison, and Tom Grant, the private detective hired by Love when Cobain had fled his LA rehab in April 1994. The film also shows how Broomfield's own attempts to interview Love were thwarted.

But as the film progresses, it broadens to show the kind of craziness that surrounds the famous – "stalkarazzi" photographers, hangers-on and other leeches – making it something of a critique of modern-day celebrity. Nor is every interviewee roped into the conspiracy: there are thoughtful interviews with Cobain's aunt Mari Earl (who plays a brief excerpt of a two-year-old Cobain singing), girlfriend Tracy Marander and photographer Alice Wheeler. And there are moments where the filmmaker himself takes the stage. Overall, it's a film with a pervasive sense of sadness and probably holds most appeal for staunch Nirvana fans or those interested in Broomfield's work.

Nirvanaology

The Beauty Process

Released on VHS 1999 (K Records/Murky Slough)

Directed, shot, co-written and co-edited by Krist Novoselic, this film is a combination tour video and rock'n'roll satire. Undeniably raw and low budget (filmed in "glorious Super-8mm" according to the credits), the film intersperses live footage of L7 with short skits about the evils of the music biz; there's a even a jab at Nirvana's own success when a focus group session test markets a snippet of "Nirvana Lite Angst cry baby middle class white boy grunge". Novoselic shot the film when Sweet 75 opened for L7 on an October 1997 tour; it's a shame his camera didn't capture the exploits of his own band, too.

Saturday Night Live: 25 Years Of Music

Released on DVD 2003 (Lions Gate)

This five-disc set features Nirvana's performance of "Rape Me" on 25 September 1993.

Everywhere But Home

Released November 2003 (Roswell/RCA/BMG)

The aptly named DVD has footage from Foo Fighters' 2002–2003 tour in support of their fifth album, *One By One*, the main concert being a high energy 7 July 2003 date in Toronto. Extras include excerpts from the 1 May show in Washington, DC, a 23 August date at Ireland's Slane Castle, and an audio-only concert from 26 August in Reykjavik; there's also "hidden" footage from a 12 July 2002 concert in Dublin.

The Work Of Director Anton Corbijn

Released on DVD 2005 (Palm Pictures)

This compilation of the filmmaker's videos has Corbijn discussing the creation of Nirvana's "Heart-Shaped Box" video, drawing on previously unseen interview footage of Cobain shot in December 1993. The accompanying booklet reproduces Cobain's sketch for the video's set.

Last Days

Released on DVD 2005 (HBO Video)

A disclaimer notes that writer/director Gus Van Sant's film was "inspired" by Cobain's life and isn't meant to be a traditional biopic. Van Sant uses the same technique he used in his films *Gerry* and *Elephant*, with the camera following the characters seemingly at random, unexpectedly moving back and forth in time, with long, static sequences where not much happens  – which viewers find either hypnotic or boring. Those familiar with Cobain's story will pick up on the many visual references: as "Blake", Michael Pitt not only looks like

Cobain, he variously wears a black slip like Cobain wore at the end of his Rio concert in 1993, the white framed sunglasses worn in much of the press coverage at the time of *In Utero*'s release, and the red-and-black striped sweater Cobain wore at various shows. And though little narrative is provided, it becomes clear that Blake is a rock star who's left rehab, has a daughter, and has a detective looking for him. But it's hard to become involved in a film where the viewer is kept at such a distance; you're never clear on what Blake's thoughts or motivations in any situation may be (it doesn't help that what little dialogue he's given is delivered in a mumble). An appearance by Sonic Youth's Kim Gordon, and voiceovers by MTV VJ Kurt Loder and Nirvana biographer Michael Azerrad add to the surreal mood.

Nirvana: Nevermind

Released on DVD 2005 (Eagle Vision)

This episode from the UK *Classic Albums* TV series offers a good overview of the album's creation. Krist Novoselic, Dave Grohl and Butch Vig are the most significant interviewees, and the sequences where Vig plays tapes from the sessions are fascinating. It's a shame more time wasn't devoted to looking at every song on the album (not to mention covering Vig's April 1990 session with the group) instead of having four journalists muse on the album's importance. Bonus features help fill out the story, covering the creation of the cover art, the "Teen Spirit" video, the recording of "Drain

You" and a performance of "Polly" taken from the Seattle 1991 show.

Skin And Bones

Released on DVD 2006 (Roswell/RCA/BMG)

Filmed in 2006 across Foos' 29–31 August dates at Los Angeles' Pantages Theater, the DVD features more tracks than the accompanying live CD. Though Grohl remarks on how odd it is to see everyone sitting down at a show, Foos have plenty of material that translates well to a more subdued setting, and the band is clearly having a good time as well. Happily, the concert footage isn't plagued by hyperkinetic editing, so you get a real sense of what it's like to see the band live. The UK version is even better, as it comes with an extra disc filmed at a 16 June 2006 show in Hyde Park, London.

Unplugged In New York

Released November 2007 (Geffen/MTV Networks/UMe)

For weeks after Cobain's death, you couldn't turn on MTV without seeing the edited version of Nirvana's *Unplugged* show. That wasn't enough for the bootleggers of course, who were soon peddling an uncut version that featured the entire performance, as well as all the between-songs chat.

Fourteen years later, an official release of the full version finally arrived. Those used to the MTV edit will be surprised at the seemingly random manner of the show, as the group discusses what song to do next, debates how to perform songs and even solicits requests from the audience, resulting in short jams on "Sliver" and Lynyrd Skynyrd's "Sweet Home Alabama" (the latter of which got a huge cheer). The mood is also far more relaxed than it appears in the MTV version, though everyone defers to Cobain's wishes. Extras include a five-song excerpt from the band's rehearsal, a behind-the-scenes look at the show from the MTV progamme *Bare Witness*, plus the original MTV edit of the show.

Kurt Cobain: About A Son

Released on DVD 2008 (Shout! Factory)

Though some were frustrated that director A.J. Schnack didn't produce a more traditional documentary, others were won over by his idiosyncratic approach. Schnack has his camera drifting languorously through the three main places where Cobain lived – Aberdeen, Olympia and Seattle – with the sole narration provided by the interviews Cobain did with Michael Azerrad for *Come As You Are*.

Hearing Cobain speak at such length is a surprisingly intimate experience, even if you're already familiar with Azerrad's book. There's no footage of Nirvana, and no still pictures of Cobain until the end. Nor is there any Nirvana music on the soundtrack, which draws instead on songs that influenced Cobain (the Melvins, the Vaselines, Queen, R.E.M.); the film's atmospheric original score was written by Steve Fisk (one of Nirvana's producers) and Benjamin Gibbard (of Seattle band Death Cab For Cutie). Cobain offers a highly subjective account of his life (with many false claims and exaggerations), but it's nonetheless the truth he wanted put on record. And since most of the interview clips you hear in other documentaries are brief, it's mesmerizing to be able to listen to his dry, late-night drawl for ninety minutes. Bonus features provide background info, such as the fact that the film's opening sequence includes shots looking out of the window of the house where Cobain and Azerrad did their interviews.

Tributes and covers

Tribute albums

Nirvana tribute albums take one of two approaches: covers done in an alternative rock style or the "novelty" of reworking alternative rock songs as lounge/semi-classical background music. Most releases are for completists only.

Grunge Lite

Sara DeBell (C/Z Records, 1993)

One of the best Nirvana tributes was, naturally enough, a homegrown effort. In the wake of the grunge explosion, Seattle musician Sara DeBell holed up in her apartment and created Muzak-style instrumentals of songs ranging from "Smells Like Teen Spirit" and "Negative Creep" to Pearl Jam's "Even Flow" and Mudhoney's "Touch Me I'm Sick". "We had to put it out before K-tel did," a C/Z representative cracked at the time. The inner

sleeve makes further comment on grunge hype via a picture of a herd of sheep wearing flannel; coincidentally, "Sheep" was briefly considered as the title for Nirvana's second album.

A Tribute To Nirvana

Various artists (Tribute Records, 1995)

This set emerged from Sweden and features serviceable – if occasionally odd – versions of Nirvana songs by bands with names like Calcutta Anazamama ("Smells Like Teen Spirit"), Wasted Youth ("Floyd The Barber"), Melanie's Breast ("Heart-Shaped Box") and NME Within ("In Bloom"), in a variety of rock styles.

Angels Bleed: Songs Of Tribute... From Seattle And Beyond

Various artists (Reversing Recordings, 1996)

Not all songs on this album reference Cobain's death directly, but all are concerned with issues of pain and loss. Artists include Snow Bud ("Your Baby's Gone"), Sanctus ("Life Signs") and Wrick Wolff ("Kurtsey, Bow And Scrape"). The disc was also a fundraiser, with profits earmarked for "chronically depressed young people who cannot afford treatment".

Smells Like Nirvana: A Tribute To Nirvana

Various artists (Dressed To Kill, 2000)

One of the more forgettable collections, featuring artists like Beki Bondage ("Lithium"), Dead Sex Kitten ("On A Plain"), and the more creatively named Artist Formerly Known As Ponce ("All Apologies" and "Rape Me").

Smells Like Bleach: A Punk Tribute To Nirvana

Various artists (Cleopatra, 2000)

This album is a rarity among Nirvana tribute releases, featuring artists you'll actually have heard of. Dee Dee Ramone covers "Negative Creep", DOA takes on "All Apologies", Agent Orange performs "On A Plain" (not "Serve The Servants", as the original cover stated). Flipper chose to cover "Scentless Apprentice", little suspecting that six years later they'd be performing the song with one of its co-authors when Krist Novoselic joined their line-up. Liner notes are by Dave Thompson, who wrote the first posthumous biography of Kurt Cobain, *Never Fade Away: The Kurt Cobain Story*.

The Cocktail Tribute To Nirvana

Various artists (Vitamin Records, 2001)

Nirvana music for lounge lizards.

Nearvana "San Francisco"

Various artists (Tinnitus Records, 2002)

A mixed bag of Nirvana covers by San Francisco/ Bay Area artists. Some of the highlights are The Reducer's Sleater-Kinney-esque "Polly", Violet Discord's "Lithium", seemingly channelled by The Fastbacks, and Jojo's "Frances Farmer Will Have Her Revenge on Seattle", not least because it's a song notable for its absence on other tribute compilations.

The String Quartet Tribute To Nirvana

Tallywood Strings (Vitamin Records, 2003)

Nirvana songs with a semi-classical touch. There were subsequent "String Quartet Tributes" to *Nevermind* and Foo Fighters.

Guitar Tribute To Nirvana

Various artists (Tribute Sounds, 2004)

Fair-to-middling collections of guitar-based renditions of Nirvana songs. There's a Foo Fighters tribute album too.

Tribute To Nirvana: Flannel And Leather Brought Us Together

Various artists (Sonic Fuzz Records, 2004)

Covers from the likes of Stick Figure Suicide, 37 Slurp, Jettison and Common Decency. One thing: Nirvana weren't known for their love of leather.

Last Days: Tribute To Mr K

Various artists (Avex, 2006)

This Japanese release featured music "inspired by" Gus Van Sant's *Last Days*, and is often incorrectly credited as the film's soundtrack. Among the featured artists is Shonen Knife, one of Cobain's favourite bands.

Cover songs

Unsurprisingly, "Smells Like Teen Spirit" is the most frequently covered Nirvana song. One of the first covers was actually a parody – "Weird Al" Yankovic's "Smells Like Nirvana", which poked fun at the difficulty people had in figuring out what Cobain was singing; released as a single, it also appeared on his album *Off The Deep End* (Scotti Brothers, 1992). Another parody version, "Smells Like Queer Spirit", was released on the album *Pile Up* (Lookout, 1995) by San Francisco-based queercore group Pansy Division. Singer/songwriter Tori Amos's version appeared on the US version of her "Crucify" single (Atlantic, 1992). Though Cobain sarcastically called it "a great breakfast cereal version", the track was occasionally used as entrance music for the band in concert, while the band members playfully cavorted like ballerinas. The Melvins covered the song on *The Crybaby* (Ipecac, 2000), with former teen idol Leif Garrett taking the vocal. A bizarre "swing" version appeared on Paul Anka's *Rock Swings* (Verve, 2005) album, with no one sure if it was meant to be a joke or not (the album also featured covers of Soundgarden's "Black Hole Sun" and Pet Shop Boys' "It's A Sin", among others). Patti Smith performed the song on her covers album, *Twelve* (Columbia, 2007); she has also covered "Heart-Shaped Box" in concert.

Among other songs, "Afro-Celtic" singer/songwriter Laura Love covered "Come As You Are" on *Octoroon* (Mercury, 1997). Love was signed to the label by Danny Goldberg, one of Nirvana's managers.

"Lithium" was covered by a UK prog rock band also named Nirvana. In the wake of *Nevermind*'s success, the UK group had sued Cobain and co. over their use of the name "Nirvana"; the matter was settled out of court, with the US Nirvana paying the UK Nirvana $100,000 for the right to use the name. The UK Nirvana's cover of "Lithium" appeared on their album *Orange and Blue* (Edsel, 1996).

"All Apologies" is another song frequently covered on record and in concert by artists as varied as Nina Hagen, Coldplay, Herbie Hancock and Sinéad O'Connor. When Christian rock group dc Talk performed the song in concert, they altered the line about everyone being gay to "Jesus is The Way."

Velvet Revolver's cover of "Negative Creep" appears on their single "Slither" (RCA, 2004) and on a bonus disc included in the Australian edition of *Contraband* (RCA, 2004). Three members of the band were in Guns N' Roses, a group Cobain regularly disparaged.

Songs about Cobain

Dozens of songs have been written about or make reference to Kurt Cobain. One of the first to put out a tribute song was Neil Young, who had been greatly disturbed when Cobain quoted from Young's "Hey Hey, My My (Into The Black)" in his suicide note. In response, he wrote the song "Sleeps With Angels", which became the title track of his next album, released in August 1994 on Reprise. When Young was inducted into the Rock & Roll Hall of Fame in January 1995, he thanked Cobain for "all of his inspiration".

"Let Me In", on R.E.M.'s 1994 album *Monster* (Warner Bros.), is also about Cobain. He and R.E.M. vocalist Michael Stipe had tentative plans to work together before Cobain's death, and the band's bassist, Mike Mills, can be seen playing Cobain's Jag-Stang guitar in the video for the song.

Patti Smith began performing a number about Cobain, "About A Boy", in 1994, recording it for *Gone Again* (1996, Arista).

Simon Timony of The Stinky Puffs wrote the song "I'll Love You Anyway", which appeared on *A Little Tiny Smelly Bit Of...* (Elemental, 1995) in two versions: a studio version, and a live version recorded with Krist Novoselic and Dave Grohl. A re-recorded version of the song appeared on *Songs And Advice For Kids Who Have Been Left Behind* (Elemental, 1996).

Unsurprisingly, much of Hole's *Celebrity Skin* (DGC, 1998) can be read as a response to Cobain's death, in particular the songs "Northern Star" and "Playing Your Song".

A number of Grohl's Foo Fighters songs are said to be about Cobain or Love; though consistently denying there are any direct references, he conceded to *The Guardian*, "those correlations are gonna pop up every now and again [but] I still remain a little secretive about it all". But one song definitely about Cobain is "Friend Of A Friend" a song Grohl wrote when he joined Nirvana in the fall of 1990 and shared an apartment with Cobain. Grohl first released the song on his *Pocketwatch* tape (credited to Late! and released on Simple Minds in 1992), and re-recorded it for Foo Fighters' *Skin And Bones* live album and DVD (RCA, 2006).

Nirvana locations

The main locations associated with Nirvana are Aberdeen, where Kurt Cobain was born and Nirvana began; Olympia, where Cobain lived from 1987 to 1991, a key period in the band's development; and Seattle, where the band members lived after the success of *Nevermind*. Though some of the sites described here no longer exist, others remain much as they were, especially in Aberdeen. Note that some sites are private property; be considerate and take care not to trespass.

Aberdeen and around

It's not until you drive through the streets of Aberdeen that you realize how small it actually is – if you hit all the stoplights when they turn green, you can drive straight through town in about five minutes. So it's easy to get a feel for the kind of environment Kurt Cobain and Krist Novoselic grew up in.

Cobain was born at Grays Harbor Community Hospital in Aberdeen, which sits atop one of the town's surrounding hills at 915 Anderson Drive. It was a place he'd return to during homeless periods in his teenage years, having figured out the staff wasn't likely to disturb someone snoozing in the waiting room; they'd simply assume he was waiting for a relative. Cobain spent his first two and a half years in Hoquiam, then the family moved to Aberdeen, living in a house at 1210 E 1st St, a lower-middle-class area of town called "The Flats". A number of Cobain related sites are within walking distance of his childhood home, so you can explore the area at your leisure.

His first school, Robert Gray Elementary, is close by, at 1516 N B St. Two blocks from his home, E 1st St turns into Young St, which crosses the Wishkah River. One of Cobain's hangouts was under the bridge, and today you'll find graffiti from fans around the world, along with a sign tacked on one of the bridge supports reading "In Memoriam 'From the Muddy Banks of the Wishkah'"; it's generally the first stop Nirvana fans make when they come to town. A few blocks west, at 1000 1/2 E 2nd St, is a small white shack Cobain lived in with Matt Lukin from September 1986 to May 1987. It was here that the band that became Nirvana took shape, with Cobain, Krist Novoselic and their first drummer Aaron Burckhard using the shack as a rehearsal space. The shack has become increasingly decrepit in recent years, with trash inside indicating that it's occasionally used as a crash pad.

Both Cobain and Novoselic attended J.M. Weatherwax High School – more commonly

One of Cobain's hangouts, the bridge over the Wishkah now bears an "In Memoriam" sign.

referred to as Aberdeen High School – at 414 N I St. After dropping out, Cobain worked briefly at the high school as a janitor. On the night of 5 January 2002, the Weatherwax wing of the school, built in 1909, burned down. It was later discovered that the fire had been started by a student and his friend, while attempting to destroy some of the student's school records; one can imagine the incident giving Cobain a chuckle. A new high school, which opened in the fall of 2007, was built two blocks away at 410 N G St.

The building at 107 S M St was the location of Maria's Hair Design, the beauty salon owned by Novoselic's mother. Nirvana would practice upstairs when the salon was closed. Next to the salon, on the corner at 401 W Market St, is Judy's Antiques & Collectibles, which Cobain and Novoselic would scour for records and books, Novoselic in particular examining any instruments that happened to be in stock. Across the street at 320 W Market St is the former site of the local YMCA, where Cobain worked briefly as a janitor and occasionally filled in for instructors. Novoselic was more gainfully employed at a Taco Bell then located at 810 E Wishkah St, and the Foster Painting Company at 411 S Jefferson St.

A few blocks east, at 121 E Market St, is the Aberdeen Timberland Library, where Cobain spent many hours, often when he should have been in school. Both Cobain and Novoselic took guitar lessons at Rosevear's Music Center at 224 E Wishkah St. Today, a star with Cobain's name can be found in front of the store, and a nearby tree is surrounded by a fence decorated with Cobain's silhouette.

Cobain's first home of his own was an apartment on the northeast corner of W 3rd St and N Michigan; the building is no longer standing. Dale Crover's former house, not far away at 609 W 2nd St, was where the Melvins rehearsed and became another hangout for Cobain and Novoselic.

The band would practise above the former beauty salon run by Maria Novoselic.

Nirvana never played a show in Aberdeen; the closest they came was a show on 21 December 1988 at the Eagles Lodge at 220 5th St in Hoquiam. It's been said that after this show, Cobain and Novoselic gave an impromptu performance at The Pourhouse, an Aberdeen tavern at 506 E Wishkah St; they certainly drank there over the years, and it remains a popular Aberdeen watering hole. Novoselic performed with the Melvins in an ad hoc group at Aberdeen's now closed D&R Theater at 205 S I St in 1984.

As you leave Aberdeen heading west, after crossing the Wishkah River, Morrison Riverfront Park is on the right at 1401 Sargent Blvd; on 9 April 1994, a memorial for Cobain was held here.

Montesano and Raymond

After his parents' divorce, Cobain lived with his father at 413 Fleet St S in Montesano, eleven miles east of Aberdeen. Cobain attended Beacon Elementary School at 1717 E Beacon Ave and later Montesano Junior High and High School, both located at 303 N Church St. And it was in Montesano that Cobain discovered what he called his "special purpose" after witnessing an impromptu concert by the Melvins behind the Montesano Thriftway, at 211 E Pioneer Ave, in the summer of 1983.

Four years later, Nirvana played their first show at a party at 17 Nussbaum Rd in the small town of Raymond, 29 miles south of Aberdeen.

Where Did You Sleep Last Night?

In *Rolling Stone*'s first cover story on Nirvana, published 16, April 1992, author Michael Azerrad said that Kurt Cobain had "lived under a bridge in Aberdeen", referring to the Young Street Bridge, which crosses the Wishkah River. He later amended this statement in *Come As You Are*, saying Kurt merely slept under the bridge "sometimes", but the debate over whether or not he did indeed stay there has continued. Charles Cross's *Heavier Than Heaven* quotes Krist Novoselic and Cobain's sister Kim as saying Cobain never "lived" under the Young Street Bridge, two blocks from his childhood home, he just "hung out" there – and surely the leap from "hanging out" to "sleeping there on occasion" is not a big one. Others have said he actually stayed under the Sixth Street Bridge, by Aberdeen's Canyon Court residences; this is where Aberdeen Police Captain Mike Haymon told Aberdeen's *Daily World* Cobain dumped a tent he had stolen from Haymon's backyard.

While it's true inclement weather undoubtedly drove Cobain to seek shelter indoors during his homeless periods, it's not unreasonable to think he spent the occasional night under both bridges, as well as innumerable other places around Aberdeen. Cobain himself told Azerrad, during the interview sessions for *Come As You Are*, he only slept under the bridge when he'd worn his welcome out after crashing at different friends' houses for months, which would seem to settle the matter. Ultimately, Cobain drew on his experiences of homelessness – wherever they were spent – in writing the haunting song "Something In The Way".

Olympia

In May 1987, Cobain moved into the apartment of his girlfriend, Tracy Marander, at 114 Pear St in Olympia, fifty miles east of Aberdeen. The city is not only the capital of Washington State, but also home to the progressive Evergreen State College, and Evergreen would play a not inconsiderable role in Nirvana's career.

Cobain's first live performance was at GESCCO (Greater Evergreen Student Community Cooperative Organization), and Nirvana also played a show at the venue, located at the corner of 5th Ave and Cherry St. The college itself, at 2700 Evergreen Parkway NW, was also the site of a number of Nirvana shows, particularly at, or in front of, K Dorm;

and they played an anti-war benefit at the library on 18 January 1991. The band also appeared on the campus radio station, KAOS, in 1988 (Cobain made a solo appearance in 1990), recording some tracks in the music building in 1989, and returned to tape some videos there in 1990.

Grohl's first show with Nirvana was at the now-closed North Shore Surf Club, 116 E 5th Ave. Grohl lived with Cobain at Pear St for a few months, across the street from the Washington State Lottery building, at which the two would occasionally shoot their BB guns. They were often seen at the now-closed record store Positively Fourth Street at 208 4th Ave W, selling Nirvana T-shirts and records. The Capitol Theater, at 206 E 5th Ave, has hosted

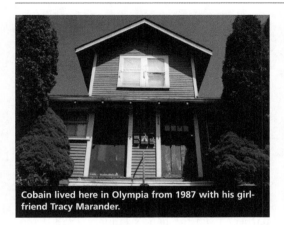
Cobain lived here in Olympia from 1987 with his girlfriend Tracy Marander.

many alternative rock shows over the years, and on the opening day of the first Yoyo-A-Go-Go festival, 12 July 1994, Grohl and Novoselic gave their first live performance since Cobain's death, backing The Stinky Puffs.

Seattle

Ironically, though lumped in with other "Seattle scene" bands, no one in Nirvana lived in the city until after the success of *Nevermind*. But they had been playing Seattle clubs since 1988.

Many places associated with the band are now gone, and unlike Aberdeen and Olympia, which retain a small town feel, Seattle has undergone extensive development since the 1980s. The first studios the group used, Reciprocal Recording (formerly at 4230 Leary Way NW) and The Music Source (615 E Pike St) no longer exist. Many clubs are gone as well; only the truly

dedicated will want to see the former locales of Squid Row (518 E Pine St), the Annex Theatre (1916 4th Ave), Motor Sports International Garage (the southwest corner of Stewart St and Yale Ave) or The Underground (4518 University Way NE). Nor is The OK Hotel (formerly at 212 Alaskan Highway S) standing, a casualty of Seattle's 2001 earthquake. This was not only the site where the band debuted "Smells Like Teen Spirit" (footage of which appears in both the film *Hype!* and on the *With The Lights Out* DVD), but it also appeared in the film *Singles* as the "Java Jive" restaurant. Some sites remain open as other businesses, allowing visitors a look inside. The Vogue, at 2018 1st Ave, is now a hair salon called Vain, its layout not too dissimilar to the club's. The King Theater, 601 Blanchard St, where Nirvana played a benefit show for the Mia Zapata investigative fund in 1993, is now The King Cat Theater, hosting music and theatrical events.

In Seattle's historic Pioneer Square neighbourhood, long home to many clubs, one venue where Nirvana performed is still in operation: the Central Tavern at 207 1st Ave S, which also held the management offices for Soundgarden and Alice In Chains for a time. Union Station, a former railroad terminal at 401 S Jackson St, was where the band opened for the Butthole Surfers in October 1988, and still hosts occasional functions. Nirvana's final show in the area was at another unusual venue, the former ferry terminal Pier 48 at 101 Alaskan Way S; here, on 13 December 1993, they were filmed for MTV's *Live and Loud* show, to be broadcast on New Year's Eve.

The picture of a multistorey office building in the *Sub Pop 200* booklet captioned as "Sub Pop World Headquarters" wasn't just another example of the label's penchant for hype; the company really did have an office in the Terminal Sales Building at 1932 1st Ave, eventually moving into the penthouse and expanding into a warehouse space on a lower floor (they have since moved). One block north at 1932 2nd Ave is The Moore Theatre, where Nirvana played twice: once at the first Sub Pop "Lame Fest" in 1989, and again the following year, when they opened for Sonic Youth.

The Crocodile Café (2200 2nd Ave), where Nirvana opened for Mudhoney in 1992, closed in 2007, but at the time of writing was scheduled to reopen during 2009. Nirvana never recorded at Bad Animals Studios, 2212 4th Ave, but tracks from *In Utero* were remixed at the studio, and work on the box set *With The Lights Out* was also done here. Three blocks away, C/Z Records was located at 2028 5th Ave, on the second floor of the building, right next door to *The Rocket* magazine offices.

Of the few clubs where Nirvana played that are still in existence, El Corazon, at 109 Eastlake Ave E, was where Grohl played his first Seattle show with Nirvana, in 1990, when it was called The Off Ramp Café. Grohl also played the club (then called Graceland) in 2002 when he drummed for Queens of the Stone Age, and Novoselic appeared here with Eyes Adrift on Halloween the same year; he's since played the venue with Flipper. And Re-bar is still around, at 114 Howell St; it's

where *Nevermind*'s record release party was held on 13 September 1991. Around six weeks later, the band played a triumphant homecoming show at the Paramount Theatre, 911 Pine St. The show was filmed and recorded; select songs have been released on various singles and promos, and footage from the show appeared in Nirvana's "Lithium" video.

The University of Washington, whose main entrance is at NE 45th St and 17th Ave NE, was home to radio KCMU in its Communications building; the station was possibly the first to play a Nirvana song on the radio – "Floyd The Barber" from the band's January 1988 demo. The band also played two shows at the Husky Union Building (HUB) in 1989 and 1990. In the same neighbourhood, on 16 September 1991, Nirvana played an in-store appearance at Beehive Music & Video, formerly at 815 NE 45th, then signed copies of *Nevermind* for attendees. To pluck up their courage before the show, the group went across the street to the Blue Moon Tavern at 712 NE 45th for a few drinks. The tavern is one of Seattle's most legendary counterculture establishments, including writer Tom Robbins and poet Theodore Roethke among its regulars, while notable visitors have included Allen Ginsberg and Dylan Thomas.

The Seattle Center, bordered by Mercer St to the north, Denny Way to the south, 5th Ave and 1st Ave to the east and west, was built for the 1962 World's Fair (and featured prominently in the 1963 Elvis Presley movie *It Happened At The World's Fair*). The primary concert venues have undergone many name changes. When Nirvana first played on the grounds on 11 September 1992, they appeared at the Coliseum; when Grohl later played the venue with Foo Fighters, it had been renamed Key Arena. On 7 and 8 January 1994, Nirvana played their last US dates at what was then called the Arena; today the abandoned venue is called the Mercer Arena and is rumoured to be in for a redesign. On 10 April 1994, a citywide memorial was held for Cobain at the Center, at what was then the Flag Plaza; the area has since been substantially redesigned. The grounds are also home to Seattle's rock'n'roll museum, the Experience Music Project, where you'll find numerous Nirvana artefacts on display. While Cobain's public memorial was held at the Center, a private memorial service for his family and friends was held at the Unity Church (For Truth) a few blocks away at 200 8th Ave N.

Cobain's first home in Seattle was at 11301 Lakeside Ave NE; the "Sliver" video was shot in the garage. In January 1994, he moved into a large house at 171 Lake Washington Blvd E. He was sometimes seen at restaurants in the area along nearby Madison St, including the International House of Pancakes at 950 E Madison St, Taco Time at 1420 E Madison St, and, one of the last public places he was seen, Cactus at 4220 E Madison St. Viretta Park, next to his last home on Lake Washington Blvd E, is where you'll find the most visible reminder of his presence. Messages to Cobain are written on the park's benches, and on the anniversary of his death fans congregate in the park.

Websites

Do a Google search for "Nirvana" and you'll get over 42 million results, the majority nothing to do with the band; add "Kurt Cobain" to your search and the number drops down to the far lower but still overwhelming number of 3.3 million. None of the official Nirvana sites is particularly inspiring, however. **Geffen.com/nirvana** has a timeline that runs to 1996, along with info on the band's releases and eight videos; **myspace.com/nirvana** provides links to buy the band's releases; and in 2008 you could still visit promotional websites for *With The Lights Out*, *Sliver: The Best Of The Box*, and the *Live! Tonight! Sold Out!!* DVD. Fortunately, there are other Nirvana websites run by dedicated souls whose zeal and eye for detail elevates them above mere fandom.

Nirvana websites

livenirvana.com Though much of the site is dedicated to the discussion and documentation of live audio and video recordings, you'll also find complete studio and tour histories, equipment and song guides, photo archives, a day-by-day history and much more, along with a very lively forum.

nirvanaclub.com is the best site for Nirvana news, regularly breaking stories on new releases and frequented by band members. There's an archive with hundreds of Nirvana-related articles, as well as interviews exclusive to the site, an excellent section on *With The Lights Out*, photo galleries, sound and video clips, music tabs, a forum and chat room.

nirvanaguide.com has detailed listings for every known Nirvana live performance (including pictures of the show, concert posters, ticket stubs and other emphemera), noting which material has been released – officially or otherwise.

kurtsequipment.com, though it hasn't been updated since 2002, tells you all you'd want to know about the gear Cobain used onstage and in the studio, with substantial input from the band's guitar tech, Earnie Bailey.

sliver.it/nirvana is an extensive discography of Nirvana releases around the world, illustrated with numerous pictures. Included are sections devoted to promos, side projects, memorabilia and counterfeit items. The site is also assembling a list of everyone who owns a copy of the limited edition "Love Buzz" single.

crimson-ceremony.net/pr3 takes you through the entire process of creating a Nirvana release, with information on mastering, matrix codes, artwork, test pressings, promos and more. It's also the best place to get information on what would have have been *In Utero*'s last single, "Pennyroyal Tea", which was recalled after Cobain's death.

Foo Fighters websites

foofighters.com is the band's official site and packed with info. The discography has listings on many (though not all) of the band's albums, singles and compilation appearances, along with a song list detailing which release the track appears on, lyrics, and the date the song was first played live. There's a news section, message board and store, and fans are invited to share photos and reviews. The media section has few offerings, but one suspects that will change.

foofighterslive.com was launched in 2007, and has already set itself a high standard, as you'd expect from fans who met up via the livenirvana.com site. The Live Guide endeavours to document every Foo show from 1995 onwards, and there's also a session history, DVD guide and forum.

fooarchive.com has an ever-expanding collection of print and radio interviews, a comprehensive news section, and a "Grohl-O-Meter", with Grohl quotes on subjects from A to X (he hadn't spoken about anything beginning with Y or Z at the time of writing).

Other sites

Krist Novoselic has run various websites since Nirvana. **murkyslough.com** hasn't been updated since 2007 and offers only a few sound clips. At the time of writing, Novoselic was blogging for the *Seattle Weekly*, with his column "Krist Novoselic: Contention and Conscious" covering politics, music and other topics at **blogs.seattleweekly.com/dailyweekly /krist_novoselic_contention_con**. Like murkyslough, the unofficial **novoselic.com** site hasn't been updated since early 2007, but it still has some useful information, including bass tabs.

myspace.com/beforecars is the site for Chad Channing's latest band, with news and song clips.

jackendino.com has an extensive Nirvana FAQ, as well as updates on his current projects (including recording the post-Nirvana bands of Chad Channing and Krist Novoselic). You can hear Endino's own recordings at **myspace .com/jackendino**.

kurtcobainmemorial.org is the site of Aberdeen's Kurt Cobain Memorial Project, founded to "recognize the contribution made by Kurt Cobain and Nirvana to music", and carries news of their latest projects, as does **myspace.com/kurtmemorial**.

Index

Page references to in-depth discussions of Nirvana recordings are in **bold**.

Index

Index

... presents...

"...ned recommendation and needless trivia"

...ult Movies

...include:

American Independent Film • British Cult Comedy • Chick Flicks • Comedy Movies • Cult Movi
Film • Film Musicals • Film Noir • Gangster Movies • Horror Movies • Sci-Fi Movies • Western

MAKE THE MOST OF YOUR TIME ON EARTH™